teach
yourself

psychology

teach
yourself

psychology

psychology
nicky hayes

For over 60 years, more than
40 million people have learnt over
750 subjects the **teach yourself**
way, with impressive results.

be where you want to be
with **teach yourself**

For UK order enquiries: please contact Bookpoint Ltd, 130 Milton Park, Abingdon, Oxon OX14 4SB. Telephone: +44 (0) 1235 827720. Fax: +44 (0) 1235 400454. Lines are open 09.00–18.00, Monday to Saturday, with a 24-hour message answering service. Details about our titles and how to order are available at www.teachyourself.co.uk

For USA order enquiries: please contact McGraw-Hill Customer Services, PO Box 545, Blacklick, OH 43004-0545, USA. Telephone: 1-800-722-4726. Fax: 1-614-755-5645.

For Canada order enquiries: please contact McGraw-Hill Ryerson Ltd, 300 Water St, Whitby, Ontario L1N 9B6, Canada. Telephone: 905 430 5000. Fax: 905 430 5020.

Long renowned as the authoritative source for self-guided learning – with more than 40 million copies sold worldwide – the **teach yourself** series includes over 300 titles in the fields of languages, crafts, hobbies, business, computing and education.

British Library Cataloguing in Publication Data: a catalogue record for this title is available from the British Library.

Library of Congress Catalog Card Number: on file.

First published in UK 1994 by Hodder Education, 338 Euston Road, London, NW1 3BH.

First published in US 1994 by Contemporary Books, a Division of the McGraw-Hill Companies, 1 Prudential Plaza, 130 East Randolph Street, Chicago, IL 60601 USA.

This edition published 2003.

The **teach yourself** name is a registered trade mark of Hodder Headline.

Typeset by Transet Limited, Coventry, England.
Printed in Great Britain for Hodder Education, a division of Hodder Headline, 338 Euston Road, London NW1 3BH, by Cox & Wyman Ltd, Reading, Berkshire.

Hodder Headline's policy is to use papers that are natural, renewable and recyclable products and made from wood grown in sustainable forests. The logging and manufacturing processes are expected to conform to the environmental regulations of the country of origin.

Impression number 10 9 8 7 6 5 4
Year   2009 2008 2007 2006 2005

contents

Acknowledgements

My thanks are due to Usha Patel, Colin Smith, Graham Gibbs and Christine Sefton, whose different kinds of support helped me so much in the preparation of the first edition of this book; and to David Griggs whose support has been invaluable in the preparation of this second edition.

Dedication

This book is dedicated to Professor Steven Rose, who first introduced me to levels of analysis as an alternative to reductionism.

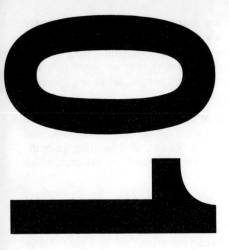

01

what is psychology?

In this chapter you will learn:
- the definition of 'psychology'
- how to describe the different activities psychologists engage in
- to identify six distinct approaches to conductinig psychology.

What is psychology? There are many ways in which I could try to answer that question. The most straightforward answer, though, is to say that psychology is about understanding people: how they think, what they say, and why they do what they do. It's about finding out what motivates people, what is important to us, and why we are all so individual.

That isn't the whole answer, of course, because there are some psychologists, such as those who work with dolphins and chimpanzees, whose main interest lies in understanding animals. However, most psychologists are interested in understanding people.

The problem with trying to understand people, though, is that people are complex, and change all the time. We learn from our experiences, we form good intentions, and we are acted on by circumstances. So what we do can be influenced by a great many different factors. Also, everyone has their own ideas and opinions about what people are really like. These ideas can influence what we do and also how we interpret what other people are doing. And since we each have had different lives, and have learned from our experiences, these ideas can be very different from one person to the next.

What this means is that it is very important for psychologists to study people in a careful and systematic way. In the final chapter of this book, we'll be looking at that in a little more detail. We'll look at how psychologists collect evidence; how they interpret their findings and try to avoid becoming too biased; and at how they manage to bring together information from so many different levels of analysis – biological information, cognitive information, personal information, social information, and cultural information. By then, though, you'll have come across quite a few different examples of psychological research, because just about all of the information in this book has come from psychological research of one kind or another.

The science of the mind

The word psychology comes from the Greek word *psyche*, which means 'the soul', or 'the essence of life' and is sometimes portrayed as a female figure representing the mind. The second part of the word also comes from the Greek language, and indicates knowledge or science. So combining the two gives us the idea of psychology as being the science of the mind.

Psychology has been through a couple of transformations over the past 150 years or so. Early psychologists spent a lot of time exploring how the mind works by thinking about it, using a method called **introspection**. However, in the first half of the twentieth century, a kind of psychology developed which took the view that if psychology was to be a proper science, then it must be objective, dealing only with information which could be directly observed and measured – in other words, with people's behaviour, not their minds. These psychologists called themselves **behaviourists**, and some of them became quite extreme in insisting that behaviour was the only thing that mattered, and that thoughts, feelings or personal experiences were unimportant because you couldn't study them directly.

Gradually, however, psychologists became better at studying experience as well as behaviour, and at conducting research which lets us discover how people think, and how we make sense of our experience. They don't do it in the same way as those early psychologists, of course, but psychologists nowadays are just as interested in understanding the mind as they are in understanding people's behaviour.

A modern definition of psychology would probably refer to it as **the scientific study of experience and behaviour**. That means that as psychologists, we are interested in what people experience as well as what they actually do. We need to put both types of knowledge together if we want to understand human beings.

Psychologists, of course, aren't the only people who are trying to understand human beings. A sociologist, for example, will try to understand human beings from the point of view of people in society, and how groups of people and social trends emerge, whereas a psychologist is interested mainly in the individual person. That doesn't mean that we can ignore society: as we will see in the next chapter and elsewhere in this book, it simply isn't realistic to try to understand an individual person as if their society or culture had nothing to do with what they were like. But it means that in psychology, we take the individual person, rather than society as a whole, as our starting point.

Understanding the individual person, though, is a pretty massive task, and it would be unrealistic to think that we know everything there is to know. When it comes to human beings, there aren't any easy answers. After reading this book, you won't find that you can understand everyone you've ever met. But what you will find, I hope, is that you know a great deal more about people than you knew before; and that knowledge may sometimes help you to understand the people around you a little better.

What do psychologists do?

Psychology, as we've seen, is the study of experience and behaviour. But it is also a profession, and professional psychologists put psychological knowledge to work in all sorts of ways. This mixture of academic and professional psychology means that psychology itself is very wide-ranging. It is also changing all the time, as psychologists learn new things and develop new methods of working, so there's always something new to discover.

That doesn't mean, though, that every psychologist has to know everything there is about psychology – that would be pretty impossible. Speaking personally, I've been studying it for nearly 30 years now, and I'm always conscious of how much I don't know! But psychologists always specialize in one way or another. Academic psychologists, for example, generally work within a very small area of psychology. Their task is to conduct research into that area, identifying the fundamental mechanisms and processes which are taking place, and exploring how they can contribute to our understanding of people.

Professional psychologsts also tend to specialize, dealing with just one area of applied psychology. They use the work of academic psychologists and also conduct research of their own, and put that knowledge to use in helping people in one way or another. Their research also feeds back into academic psychology – in fact, most areas of academic psychology have been influenced at one time or another by theories and evidence obtained from professional psychology.

Professional psychologists can be found at work in almost any area which involves dealing with people. Forensic psychologists, for example, work with police and prison staff in tackling many different aspects of crime. Sports psychologists work with coaches and competitors, developing ways of maximizing competitive performance. Consumer psychologists are at work in advertising and market research, working out how to reach new markets. In the sister volume to this book, *Teach Yourself Applied Psychology*, I described 18 different areas of applied psychology, which are listed in Table 1.1. If you're curious about these, take a look at that book.

There are other types of work that psychologists do – the 18 areas in the list are only a sample – but people who study psychology don't usually know what area of work they want to

table 1.1 areas covered in *Teach Yourself Applied Psychology*

Applied Cognitive Psychology	Occupational Psychology
Applied Social Psychology	Organizational Psychology
Applied Bio-psychology	Engineering and Design
Applied Developmental	Psychology
Psychology	Space Psychology
Clinical Psychology	Sport Psychology
Counselling Psychology	Consumer Psychology
Health Psychology	Environmental Psychology
Forensic Psychology	Political Psychology
Educational Psychology	
Applied Psychology of	
Teaching	

go into when they have finished. What they do know is that they are interested in people and want to learn more about them. Some people just study it for interest and no other reason. Others become interested in a particular topic and aim for an academic career which will allow them to do research. Some people decide that they want to go on to further training so that they can become a professional psychologist. And sometimes people feel that having a first degree or an A level in psychology is enough, and they go into careers as policemen, social workers, doctors, nurses, personnel officers or one of any number of occupations which involve dealing with people.

Whatever decision they make, most people find that having a good knowledge of psychology is helpful to them. Knowing about psychology may not give you all the answers, but it does help you to ask the right questions and to go about seeking solutions in an intelligent way. In an article I published in 1996, I listed a number of different skills which psychology graduates have, and which are useful in all sorts of working contexts. Those skills are listed in Table 1.2. As you can see, there are a lot of them; and they come about because psychology is such a complex subject to study and has so many different areas.

table 1.2 the skills acquired through psychology degrees

Literacy   Writing research reports, discussion papers and essays.

Numeracy   Statistical analysis and understanding.

Computer literacy   Using information technology of one sort or another.

Information-finding skills   Using databases, journals, libraries etc.

Research skills   Obtaining systematic scientific evidence.

Measurement skills   Operationalizing and designing complex measures.

Environmental awareness   Understanding how environments influence people.

Interpersonal awareness   Social communication and social skills.

Problem-solving skills   Sizing up situations and applying different strategies and approaches.

Critical evaluation   Appraising how adequate explanations of evidence are.

Perspectives   Exploring issues from several different angles.

Higher-order analysis   Spotting recurrent patterns and systems.

Pragmatism   Learning how to get on and make the best of things.

(Hayes, 1996)

Areas of psychology

Psychology, as we've seen, is about people. But people are complicated, and we need to gather information about them in many different ways. So studying psychology involves knowing something about each of the main areas of psychology. There are six of these, roughly speaking, and each one gives us a different kind of information, which we can use in our attempt to understand people.

One of the central areas of modern psychological knowledge is known as **cognitive psychology**. This has to do with how we gather and use information. It includes mental processes such as taking in information and making sense of it (a process we call perception), remembering things, or recognizing them, and also thinking and reasoning. These mental processes are known as cognition, which is how cognitive psychology gets its name. Psychologists studying cognition have discovered a great deal about how people's minds work, and that information is often useful when we are trying to understand why someone is acting in a particular way.

Another branch of psychology is concerned with understanding how people act when they are with other people, and it is known as **social psychology**. It ranges from looking at body language to understanding why people obey those in authority, or when they may or may not help someone in need. Social psychologists are also interested in how we make sense of our social experience. That part of social psychology is about the mental side of social life, so it is known as social cognition.

Some psychologists have been concerned with studying what makes people different from one another. Some people, for instance, seem to be more intelligent than others; some people are highly creative while other people are not, and each of us has our own special personality. We also differ in motivation: some people are keen to get ahead in life, while others are concerned mainly with establishing a happy home and family life. **Individual psychology** is concerned with what motivates people, as well as with how people are different from one another.

All this makes it seem as though understanding people is really just about looking at what they do, or how they process information. And that is a large part of it. But, sometimes, what we do or how we think is also influenced by our physical state. If we are tired or stressed, for instance, we often don't make decisions very well, or we can become irritable with the people around us. So an important part of psychology is concerned with understanding how our physiological state influences us, and this is known as **physiological psychology** or, sometimes, bio-psychology. Physiological psychologists look at areas like the effects of brain damage, how drugs work, sleep and dreaming, or understanding stress.

Each year that passes adds its store of experience and knowledge, but how do we use that experience? And do we inevitably decline as we get older? **Developmental psychology** is concerned with understanding how changes in childhood, adolescence, adulthood, and old age affect us, and what those changes actually involve. Interestingly, the picture which emerges when we really begin studying the processes of maturity and ageing are much more optimistic than society often assumes – but we will look into that in more detail in the appropriate chapter.

Comparative psychology, as its name suggests, is all about making comparisons. But what are we comparing ourselves with? As we know from evolutionary biology, human beings are a kind of animal – even if rather a special one. So that leads us to some very interesting questions about how close we are to other animals, and whether we have anything in common with them – or whether they have anything in common with us. Comparative psychologists are interested in animal behaviour in its own right, of course, but they are also interested in studying how animals interact with one another, because this might give us some clues in understanding human beings.

We can see, then, that psychology is really quite a broad topic. It also covers a great many levels of explanation, ranging from research at the molecular level as physiological psychologists investigate how drugs work in the brain, to research into the shared beliefs of whole cultures, as social psychologists investigate social representations. We'll be looking more closely at levels of explanation and also at how psychologists go about their research in the final chapter of this book. By then, I hope, you will have obtained your own ideas of what psychology is about, from the intervening chapters.

About this book

We'll begin our investigation of psychology by looking at ourselves and, in particular, how we connect with the social world in which we find ourselves, and how we understand other people. Then we will go on to explore more personal matters – emotions, states of mind, motivation and cognitions. Following that, we'll be looking at how our biological heritage influences us, in terms of evolution and also in terms of the many different ways that human beings are able to learn. Then we will look at some of the broad patterns of development which are apparent during childhood and adolescence, and on throughout our lifespans.

The next ten chapters, therefore, mainly cover psychological knowledge obtained from academic research. In the following four chapters you will have a taste of applied psychology – not in as much detail as in *Teach Yourself Applied Psychology*, of course, but enough to get a general idea of how psychology may be involved in working life, leisure, education and health, and the environment. Finally, Chapter 16 will take up some of the issues which we have glanced at here – how psychologists go about their research, the different levels of analysis which are used in psychology, and what is involved in becoming a professional psychologist.

We will begin our closer look at psychology by looking at ourselves and others, in Chapter 2.

02

self and others

In this chapter you will learn:
- why sociability in human babies is so important
- how other people can change the way we feel about ourselves
- to identify three different cultural approaches to understanding ourselves.

This chapter is about who we are and how we come to be that way. Each of us has a different life experience and we were each born with our own particular temperament and physique. These things all help to make us different from one another. Even newborn babies differ in their likes and dislikes. So we are all different from the start. But we also live in society, and as part of that, we learn how to act with other people, and how to recognize experiences that we have in common. We inherit a powerful tendency to be sociable and to learn from other people who matter to us. And that, just as much as our physical characteristics or temperament, is crucially important in who we are.

The first relationships

All over the world, babies are brought up in different ways. The experience of an Inuit child, living in a traditional community in the Arctic regions of northern Canada are widely different from the everyday experiences of an infant growing up in Papua New Guinea; and both of these are different from the experiences of a child growing up in Britain. In some communities babies are kept tightly wrapped up (swaddled), in others they wear few if any clothes; in some communities they are carried around continuously, while in others they spend most of their day in cots or beds. And in some communities they spend all their time with their mothers, while in others they are looked after by relatives, friends, or even older children.

Yet despite all these different conditions all over the world, babies grow and, if they survive, generally develop into mature, balanced adults. Human babies can adapt to a tremendous range of different environments and conditions. These differences in how they are looked after don't really matter, as long as a baby gets what it really needs for healthy development. And what it needs most of all is other people.

Human infants, when they are first born, are physically totally helpless. They have to be fed, cleaned and carried around by other, older humans, and without this they would not be able to survive. This physical helplessness continues for a very long time – far longer than in any other animal. On the face of it, it would seem as if luck, as much as anything else, is what helps babies to get through. But nature doesn't really work that way. As we will see in Chapter 8, the process of evolution means that we would develop only in a certain kind of way if it gave us an increased chance of surviving. And the human infant is actually a long way from being as helpless as it looks.

Sociability

Human infants are born supremely adapted for sociability. Being unable to move themselves, as well as being unable to cling to their mothers as many animals do, they depend completely on other people. Because of this, they are very strongly predisposed to interact with people – and this is true of babies all over the world. For example, when an infant is first born it is unable to change the focus of its eyes. However, those eyes have a fixed focus at just the right distance to allow the child to look at its mother's face while it is breast-feeding – and this is from the first day after birth.

Smiling

Human infants also begin to make facial expressions very soon after birth. These movements are often quite tiny, but their parents, who are used to the baby's face, can recognize them. A human infant inherits a tendency to smile when it sees something which resembles a human face – and as it gets older, the resemblance needs to be more and more exact. Ahrens (1954) showed that very young babies, in their first month or so, would smile when they saw an oval shape with two dots in it for eyes; but as the baby grew older, more detail was needed until by four months the infant would smile only at a real human face, or a very realistic picture.

For a parent, of course, being looked at and smiled at by your baby is an extremely special experience. It is very rewarding and so it means that the parent is more likely to want to spend time with the baby, playing with it and talking to it. And that interaction, as we will see, forms a strong foundation for the future relationship between a parent and its child.

Crying

Babies also have a very good way of summoning help when they need it. Since the human infant can't run for help itself, it needs to have a way of summoning help from its caretaker quickly. And it has. A baby's crying can penetrate for a very long distance, and people quickly learn to recognize the sound of their own baby's crying as opposed to that of any other infant.

Some psychologists believe, too, that there are special harmonics in a baby's cry which activate the autonomic nervous system, so that adults find it particularly disturbing. This means that they are particularly likely to hurry to the baby and try to calm it down. It might also account for the intense degree of frustration on the part of parents who are living with a continuously crying child, and who may sometimes become so frustrated and upset that they injure the child. We don't know whether this is really the case. We do know that people find baby cries extremely disturbing – that isn't under question – but it is possible that they disturb us because they are associated with pain and distress, and not because of the harmonic qualities of the sound.

In either case, though, the fact is that very few people can really ignore a baby crying. It is a very good way for the infant to communicate the fact that it needs help. Moreover, infants can communicate more than one message through crying. Wolff (1969) recorded baby cries and analysed them using a sound spectrograph, showing that there were at least three different types of cry, with three different patterns of sound: one for pain, one for hunger, and one for anger. And the mothers were perfectly able to recognize the message in their own baby's crying.

So even an apparently helpless infant is equipped to be sociable. It responds to the sound of people's voices, it shows pleasure when people are nearby, and it can summon help if it needs it. The baby's physical survival depends on the people around it, and so the baby needs to be able to interact with people too.

Parent–infant interaction

As it grows older, the baby's tendency towards sociability becomes even more apparent. Babies delight in even the simplest repetitive games with another person. As any parent knows, they will play games like 'peek-a-boo', or 'throw-your-teddy-out-of-the-cot-and-see-daddy-pick-it-up' for as long as the adult is prepared to carry on playing, even though they rarely show so much persistence with games that they play on their own, such as with rattles or toys.

Parents and other adults almost automatically seem to adapt themselves to these baby games. Psychologists have conducted many observations of parent–child interaction, and found that most of the things which parents and infants do when they are playing together help the baby to learn skills it will need in childhood and later life. But for many people, this is entirely unconscious: we do it automatically, without thinking.

One thing which people do when they are playing with a baby, for instance, is that they make faces. Carefully analysed video-tape of these games shows that the babies make faces too. Parent and infant imitate one another, and these exchanges can go on for some time. It is games like these which set the foundation for later social experience. Infants learn how to take turns and how to wait for the other person to respond before doing their action – which is like the turn-taking that occurs in conversation, and which even involves the same kind of timing. Moreover, they learn it very quickly: we are strongly predisposed to learn that kind of thing.

Infants are also strongly predisposed to learn to communicate. They want to do it, and try to do it very hard. Again, we help them automatically. Psychological studies of baby-talk have shown that the special way that human beings talk to babies, which is so often ridiculed by comedians, actually helps the baby to notice speech. The softened tones and higher notes that we use are particularly easy for the baby to hear, and the repetition of vowel sounds ('baa-baa') draws attention to the part of the language which the child learns to produce first.

What all this adds up to is that other people are the most important thing in a child's world. A human baby may be physically helpless, but it is not at all helpless in terms of its social abilities. It is already equipped with some social skills, and learns new ones even faster than it learns physical co-ordination. People are the most important thing in an adult's world too – at least for all of us except a few very exceptional individuals. And what infant sociability does is to form the foundation for the personal attachments and relationships which we all need in later life.

Developing attachments

It used to be believed that infants developed attachments with the people who looked after them purely because of the association with physical care and satisfying hunger. This led to a number of debates, such as whether mothers should go out to work, and similar issues. However, as a result of these debates, psychologists began to study relationship development very carefully and found that things weren't nearly as simple as that. For one thing, many babies develop special attachments to more than one person, and sometimes they will develop a special relationship with someone that they only see for a relatively short period each day. In the pioneering study by Shaffer and Emerson, conducted in 1964, the psychologists found that many of the infants in the families that they were studying had special attachments with their fathers, who were out at work all day, as well as with their mothers, who in this particular study were at home. Other babies though, didn't form attachments with their fathers. And some formed attachments with the fathers, but not with their mothers, even though it was the mother who was with them most of the time.

What made the difference? Shaffer and Emerson found, as have many psychologists since, that it was the quality of social interaction between parent and child which affected the infant's response. Babies become especially fond of parents (and other people) who are sensitive to the signals they are giving out – smiling and other facial expressions, movements and so on – and who are prepared to interact with them in their playing. They don't develop attachments to people who just care for them physically but don't play with them or talk to them.

Even though parents become attached to their infants very quickly, it takes longer for the infant to develop its own attachment. Although infants often prefer to be with one person rather than someone else, in the first few months they are rarely distressed if their special person is not present. Psychologists found that the full attachment would appear at about seven months. Then, the baby would cry if the person had to leave – although of course babies can usually be distracted quite quickly.

This attachment forms the basis of the loving relationship between parent and child which persists throughout life (if it is not actively disrupted). And that attachment, in its turn, has been based on the quality of the interactions between the parent and the baby. Of course, that doesn't mean that an attachment has to be based on that – as adopted children know, a relationship which begins later in life can be just as special. But a predisposition to interact with people, and to form relationships with the people who respond to you sensitively is one which is common to human infants all over the world. It is, quite literally, part of our heritage as human beings.

The self-concept

In later life, too, other people are more important to us than we sometimes realize. Each of us has our own, personal idea of ourselves – something which is known as the **self-concept**. On the surface, it seems as if we should develop our knowledge of ourselves from our own personal experiences of what we can do, and what we like. However, when psychologists have studied the self-concept, they have found that one of the most important factors in how we see ourselves is how other people see us.

Social relationships

As early as 1902, Cooley described the self-concept as the 'looking-glass self'. What Cooley meant was that we see ourselves as if we were reflected in the eyes of other people. We don't just think of ourselves in terms of our own personal knowledge: we judge what we are like by the way that other people respond to us, and what we think they may think.

Guthrie (1938) related a story about a group of students who decided to play a joke on a class member – a girl who was very plain and unattractive. The male students in the class took it in turns to ask her out and treated her as if she were attractive and interesting. Guthrie observed that the students who were fifth and sixth on the list were actually quite interested in taking the girl out, because by that time, she had changed considerably. The extra interest that she was receiving had raised her self-confidence and now she was interesting to talk to and took pains to make herself look attractive.

The self-fulfilling prophecy

What this shows is that sometimes other people's ideas about us may become a **self-fulfilling prophecy**. In other words, what we think about someone may come true simply because we think it. One of the most striking illustrations of this mechanism was reported by Rosenthal and Jacobson, in 1968. They had gone into an ordinary high school in America, ostensibly to test out a new kind of intelligence test. On the basis of the test which they gave (which was really just a standard one) and class marks, they chose a number of ordinary children whose performance in class was only average. They didn't speak to the children directly – instead, they let the teachers 'overhear' a conversation in which these children were named as being likely to show a sudden spurt in their academic work over the next year. The teachers also believed that the intelligence test they had used was a special one, designed to pick out these late developers.

When Rosenthal and Jacobson returned to the school a year later, they found that the children they had chosen were up at the top of their classes. Because the teachers believed that they would do well, they had given them extra encouragement. The children didn't know anything about the teachers' beliefs, but they had felt the encouragement, and worked harder. They had also become more confident about their ability to learn. So the prophecy which Rosenthal and Jacobson had made – that the children would improve during the course of the next year – had come true simply because they had said it.

Self-image and self-esteem

Many other psychologists, too, have found that the self-concept depends on the type of interaction that we have with other people and on the expectations that they have of us. The self-concept is often thought of as having two different parts. One of these is a descriptive part, which is just about what we are like: tall, being good at languages, liking sport, and so on. That part is known as the **self-image**. The other is an evaluative part, which makes judgements about whether we are good, bad, worthwhile and so on. That part of the self-concept is known as our **self-esteem**. And that is the part which can be most influential in shaping our relationships with others.

Personal relationships

Carl Rogers, the famous psychologist who is known as the father of counselling psychology, argued that our level of self-esteem depends on the type of personal relationships that we have had. People, Rogers argued, have two basic psychological needs, and will suffer psychological damage if those needs are not met. One of those needs is the need for **positive regard** from other people – affection, love, trust, and so on. Everyone, Rogers argued, needs positive regard of some kind. Even people who avoid close relationships find it important that other people should respect them. To have some kind of positive regard from other people is a very fundamental need, which has to be satisfied.

The other fundamental need which has to be satisfied is the need for **self-actualization**. Self-actualization means making real ('actualizing') the different parts of the self – in other words, exploring and developing our ideas, abilities, interests and talents. This is a fundamental need in people too: without any way of developing our abilities or skills, we can become psychologically damaged.

People self-actualize in many different ways. Many people have a hobby or an interest which takes up some of their leisure time, and this usually involves some kind of skill, or problem-solving. Fiddling with a car engine, playing video games or darts, baking, sewing clothes, or conducting a successful children's party are all highly skilled activities. We enjoy doing them, and doing them well gives us a sense of achievement and satisfaction. It helps us to feel good about ourselves.

So far, so good. Most people have family, friends and working colleagues who provide them with the positive regard which they need; and hobbies, interests and, if they are lucky, challenging jobs to satisfy their need for self-actualization. And for that reason, Rogers argued, most people have a reasonably high level of self-esteem. While they don't see themselves as being perfect, they are reasonably content with being who they are.

However, Rogers was working as a clinical psychologist and came across a lot of people who weren't in that position. In these patients, Rogers found that the two needs contradicted one another. Their need for positive regard, or approval from other people, was in direct conflict with their need for self-actualization. These people had come to Rogers because they were suffering with neurotic problems. From his clinical observations and treatments, Rogers concluded that these problems occurred because they were suppressing such an important psychological need.

Conditional positive regard

When Rogers explored the childhood which these people had experienced, he found that they all had one thing in common. They had all grown up with parents or others who had made their positive regard conditional on good behaviour. In other words, when they were naughty or had misbehaved – as children often do – they had received a very clear message that they were unloved and unwanted. 'Normal' people, though, had parents who, even if they were strict, always made it clear that they still loved their child.

Those children who had grown up with conditional positive regard were actually being given a message that it wasn't really them who was loved – it was some ideal, perfect child who was never naughty. So they grew up believing that they had to be ideal and perfect, and that if they were not, nobody would like them. What this meant was that they needed approval from other people so much that they wouldn't risk exploring their own interests, in case other people didn't like it or didn't approve. They stifled their own personal ambitions, interests or talents – in other words, their need for self-actualization – in order to be sure of social approval.

These people, as we can see, had very low self-esteem. They had developed unrealistic **conditions of worth** – that is, unrealistic ideas about what they needed to do to gain social approval or respect. And they applied these unrealistic conditions of worth when they were judging their own behaviour. Even if they were really quite successful, they still thought of themselves as failures, or as inferior to other people. Naturally, all this had made them very anxious, and eventually neurotic.

Unconditional positive regard

The solution which Rogers found was very simple. He argued that everyone needs some kind of secure psychological base from which they can develop. That base will be found in a relationship which gives them **unconditional positive regard** – positive regard which doesn't depend on how the person acts. If you really love, trust or like someone, then you accept the decisions which they make about how they are living their life. That doesn't mean, of course, that we have to condone things which are morally wrong. But we can dislike what someone does, and make that clear, without disliking that particular person. As parents do all the time.

However, Rogers found that it isn't only parents who can provide this kind of relationship. In fact, we can experience this kind of relationship at any age, and it can provide us with the security that we need to begin to self-actualize. Many people in adult life find relationships which give them that security, and begin to explore aspects of themselves which they have ignored before – like people who go to college for the first time in their thirties or forties. The important thing is to have a relationship of that kind at all – it doesn't have to be in childhood.

Rogers developed an approach to psychotherapy based on this principle. The role of the therapist, he argued, should be to provide an accepting and warm relationship for the client (he didn't approve of the word 'patient') – in other words, a relationship based on unconditional positive regard. This would give the client the psychological freedom to make their own life decisions and to develop solutions to their own problems, because they wouldn't be risking disapproval. Rogers called this **client-centred therapy**, because it is entirely based on what the client wants and does, and not on what the therapist thinks they should do. Many counselling psychologists still use this approach today.

Cultural and social influences

We can see, then, that both our social interaction and our personal relationships can have a considerable effect on how we see ourselves – on the self-concept. But our ideas about ourselves and how we are linked with other people are also shaped by the social groups and cultures that we belong to. And different cultures can make very different assumptions about individuals and what it is to be an individual human being.

Cultural contexts of self

In the Western world, it is quite common to see each person as a separate individual, who may choose to link him/herself with some kind of social group if they want to. This model of the individual person has a long history: ultimately, it goes back to the philosophical systems of the ancient Greeks, and was reinforced by later philosophers such as Descartes, in the seventeenth century. The idea is also apparent in European history. The Protestant reformation, for example, emphasized the individual's own direct responsibility and conscience in religion, rather than the responsibility of the priesthood to interpret religion for the community.

It is open to question, though, whether any human being really can be such an entirely separate individual as all that. Most of us exist within a network of communities and social expectations: family, friendship groups, and occupational groups. Many people seek out communities to belong to: religious groups, communes, volunteer groups. In other words, we don't really exist as independent individuals: we live within social networks and groups. As we will see later in this chapter, belonging to these social groups can form a very important part of our sense of identity.

We do, though, tend to believe that it is important to be an individual. Being an individual involves making one's own decisions about one's life, partners, friends and career. And it is this belief which makes the Western approach rather different from most of the other cultures in the world.

Self embedded in community

For example, in most of the traditional African cultures, and in Native Australian cultures as well, the person is seen as being primarily a member of the community. That doesn't mean that they are not seen as being an individual person, but it does mean that how they live their life concerns the rest of the community as well, and isn't just their own responsibility. Individualism which doesn't concern itself with the community as a whole is seen as being irresponsible, and pretty well uncivilized.

When the Native Australian rock group Yothu Yindi began to have commercial success with their records, for instance, the decisions about how the group's career should go were all taken by the group's tribal community. As spokespeople for their culture, the members of the band had no wish to do anything else. The prominence of the band had brought increased acknowledgement and recognition of Native Australian culture to white Australian audiences (and later to worldwide ones). To the members of the group, it was important that they remain a part of their culture, rather than abandoning it and chasing success as individual musicians.

In other words, they regarded being part of their community an important part of being themselves – not just an optional extra. To people from such cultures, the idea of acting as an individual, separate from family, community and social group is simply unrealistic – and selfish, too. According to Mbiti (1970), the individual self is firmly located within the collective self of the tribe or people, and to try to separate them is to imply that the person operates only with half an identity.

Layers of self

A different concept of the self is apparent in Hindu belief systems. Bharati (1986) described how Hindu belief is centred around the idea of the self – but not the individual self-concept as it is in Western cultures. Instead, according to Hindu thinking, the innermost self or *atman* is at one with God: it is a central, spiritual self which everyone possesses, but which can be reached only through meditation and other techniques. Other, more superficial parts of the self also contain more superficial qualities like personality, and negative emotions such as jealousy or greed.

For the most part, therefore, what someone sees as their self-concept is really these outer layers of personality, and not their true, inner self. Only those who have disciplined themselves, through yoga or meditation, have access to the *atman* and can experience the true unity of the self and God.

So this idea of the self, too, is very different from the idea of the individual which is maintained by Western cultures. Although this view is not based on the importance of the culture and community, it still maintains the idea that there are other dimensions to the self: that there is more to being human than simply our own individual wishes and emotions.

The private self

Even within highly industrialized societies, there are different ideas of the self. Japanese people, for example, see the self as operating within a social context – but not a context of traditional family or tribe. Like city-dwelling Westerners, Japanese people may be meeting strangers all the time, but Japanese society places a great deal of emphasis on social consideration and social harmony. In order to maintain this, people are expected to keep inner emotions private, and to act in a socially acceptable manner at all times. Azuma, Hess and Kashiwagi (1981) described how this idea is apparent even in the experiences of a very young child in Japan.

At the age of two or thereabouts, as many parents know to their cost, children often become very wilful, insisting on getting their own way at every opportunity – or trying to. It is at this time that they have to learn social responsibility – or at least, that they cannot always have their own way in everything. Different cultures go about teaching this in different ways. Among traditional families of the Shona people of Africa, for instance, children of this age go to live with their grandmother, and stay with her until they are about five. So the more experienced family member is the one who tackles this difficult part of child-rearing. Western parents tend to confront their children, refusing to co-operate until the child eventually learns that it must moderate its behaviour.

A Japanese mother, though, doesn't tend to confront an egocentric two-year-old directly. Instead, she 'suffers' her child, making it very clear that its behaviour is causing her pain and distress. In this way, the child is brought to realize that its actions have social and emotional consequences for other people, even from a very early age. It is encouraged to feel responsible for the suffering that it has caused, and also guilty, so it learns self-control as a way of not causing the suffering and not having to feel the guilt. These messages are consistent throughout childhood and leave powerful influences on the adult's behaviour.

A Japanese person, then, is still regarded as an individual, but in a different way from Westerners. The self is essentially private, and the individual has extremely important social responsibilities which cannot be avoided. This means that, for the most part, personal wishes, emotions, and impulses need to be kept in check. The self is not independent of other people because it is easily able to cause grief or pain to them, through inconsiderate behaviour. Social interaction has to be managed in such a way as to minimize that grief or pain, and so minimize the guilt which the individual would feel for having caused it. The self is seen as existing in a social context, with social requirements, meaning that it often has to be kept private, or even secret.

We can see, then, that people in different parts of the world – and also in different subcultures within Western countries – have very different ideas of what it is to be an individual person. The idea of the individual as entirely separate from others is really quite an uncommon one. And even in Western cultures, we are not quite as immune from the influence of other people as all that.

Social identification

There is another way, too, in which other people affect the way that we see ourselves. We are all part of society, and each of us belongs to some social groups of some kind. Social groups can be large-scale, like gender or ethnic background groups; they can be medium-scale, like being an accountant or a machinery tuner in a mill; or they can be small-scale, like being a member of a local astronomy club. But whatever the size, belonging to different social groups has an influence on our sense of identity.

Social identity theory began in psychology with the work of Henri Tajfel, and has become a very useful way of understanding many important things about how human beings act. Tajfel pointed out how the social groups which we belong to exist in the real world, and vary in terms of things like how powerful they are, how widely known they are, and how much prestige there is in belonging to them. Because we all live in the real world too, we are aware of these differences. So, for example, if we belong to a local astronomy society and are aware that, in that local town, the astronomy society is quite respected, then we would feel proud of belonging to it.

Moreover, belonging to that particular social group would be part of our own identity – part of who we are. Sometimes, we would interact with other people as a member of that group, for example, speaking up for the group, or giving the members' point of view when we were talking with someone who didn't belong to it. We can slip into that particular social identity when it seems to be relevant.

At other times, a different social identity might be the relevant one. An argument about who should do the washing up might begin as just a discussion between two partners. However, if one of them makes a remark about gender, it can rapidly change from being a personal argument, to a confrontation between 'men' and 'women', with each person arguing as a representative of their gender group, rather than as their individual self.

Categorization and self-esteem

We all have a number of different social identities. According to Tajfel, social identities come from our basic human tendency to sort things into different categories. We categorize other people as well as other things: this person is a typical Volvo driver, that person is a rock fan, and so on. And we include our own groups – the ones that we belong to – in the classification.

However, there is more to it than that, because it is also a basic human tendency to look for sources of positive self-esteem. In other words, it is important for us to feel good about our own groups – we need to be able to feel proud of belonging to them. If our group doesn't have much status, then we often try to redefine it so that we can see it as more important. But if we can't do that, then we will try to leave the group, or at the very least, pretend that we are not like the other members of it.

For example, imagine that you are a teenager and have a particular hobby, say, trampolining, which you really enjoy. Moreover, you are really getting quite good and have passed various certificates. But then you join a new school and it becomes apparent that your new friends there see it as an inferior kind of sport. What would you do?

Actually, there are several possibilities which are open to you – and all of them amount to ways of keeping positive self-esteem. You might leave the trampolining group altogether and look for some other hobby which will be a bit more respected. You might claim that you only go because of parental pressure, or because your younger brother likes to go and you have to take him, or something like that. That would be distancing yourself from the group – implying that you aren't really like the others.

Changing the status of the group

Alternatively, you might try to get your friends to change their view of it, for example by pointing out that it actually involves a very high level of skill. Or you might argue that it is a great deal better than other kinds of recreational activity that some people do. Both of these are attempts to change the perceived status of the trampolining group, so that it becomes more respected. Or you could change your friends and associate only with other people who also do trampolining and know how skilled it is.

This is a fairly small-scale example, but exactly the same processes take place in larger social groups too. It is now much easier for a black child, for example, to grow up being proud of being black than it was 50 years ago. There are far more black people doing responsible, professional jobs, or holding highly respected positions in society than there used to be, which helps. There are also many people in the public eye who are proud of being black, and ready to say so.

This is because over the past 50 years a great many black people have been deliberately changing the perceived status of their group, by challenging stereotypes and discrimination whenever they encounter it. This has had its effect. There is still racism, of course, and still a lot to do, but the general view in Western society is very different from the view which was commonly held – even by black people – 50 years ago.

We can see, then, that who we are and how we see ourselves, is very closely linked with the ways in which we interact with other people. We all have our own personal likes, dislikes, talents and personalities. But we also exist in a network of social interaction, and have done so since we were very small babies. Other people's reactions and ideas matter to us, and they influence how we go about acting in life. Our cultural background also shapes how we see ourselves, and so do our social identities. None of us is totally patterned by these social influences – after all, everyone is different – but we are not totally independent of them either.

03

understanding other people

In this chapter you will learn:
- how children develop social sensitivity
- to identify at least two ways of analysing communication between people
- a psychological reason why we might disobey an order we do not agree with.

In the last chapter, we looked at how belonging to social groups can influence our sense of identity, and our dealings with other people. In this chapter, we will look more closely at the branch of psychology known as social psychology – the study of how we interact with other people. We will look at how we communicate with other people, why we sometimes help others and sometimes don't, and when we are likely to co-operate or obey. There are other aspects of social psychology in other chapters, as well – for example, in Chapter 4 we will be looking at some of the social influences involved in our experience of emotion, and in Chapter 6 we will be looking at social motivation. Human beings are social animals and so social influences affect just about everything we do, in one way or another.

Co-operation and compliance

Other people are very important to us in all sorts of ways, sometimes even when they aren't actually present. For example, we often regulate what we do by imagining what other people would think if they knew about it. That type of social influence is very strong, even when we are alone and nobody else would know. It has become **internalized**, as part of the way that our minds work. We don't actually have to see someone react to what we are doing: we use what we know about people to predict or imagine how they will respond.

The predictions we make aren't always accurate, either. For example, people often avoid disagreeing openly with someone else because they imagine that doing so will have more dramatic consequences than it really would. They think the other person might become upset or angry. In fact, we seem to spend a lot of time avoiding other people's imaginary anger, although if we do actually confront someone and disagree with them, it isn't nearly as difficult as all that.

Conforming to the majority

Asch (1952) showed just how hard we try to avoid disagreeing openly with other people. He set up a situation in which several people were asked to sit in the same room and to judge whether various lines they were shown were longer or shorter than a test line. The tasks were very easy, but most of the people in the room were actors who had been told to give obviously wrong answers. One unsuspecting person was the real research participant on each occasion. That person could see what the right answer was, but also heard all the other people in the room giving the wrong answer – and the same wrong answer at that! So the participants were forced into a situation where they either had to disagree with the others or lie.

Asch found that about a third of the time the research participants would give the same wrong answer as the others. And even when they gave the right answer, it was clear that they found disagreeing with the others very difficult. They became extremely nervous and tense just before it was their turn to speak, regardless of whether they told the truth or not. Later, they said that they had given the correct answer only because they knew it was an experiment and they felt it was their duty to report it accurately. Clearly, disagreeing openly with other people is something they found very difficult.

A later study of the 'Asch effect', conducted by Perrin and Spencer (1980) found that fewer people actually lied, but that they all became just as anxious. Perrin and Spencer suggested that perhaps fewer people lied because modern people are more independent and less likely to conform to other people. But other researchers challenged this idea on the grounds that when they, too, had repeated the study, they had found the 'Asch effect' to be as strong as ever.

The debates about how much people actually conform and how much they don't, continue. But all of the researchers, no matter when they did the study, found that openly disagreeing with other people was deeply stressful. Their research participants reported that they only did it because they believed it was important to tell the truth for the experiment. It isn't at all easy for human beings to disagree openly with other people.

Minority influence

Sometimes, though, it's important to disagree. All the great social reforms which took place in the eighteenth century, for instance, began as the dedicated campaigns of a handful of people who saw something wrong, and did not let it rest. Slavery was widely accepted in Europe in the eighteenth century, for instance, but as a result of consistent campaigning the slave trade was made illegal near the beginning of the nineteenth century, and the owning of slaves became illegal a few years later.

So it's clear that sometimes a minority can have quite a lot of influence. Moscovici and Nemeth (1974) showed that if just a few people stick to a particular view, which they are convinced is right, then over time they can have a great deal of influence on a larger group. The important thing, though, is that those people who are in a minority and trying to influence the majority should be seen to be consistent, and to be resisting social pressure. If we see people acting like that, we often become curious about why they are doing it and so we are likely to think more seriously about what they are saying than we might have done.

Understanding other people

We actually spend quite a lot of time thinking about what other people are going to think, as the study of conformity shows. In other words, we are aware that other people have minds of their own, and we use our social experience to guess how they will use those minds. From a very young age, we develop what is known as a **theory of mind** – an awareness of other people as thinking, feeling individuals – which we use to interact effectively with other people.

The child's theory of mind

But how does that theory of mind develop? As most mothers know, a two-year-old isn't really aware that other people have minds or needs of their own. Bringing up children at that age can often become a battle of wills, as the infant insists that the world must conform to its own demands, while the parent insists that the child must learn to act in socially acceptable ways. It can be an exhausting time, particularly because the child doesn't seem to have any idea about how the other person might be feeling.

Yet, by the age of five, children are very well acquainted with the idea that other people may think differently from them, that they have good and bad moods, and can be upset or made happy by the child's actions. It's obvious that something happens during this time which allows the child to become much more socially sensitive. Between the age of three and four the child develops its own theory of mind. It becomes aware that other people think and see the world differently and that its own experience isn't necessarily shared by everyone else.

Perner, Leekam and Wimmer (1987) looked at how three-year-olds understand what other people believe. The three-year-old would be in a room and aware that a friend was waiting outside. Then the child was shown a Smarties tube and asked what was in it. The child, naturally, would answer 'Smarties'. The tube was opened and the child saw that it actually only contained a pencil. Then it was closed again and the children were asked what their friend would think was in the box, if they came into the room now.

There was a difference in children's answers, depending on how old they were. Those who were just three gave one type of answer, whereas those who were nearly four gave a different one. The older children could predict what their friend would think and said that the friend would believe that the box contained Smarties. The younger children, however, said that the friend would think that the box contained a pencil. Because they hadn't yet developed a theory of mind, they couldn't imagine that the friend would think differently.

Having a theory of mind – being able to put ourselves in someone else's place, mentally – is the basis for almost all social interaction. Harris (1989) discussed how this seems to be the problem with autistic children. They can often talk and do everything that is needed for social interaction, and yet they don't interact socially. They also fail on tests like the Smarties experiment. Harris suggested that autistic children simply don't have a theory of mind, which is why they can't really communicate or make contact with anyone else.

Communication

The experience of autistic children shows us how one of the most important aspects of interaction is the way in which we communicate with other people. Deliberate communication depends on being able to guess what the other person will think, so that we can make our messages clear. If we don't know that the other person is thinking independently, we can't engage in the give-and-take which conversation needs.

Non-verbal communication

Communication isn't always deliberate, though. We pass information to one another in all sorts of ways, and sometimes we may not even realize that we have done it. We influence other people by what we say, of course, but also by how we say it, and the context in which we say it. This type of communication is known as **non-verbal communication** – communication without words.

As a general rule, we use these aspects of communication automatically, without particularly thinking about them. For example, imagine that one day you came into work and were told to go to the general manager's office. When you arrived there, you would be trying to understand what the manager was trying to communicate to you. The first thing you'd want to know, of course, is whether there was trouble coming. You might also be curious about the whole action, if it was unusual for the general manager to summon people like that. And you'd probably be rather anxious.

There are several features of that situation which are forms of communication. In fact, the actual words that the manager used would be only a small part of what was being communicated. You would listen to them, of course, but you would also be taking notice of all of the other messages which were being transmitted as well. We are all experts at non-verbal communication, even if we don't always realize it.

You would, for instance, be getting messages – consciously or unconsciously – from the manager's body language. You'd notice whether she seemed angry, or tense, or worried, and you'd pick up on that without any words being said. If she smiled at you as soon as you came through the door, you would be reassured because that would be a non-verbal message to tell you that you, personally, weren't in trouble.

You'd also be taking notice of the particular tone of voice which she used because that's another important signal. Facial expressions, posture, gestures and tones of voice are all important indicators of our feelings and attitudes. In any interpersonal situation it is important for us to pick up on feelings and attitudes, if only so that we can get some idea as to how we should be responding to them.

Signs and symbols

There are other messages in that situation, too. Human life is full of signs and symbols which convey different meanings to us. For example, the fact of being summoned to the general manager's office is in itself a message. Who says and does what and to whom is often a communication about power. If the general manager had come to see you, at your workplace, that would give an entirely different message, and would be a signal that, on this occasion, the manager wanted issues of power left out of the discussion, or at least minimized. In the normal run of things it would signify that she wanted to consult with you, or gain your opinion.

But being summoned to the office is quite different. It is a message about who is in control of the interaction: who has the power. Similar messages are also communicated by the layout of the office and where people sit. Typically, a general manager sits behind a large desk – a symbolic barrier, as well as a symbol of power – and has access to all sorts of devices which can be used to control the situation: telephones, computers, intercoms and the like. The person who has been summoned, however, has nothing like that to hand.

This example is only the tip of the iceberg. Non-verbal communication has been studied extensively by psychologists because there are so many different ways in which we communicate messages to one another, and so many messages contained within any episode of human interaction.

Believing non-verbal signals

One of the most interesting findings has been that people tend to believe non-verbal communication far more than they believe the words that we actually say. In one study, Argyle, Alkema and Gilmour asked actors to communicate different messages to people. Following that, the people (not the actors) were asked to report what they had been told. The actual words of the messages were either friendly, hostile or neutral. The non-verbal manner in which the actors delivered the messages could also be friendly, hostile or neutral, but the two didn't always match up.

When the actor's manner and words carried the same implications, there was very little misunderstanding of the message, which wasn't surprising. But it was different when the actor's non-verbal communication contradicted the words that they actually said. When that happened, the researchers found that people were four times more likely to take notice of the non-verbal communication, than the actual words which were used.

Discourse analysis

It's apparent, then, that we are very prepared to take in non-verbal information, and that we consider it important. But we do listen to what people say as well, and again we may take in more than we realize. People often convey quite a lot of extra information in the actual words that they choose, as well as the way in which they say them. Looking at how people express themselves has become a major source of interest in modern psychology. It's known as **discourse analysis**, because the researchers who are doing it are analysing the patterns of discourse or conversation.

For example, Beattie and Speakman (1983) showed how people who are discussing complex topics like politics or the state of society often try out different images, and then settle on a single metaphor. Using the same type of image helps them to picture the problems that they are discussing and identify possible solutions. One common metaphor which people use in that context, for example, involves describing the country's economy as if it were a sick person, by using phrases like 'an ailing economy' or the need for an 'injection' of capital, as if capital is a kind of medicine which will help to 'cure' the problem.

The sickness metaphor isn't the only one people use. A different group of people might refer to the economy as if it were, say, a garden, and talk about 'cultivating growth', or 'pruning surplus expenditure'. That particular metaphorical frame for a conversation would lead to different conclusions than a metaphorical frame based on illness, because a garden is something which has to be consistently cared for and looked after, while an illness has to be cured. The metaphors which people use actually contain different theories about what a 'normal' economy is like. So by listening to the pattern of words which people use, we can get an insight into how they understand or make sense of the problem that they are discussing.

Attributions and explanations

Another part of discourse analysis involves looking directly at the explanations which people give for why things happen. We all have to make sense out of our social experience, and explanations are an important part of that. We don't just accept what happens to us passively – we try to work out why it has happened, and whether we could have done anything about it.

Finding a reason why something has happened often involves making decisions about intentionality: did so-and-so do that deliberately, or was it just an accident? We also draw on our knowledge of other people and on more general social explanations and assumptions in forming these explanations.

The process of ascribing reasons for why things happened and why people acted in certain ways is known as **attribution**.

In Chapter 4 we will look at how the different kinds of attributions people make can influence our behaviour. As we will see, people who are chronically depressed often have a depressive attributional style, which means that the explanations they give for why things happen are always the kind of explanations which will make them feel helpless and out of control. Other people tend to use different kinds of explanations, which allow them to see themselves as able to act positively and to be in control of things.

One of the interesting things about how we use attributions is that we tend to judge other people's actions differently from the way we judge our own. When we are giving reasons for what we do, we make what are known as **situational attributions** – in other words, we give reasons which are to do with the situation. For example, Nisbett *et al.* (1973) asked college students to write a paragraph explaining why they had chosen to study their particular course at college. The students all gave situational reasons, such as saying that doing the course would help them to get a better job.

But when we are judging someone else's actions, we generally use **dispositional attributions** – we conclude that the reason why they are doing something is because of their personality or character. When the same students were asked to explain why their best friend had chosen to study that particular course, they gave dispositional reasons, such as 'he's good at maths', or 'he likes studying rocks'.

Our tendency to make dispositional attributions about other people is very strong. It's known as the **fundamental attribution error**, and we do it even when we know that the situation is really the most important thing. Ross, Amabile and Steinmetz (1977) asked people to observe a quiz game. They also observed how the people playing the game were chosen: it was entirely random whether someone acted as a contestant or as the quizmaster. The quizmasters had free choice of subject, so they could choose topics that they knew about. But even though the observers knew that, they always judged the person asking the questions as having a greater general knowledge than the contestant. They knew about the situational factors, but still believed that the person's disposition was more important.

Social representations

The types of reason that we use to explain why things happen are not always entirely personal. Often we will adopt explanations which are shared by other people as well, or which are held to be true by society in general. These shared explanations are known as **social representations** and can be a very powerful influence in society. A social representation is a kind of theory about why things happen, but it is shared by a lot of people, rather than just one individual.

The social representations that we share influence how we act. For example, in a study of medical social representations, Herzlich showed how some doctors tend to see all problems which are brought to them as having physical causes, while other doctors see many problems as having psychological causes. They recommended entirely different forms of treatment for the same kinds of problem, depending on which social representations they held.

Cultural differences in social representations

Social representations are also influential in determining social policy. For example, in Britain, the prevailing social representation is that people become criminals because of something inside themselves – because they are inherently bad in some way. This means that we tend to ignore, or discount, serious attempts to rehabilitate criminals, because we don't believe it will work. And even when we try a rehabilitation scheme, we don't usually give it enough time or resources for a long-term effect.

However, other societies have different social representations. Unlike Britain, for instance, American society has a general social representation that people can change – that they don't stay the same all their lives. (That doesn't mean that everyone in America believes that, of course, but it means that most people do, or at least that social policies have been based on that idea.) So in America, rehabilitation units attempt to develop re-education programmes which will help criminals to change their ways.

I remember once being at a conference on child abuse and watching an argument between an English and an American professional working in this area. The American woman ran a rehabilitation centre for young men who were sexual abusers of children. The centre had a very intensive treatment programme which took a couple of years to complete. It was carefully worked out and was very arduous to go through, but it also had a very high success rate.

The argument between the Englishwoman and the American, though, wasn't about exchanging information about the programme. Essentially, it was a clash of social representations. The Englishwoman simply did not believe that child sexual abusers could change their ways, and the American woman knew, from her own experience, that they could. So she became very frustrated with the discussion and ended up almost jumping up and down (though not quite – it was a professional conference, after all!) because she couldn't understand why she was unable to get her point across.

People with different social representations often end up talking past one another, like those two women. Di Giacomo (1980) looked at the social representations held by student political leaders in a Belgian university in the 1970s, and compared them with the social representations shared by most of the ordinary students. Di Giacomo found that the two groups had very different social representations, and so they entirely failed to understand one another.

In some ways, Di Giacomo reported, it was almost as if the student leaders were talking a different language from the ordinary students. They would use phrases like 'student–worker solidarity', but the majority of the ordinary students couldn't see what students and workers had in common at all. So to them, the idea of solidarity between students and workers didn't make much sense. As a result, when the student leaders tried to mobilize the students in a protest movement they failed to get enough support for the movement to be successful.

Helping other people

How we explain things to ourselves also has quite an influence on how we interact with other people. For example, if we come across someone who is asking for help, whether we actually step in and help them or not depends on how we define the situation. If we conclude that the situation isn't really serious, then we are much less likely to help the person than if we define it differently.

Darley and Latané (1970) conducted a study in which an actor went up to people passing by on the street and asked them to give him ten cents. People responded differently, depending on what the actor said about why it was necessary. As you can see from Table 3.1, the more 'worthy' the person's cause seemed to be, the more likely people were to give him the money.

table 3.1 reasons for helping

Reason	Percentage of people asked who gave money
No reason given	34%
Money needed for a phone call	64%
Wallet stolen	70%

(adapted from Darley and Latané, 1970)

The way other people act – other bystanders, that is – also influences whether we are likely to offer help to strangers. The same psychologists set up a situation in which people who were sitting in a waiting room heard a crash from the next room, and a woman's voice crying out for help. When someone was waiting alone, they were very likely to go into the next room to see if they could help – in fact, 70 per cent of the people in that situation did so. But if there were three other people in the waiting room as well, then they were much less likely to go and help. Only 40 per cent of the research participants offered help under those conditions.

When they were interviewed afterwards, the people participating in the study said that they had taken their cues from the other people around. Because they seemed to be reasonably calm, the person had come to the conclusion that the situation wasn't really serious and so hadn't bothered to do anything. They had redefined the situation to themselves, so that it seemed as though help wasn't really needed after all. Also, they felt that the responsibility was somehow shared with the other people around, so it was less important that they offered their personal help than it was when they were alone.

We can see, then, that whether we actually exert ourselves to go and help someone depends on how we explain what is going on to ourselves. Having an unclear situation, or having other people around, can make a difference. Nonetheless, if we are sure that someone really does need help, we do tend to help them. In a study on the New York subway, Piliavin *et al.* found that commuters would usually help someone who collapsed on the train. If the person seemed to be ill, he was helped 95 per cent of the time, and even if he seemed to be drunk, people helped out on half of the occasions that he 'collapsed'.

Obedience

As we saw earlier in this chapter, co-operating with other people is something which we tend to do almost automatically – at least when those other people are present. When we're away from other people, or after we've had time to think about it, whether we co-operate or not may be quite another matter. But the tendency to avoid disagreement and confrontation is strong, and some studies show that even if other people aren't present, we may still be likely to go along with what we think other people might say.

In 1954, Crutchfield reported a study that was conducted during a management training session, with a number of military officers. It was a replication of the study by Asch, which we looked at earlier, in that people were asked to give answers to a set of very easy problems, while believing that other people also taking part were all giving the same wrong answer.

In Crutchfield's study, though, the other people were not physically present. The research participants worked in booths, with a display of lights in front of them which supposedly told them what the other people had chosen. (The lights were rigged, of course, so that they implied that the others had got the answer wrong). But even though the other people doing the study weren't actually there, so there was no need to confront them face to face, the research participants still conformed to the majority view half of the time.

Of course, it is always possible that this is a higher figure than we might normally get in those circumstances, because of the research participants all being military personnel. It's possible that, because of their training, they valued conformity more than other people would. But at the same time, they also valued accurate perception and knew that the answers they were giving were wrong. So it does seem as though our tendency to conform to other people is more than simply avoiding face-to-face interpersonal conflict.

Obeying authority

But what happens when that type of situation could mean that we end up doing something which is morally wrong? We usually obey authority figures, sometimes even if we disagree personally with what they are asking us to do. But would we obey them if they were asking us to, say, give someone a lethal electric shock? The social psychologist Milgram asked that question to a sample of psychologists, psychiatrists, and other people in the early 1960s. All of them were positive that only a very small minority of people – fewer than 3 per cent – would be prepared to kill or seriously harm another person in obedience to the demands of a psychological experiment.

So Milgram decided to set up the situation. Not to kill people, but to set it up so that people would believe their actions were being seriously harmful, even though nobody would actually be hurt. He advertised for volunteers and, when they arrived, they were told that it was an experiment about punishment and learning. The volunteers were to act as 'experimenters', and to give increasing electric shocks to a 'subject' in the next room by pressing switches each time the 'subject' got an answer wrong.

The switches were clearly labelled as being of increasing severity, and went up to 450 volts; and the 'subject' (who was really an actor) said at the beginning of the study that he had a weak heart. Both the labels on the switches and the sounds which came from the other room implied that the person was in serious pain as the voltage increased, before the victim fell ominously silent. Even then, the 'experimenter' was told to keep giving the shocks by a grey-coated supervisor who oversaw the whole operation and insisted that they should continue.

Milgram found that nearly two-thirds of the people he tested would carry on obeying the supervisor even to the very highest shock level. That didn't mean that they liked doing it: they would argue and point out that the 'subject' needed help, and try to refuse to do any more. They became very distressed indeed. But the supervisor would insist that they continue, and in the end they would obey.

People who disobey

A third of the people in the study, however, refused to obey once things reached the point where they felt that the 'subject' was in danger. They would simply and calmly refuse. When they were interviewed afterwards, these people generally turned out to have had some previous experience with unthinking obedience and what it could do. One of them had been brought up in Nazi Germany, for instance. These people made disobeying, and acting in accordance with their own conscience, seem a very ordinary thing to do. They simply made up their minds that to go any further would be wrong and ignored all of the pressure which was put on them to continue.

It's apparent, therefore, that we can either act as independent people in accord with our own conscience, or we can simply do what we are told. But in many ways, we are trained to do what we are told far more than we are encouraged to act independently. Throughout school we are trained to obey authority and in later life, too, there are people whom we are expected to obey without question, such as police officers. When this goes together with our natural tendency to conform to other people, we can see why most people would obey in a situation like that, even if they didn't want to.

There were a lot of things about the situation which encouraged obedience, too, such as the way that each electric shock was only a little bit stronger than the one before. That made it very hard for someone to draw a line and say, 'I won't go any further', because what they were being asked to do next wasn't very different from what they had already done. The people who were aware of the dangers of unquestioning obedience, though, stopped anyway when they felt they had gone far enough. They knew, in their own minds, that to go further would be wrong and that was enough. They didn't feel any need to justify or rationalize what they were doing.

Obedience in everyday life

Unthinking obedience can happen in real life, too. Hofling and others (1966) set up a study in a hospital. Nurses working on night shift were telephoned by a doctor whom they didn't know and asked to administer medication to a patient. They were told to go to the drugs cabinet and find a medication, which was labelled 'Astroten'. On the label it said very clearly that the maximum daily dose was 10 mg but the doctor asked the nurse to administer 20 mg.

Even though it violated several hospital rules – doctors were not supposed to give orders by telephone, for instance – 95 per cent of the nurses in the study were prepared to administer the medication. They were stopped at the last minute by a staff psychiatrist who had been observing what was going on in secret. The problem was, that in real life, the hospital doctors were accustomed to breaking this type of rule, and because of the hierarchy of power and their training, it was very difficult for a nurse to disobey a doctor.

Rebellion

It may be difficult, then, but we do disobey sometimes. Gamson, Fireman and Rytina set up a study in which people were asked to take part in a marketing research exercise. This involved filming a group discussion about a case of a manager of a petrol station who was in dispute with the franchise company. The research participants were told that the company said they wanted to revoke his franchise because he was living with someone and was not married to them; but the manager said it was because he had publicly criticized their pricing policies.

As the people in the study discussed the case, they were frequently asked to argue a particular case in front of the video camera. For instance, at one point, three members of the group were asked to argue as if they were personally insulted by the manager's behaviour. It soon became apparent that the group was actually being asked to provide video-taped evidence which could be used by the company to discredit the manager. At the end, they were asked to sign an affidavit giving the company the right to use the video-tapes as evidence, in any way it wanted to.

It was obvious to the groups that they were being manipulated and most people, at that point, refused to co-operate and sign the affidavit. In 16 of the 33 groups, all of the group members refused to sign, and in eight more groups the majority of members refused. Even in the groups where most people signed, there was a strong minority who refused to co-operate any further. So it's apparent that we will refuse to obey other people if we are clear enough about what is going on and how we are being manipulated.

When do we stand up for ourselves?

So why is it, then, that people will sometimes stand up for their own beliefs and at other times simply go along with what they are told? One of the answers is to do with **social expectations**. In Chapter 2, we looked at how powerful expectations can be, and how simply expecting something to happen can sometimes become a self-fulfilling prophecy. A self-fulfilling prophecy, as we saw, comes true simply because we expect it to, and act as if it already is. So that is one factor which is at work here.

Another factor, as I've already discussed, is the power of our previous training. We learn to obey people who are in charge and to do what we are told. This can be a powerful form of social conditioning: many people become very distressed at the thought of disobeying someone who is in authority, even when they know it is the right thing to do. Our early learning has taught us that, and it remains a powerful influence throughout our adult life.

It is reinforced, too, by the way in which people communicate. As we've seen, the way people use words, and the actual words that they use, encourage us to see possibilities in certain ways. Non-verbal dimensions of communication also reinforce those messages. It was no accident that the supervisor in Milgram's study wore a grey lab coat and acted in a distant, official manner. It made his authority seem even stronger.

Social scripts

Then there are the **social scripts** which are present in most situations. As we grow up, much of what we learn is about acting in the ways that society expects. We learn about social roles and how to behave in a way that fits in with the part we are playing. We also learn to conform to social scripts, which give the pattern of how people ought to behave. If we go to a restaurant, for instance, there is a definite script which tells us when we should do certain things and when we can expect things to happen. We'd be deeply disconcerted if the waiter brought coffee before the main course, for instance, and we would wonder what was going on.

Other social situations, too, have their own scripts, and sometimes these can cause us to act in unusual ways. Orne (1972) showed how normally, if you ask people to add up a set of numbers on a piece of paper and then tear the paper up and throw it in the bin, they will refuse. They might do it once or twice, but no more. But if you tell them that it is part of a psychology experiment, they will do it over and over again. In Orne's study, one research participant even had to be stopped after several hours because the experimenter wanted to go home!

So we weigh up the situation that we are in and match what we do to what we think that situation requires. The attributions and explanations that we make influence how we understand what is required and our social schemas and social representations guide our choice of actions. We interpret and analyse the situation that we are in, and that, too, influences how we behave.

Our social behaviour is complex, and draws from many levels of explanation and different kinds of experience. We are influenced by our early conditioning, by non-verbal and verbal communication, by our social roles and social scripts, by our personal attributions and by social representations. We are also influenced by the emotions that we experience and we will look more closely at these in the next chapter.

04

emotions

In this chapter you will learn:
- eight different types of positive emotion
- the difference between fear and anger
- outlines of four techniques for coping with stress.

If you were to survey a number of people about what makes a human being different from a computer, the chances are that one reply would overshadow all the rest: emotion. Human beings are very different from machines. We have other dimensions to our experience – we feel things. We become happy or upset or thrilled or furious – and we're not always particularly rational about how we do it. In this chapter, we will look at the psychology of emotions and at how psychological knowledge has been used to help people to cope with anxiety and stress.

Happiness and love

When we think of emotions, it is generally the unpleasant ones which come to mind: fear, anger, anxiety and so on. Partly, that's because we live in a society which tends to emphasize those much more than the positive ones. Films, news and TV dramas all emphasize negative emotions and ignore positive ones. So we tend not to notice the positive emotions that we feel, or to dismiss them as not really important.

People who give up smoking, for instance, often notice that they become more easily irritated. But they overlook the fact that they also become more able to smile, and that they laugh more easily. Both of these have the same physical origin – they are to do with getting the nicotine out of the body (we will look at this more closely in Chapter 5) – but we notice only the unpleasant side, because that's how our perceptions have been shaped by modern society.

Positive emotions

In reality, the positive emotions which we experience are just as rich and varied as the negative ones, if not more so. Argyle and Crossland (1987) explored some of the dimensions of positive emotions by asking people to imagine themselves in each of 24 different situations (Table 4.1). They were asked to describe how they would feel if they were in a certain situation and to say whether the feeling produced by the situation was like the feelings produced by any of the other situations on the list.

table 4.1 situations producing positive emotions

Spending a good social evening with friends.
Receiving an unexpected compliment which means a lot to you.
Getting involved in a thriller on TV.
Feeling overwhelmed by the beauty of nature.
Getting on well with your loved ones.
Solving an important personal problem.
Listening to a beautiful piece of music.
Engaging in a favourite hobby (not sports).
Having a rewarding conversation.
Doing some sort of commitment activity (e.g. charitable work etc.).
Feeling popular at a social gathering.
Being a success at something important to you.
Being absorbed by your work.
Meeting an interesting new person or people.
Engaging in a favourite sporting activity.
Being successful at work.
Reading a good book.
Doing some enjoyable physical work.
Buying yourself something you have wanted for ages.
Spending some time thinking about the good things in life.
Being given a valuable present by someone dear to you.
Having a long hot bath, or pampering yourself some other way.
Spending a memorable evening at a cinema/theatre/concert.
Having a quiet drink with friends (non-alcoholic or alcoholic).

(adapted from Argyle and Crossland, 1987)

Types of positive emotion

By combining the different descriptions and analysing what they had in common, Argyle and Crossland found that there seemed to be roughly eight kinds of positive emotion which were being described. Looking at these can make us realize just how varied our experiences can be. The first emotion on their list (although they were not arranged in any particular order) was the feeling of a sense of one's own **potency** – feeling capable and able to do whatever is needed. A second one was a **sense of spirituality** or wonder, which might be part of the feeling involved in listening to a particularly beautiful piece of music, or enjoying nature. Feeling **contentment** was also on the list, as was the feeling of being **relaxed**, which isn't the same thing at all.

Another positive emotion which people reported was referred to as **self-indulgence** by the researchers. We usually see self-indulgence as a selfish thing, but it is not always the case. The self-indulgence you experience when having a long hot bath or when pampering yourself, for example, isn't selfish in the sense of keeping something for yourself and not letting other people have it, but it is a pleasure which is personal and not to do with sharing. Some other positive emotions, though, are to do with sharing, or with caring for other people, and the researchers referred to these as **altruism**.

Being interested in something, or fascinated by a hobby, is also a kind of emotion which people enjoy experiencing. Argyle and Crossland referred to this as **absorption**. The eighth positive emotion which they identified is that of **exhilaration** – the sort of emotion one would feel when excited about something, or thrilled by an unexpected pleasant experience.

Dimensions of positive emotions

Argyle and Crossland used these eight emotions as the basis for further research, and came to the conclusion that they could be distilled into four basic dimensions which could be used to classify positive emotions. The first of these dimensions is to do with how involved we are in what we are doing. When we are having a quiet drink with friends, we tend to be less absorbed than if we were reading a good book or solving an important personal problem. We take things more lightly, and don't plunge into them as deeply.

The second dimension is about how potent or effective we feel ourselves to be. Some experiences require us to use our abilities fully, in order to achieve success, and those can be very satisfying. But other equally pleasant experiences don't require the same kind of personal achievement. That type of experience simply isn't relevant when we are socializing with friends or going to the cinema or a music concert. So positive emotions can vary depending on how much they involve a feeling of potency on our part.

The third dimension has to do with whether our attention is focused on social circumstances, as it might be when we are in conversation with friends or meeting new people, or whether we are simply having personal and self-indulgent experiences of the type that we looked at before. Some positive experiences seem to direct our attention outwards, to other people, while others direct it inwards, towards our own selves.

The fourth dimension which Argyle and Crossland identified seems to be to do with how intense the experience is considered to be. Some experiences are really quite lightweight: having a hot bath or watching a TV thriller are pleasant, but they are not desperately serious activities. Some positive emotions, though, are to do with what people see as more serious things, and in Argyle and Crossland's research, these included solving an important personal problem, getting on with loved ones, and feeling overwhelmed by the beauty of nature.

We can see, then, that there is a much larger range of positive emotions than we sometimes realize. There are others, too, which aren't on this list. However, our tendency to notice only the unpleasant emotions like anger or fear, or to regard them as somehow more important than the positive ones, has meant that this aspect of human experience has often been ignored or neglected in our modern society.

Loving

One positive emotion which hasn't been neglected, though, is love. We hear about love all the time, through the mass of romantic images in the media. But how far does the public image of 'love' actually reflect the reality? What is really involved in the experience of love, and what is the difference in the love between a couple who have been married for 30 years, and that between two starry-eyed teenagers. Are there different kinds of loving?

Love and limerence

It seems that there are. A number of psychologists have investigated different kinds of love and have concluded that we often use the same word to describe some very different emotions. One of the most useful distinctions was made by Tennov (1979) who argued that love, as a long-term emotion, was actually very different from the short-term, intensive infatuation which we also call love, or being 'in love'. She suggested that it would be more appropriate if we used the term **limerence** to describe the intensive experiences, and kept the term love to refer to the attachment involved in longer-term affections and partnerships.

Limerence, according to Tennov (and a vast number of writers, playwrights and musicians), is an intensive, all-consuming passion, which has a very strong element of fantasy in it. The person becomes totally obsessed with their idea of their loved one and spends a great deal of time thinking about them and daydreaming. Often, these thoughts are focused around tokens of some kind, such as a letter, a lock of hair, or a photograph.

Perhaps the most distinctive feature of this emotion is that it involves a state of intensive longing for the person. Because of this, Tennov argued, it is quite important that the person should be unreachable in some way – otherwise the emotion isn't likely to last very long. When two people experiencing limerence are together all of the time, the emotion tends to die away because it is not being fed by their longing for one another.

That isn't necessarily a bad thing, of course. In many cases, the period of limerence represents an initial blissful period, which is then gradually replaced by a deeper kind of loving, which becomes a basis for a long-term partnership. But some couples find that they have relatively little in common once the period of intensive limerence is over. The problem, of course, is that those experiencing limerence can't imagine it ever being over, so it is quite possible for them to make serious commitments, like marriage, while they are in this state, and then to regret it later.

The fact that limerence can be perpetuated as long as the couple are prevented from being together as much as they would like, explains why parental opposition to love affairs so often has the opposite outcome to the one which they intended. Forbidding the relationship has the effect of increasing the longing which the two people feel for one another, and so can make their attachment stronger. A more sensible course would probably be to make sure that the two people spent as much time together as possible, to see if they would still be likely to form a lasting attachment once the period of limerence is over.

Dimensions of love

Sternberg (1988) accepted Tennov's idea of love and limerence and went on to look at what seems to be involved in the longer-term emotion which we also call 'love'. He surveyed 80 people between the ages of 17 and 69, asking them about the relationships which they were experiencing at the time, and ones which they had experienced in the past. From this and other data, Sternberg concluded that love seems to consist of three underlying dimensions, with different proportions of these dimensions producing different kinds of love. These dimensions are intimacy, passion, and commitment.

The **intimacy** dimension is all to do with how closely the two partners share in one another's lives. But it is much more than simple physical closeness. The intimacy dimension includes aspects of the relationship such as how well the two people communicate, how much they understand one another and whether they are able to give each other emotional support. It also involves things like whether the two people really try to help one another, and whether each member of the partnership genuinely tries to promote the welfare of the other person.

The **passion** dimension in loving isn't just about physical passion, although of course it does include it. But passion, in Sternberg's terms, involves other kinds of emotions, desires and needs as well. For example, it would include whether the relationship satisfies nurturing and caring needs, or whether the members of the partnership feel able to satisfy their needs for personal fulfilment or self-esteem. Maslow (1954) suggested that for some people (although not for others), loving is a way of compensating for their personal deficiencies. Sternberg would see this as part of the passion dimension in a relationship, too.

The third dimension in a loving relationship is **commitment**. Like the other dimensions, this has more than one side. A short-term commitment to the relationship as it stands isn't the same as a long-term commitment to building a lifelong partnership. And the long-term commitment which two people bring to a relationship is vital, because it is only that which will keep them together during difficult times. Most couples who have been together for two or three decades report at least one bad period when they felt like giving up on the relationship altogether, but didn't because of their long-term commitment. Because they saw that time through, instead of giving up, the relationship was strengthened, and they became able to enjoy one another's company again.

Different combinations of these dimensions produce different kinds of love. For example, the kind of long-term **companionate love** which develops beween two people who have been together for many years is often one which is high in intimacy and commitment, but perhaps less so on the passion dimension. **Romantic love,** on the other hand, tends to be high on intimacy and passion, but doesn't involve as much commitment. Sternberg referred to the kind of love which involves all three dimensions fully as **consummate love.**

Love over time

Using his sample of 80 people of different ages, Sternberg also investigated how loving relationships change over time and, in particular, what kinds of things became more or less important as the relationship developed. People in long-term relationships identified five things as important – that is, they believed that five things mattered more in the long-term than in the short-term. These are listed in Table 4.2. Interestingly, the last one in the list – having a similar intellectual level – seemed totally unimportant to those whose relationships had been going only for a few years, but was seen by people in long-lasting relationships as essential.

---

table 4.2 important factors in long-term relationships

Having similar values.
Being willing to change in response to the other person.
Being prepared to put up with the other person's flaws.
Having matching religious beliefs.
Having an equal intellectual level.

(Sternberg, 1988)

Some things, though, became less important with time, including how interesting the other person seemed to be, and how attentively each person listened to one another. Some became more important during the first few years of the relationship but then declined or mattered less as time wore on. These included physical attractiveness, the ability to make love, the ability to empathize with the partner, and expressing affection towards one another. It isn't really possible to tell, though, whether these things really became less important, or whether the couples in the long-term relationships took them so much for granted that they stopped noticing them at all.

The positive emotion which we refer to as love actually incorporates many different kinds of experiences. Taking these together with Argyle and Crossland's work, we can see that our positive emotions in general represent a very rich part of human experience, and one which we need to recognize much more clearly.

Fear and anger

Not all our emotions are positive, though. In fact, some of them, like anger or extreme fear, can be extremely destructive. Since the earliest days of psychology, psychologists have been interested in these negative emotions. In particular, they were interested in how the emotion that we feel connects with the physical sensations that we also experience when we are frightened or angry.

Physical aspects of fear and anger

Both anger and fear are very active emotions. If you are angry with someone, your muscles tense up and you become restless: some people will even stand up and pace around the room as a way of helping to control the tension. Similarly, if you are frightened your muscles become tense and you may make small involuntary movements which express that tension. The two types of tension aren't the same, of course, but they do have quite a lot in common. They are quite different from the quiescent emotions, such as depression, which involve listlessness and apathy rather than tension and activity.

The 'fight or flight' response

In part, the tension that you feel when you are afraid is a survival response, and one shared by all mammals. In the natural world, if an animal is threatened by something so that it becomes frightened, then there are only two options. It can stay and fight, in which case it will need all the strength it can muster, to win, or it can run away, in which case it will need all the strength it can muster, to escape. In either case, therefore, the animal will need all its strength because holding anything back isn't much use if you end up dead. So the animal's body goes into overdrive, to give it as much energy as possible; and this is known as the 'fight or flight' response.

Most of the time, we use only a small proportion of our potential strength and energy. However during the fight or flight response, the body changes the way in which it operates physically in several different ways, all of which help to release more energy to the muscles. Physical energy comes from a chemical reaction between oxygen and forms of glucose, or blood sugars. Both of these are carried in the bloodstream to the muscles where, effectively, the sugar is 'burned' to produce energy. This process takes oxygen, so muscles that are in action need to have a continuous supply of fresh oxygenated blood if they are to work properly.

As a result, many of these physical changes are concerned with getting oxygen into the bloodstream. We breathe more deeply and more rapidly, increasing the oxygen supply entering the lungs. Blood pressure increases, carrying blood around the body more quickly, and extra red blood cells (which carry oxygen) are released into the bloodstream.

Some changes are concerned with getting more 'fuel' to the muscles. Stored fats are converted into blood sugars and released into the blood. The digestive system begins to work differently, ignoring long-term digestion and increasing the digestive processes for rapidly acting foods such as sugars. Saliva in the mouth changes in the same way, so that we can metabolize rapid-energy foods quickly.

Another set of changes is designed to protect us from injury as much as possible. The amount of vitamin K in the blood increases, making the blood more able to clot quickly if there is an injury. Also, if we are very frightened, blood vessels close to the surface of the skin shrink, making us paler and minimizing the amount of blood we are likely to lose if we are injured. Blood supply to the internal vital organs of the body, on the other hand, increases.

We also have some left-over responses designed to protect us by making us look more fearsome. In many animals, their fur stands on end as part of the fight or flight response, making them look bigger and potentially more dangerous. Humans have lost their fur, but the hairs that we have left still try to stand on end. Unfortunately, instead of making us look more frightening, all this actually does is give us goose-pimples.

We can see, then, that the fight or flight response is a very powerful reaction, which serves an important survival function – at least, when we are faced with threats that require physical action. It isn't quite as helpful when we are faced with non-physical threats, such as anxiety about the mortgage, or a fear of failing exams. Because these threats don't require physical action, we don't have a way of using up that energy, and can quickly become stressed. We will be looking at this problem later in this chapter.

Arousal

There are lesser degrees of the fight or flight response, too. When our attention is caught by something, or when we feel anxious about something, we experience the same kinds of physical changes but to a much lesser degree. The changes are strong enough to be measured, though, using sensitive detectors that will identify changes in pulse rate, heart rate, sweating, blood pressure and the like. A machine which measures several of these changes is known as a **polygraph**. Some people, such as police conducting interrogations, use polygraphs as lie-detectors because they can detect the slight anxiety which people feel when they tell a lie. Other machines can analyse slight changes in the voice caused by anxiety, which can sometimes be useful for detectives monitoring anonymous telephone calls.

The general name which we give for this kind of physical state is known as **arousal**, because it seems as though lots of physical activities have all been aroused at the same time. The type of arousal which we experience for fear is slightly different from the type we experience when we are angry, but the two conditions have a great deal in common.

Distinguishing between fear and anger

In 1953, a psychologist named Ax conducted a study to investigate the difference between fear and anger. Ax connected people up to an impressive-looking machine, so that they had wires and connectors all over the body. Then, when they were fully connected up, a technician came rushing into the room saying 'Hold it! There's a short-circuit in the apparatus'. That was the fear condition. In the anger condition, the person was wired up and then left alone with a technician who grumbled about the study and insulted them.

Incidentally, it wouldn't be possible for a psychologist to conduct this sort of study nowadays. There are very strict rules about ethical principles which have to be observed while conducting psychological experiments. It is not permitted to cause people who are participating in the research any pain or distress (mental or physical) at all. It also isn't permitted to deceive people, except under very special circumstances and with special permission from an ethical committee, and then only as long as they are told the full truth at the earliest possible moment. However, when Ax was doing this research, these conditions didn't exist.

Biochemical aspects of emotion

Ax found that that there were distinct physiological differences between the kind of arousal produced by fear, and that produced by anger. These differences seemed to be the result of different hormones and brain chemicals which were involved in the two emotions. Both fear and anger involved a chemical named adrenaline (or epinephrine in America), but anger also involved another one, known as noradrenaline (or norepinephrine).

Adrenaline and noradrenaline are both chemicals which are used by the body to stimulate a special part of the nervous system, known as the **autonomic nervous system**. This consists of a network of nerve fibres, running to all the internal organs of the body. When part of the autonomic nervous system is stimulated – a part known as the sympathetic division – the body experiences arousal. However, when the other part, known as the parasympathetic division, is stimulated, the body becomes quieter and less active The parasympathetic division seems to be involved in quiet emotions such as depression or sadness.

Which comes first?

The next question is which comes first? If physical changes happen when we feel emotions, does that mean that our emotions are caused by these physical changes? One of the early psychologists, William James, thought so. He described what happens when you trip going down the stairs and catch hold of the bannister to save yourself. During that first second, James pointed out, you simply react and do what is needed to survive. However, a couple of seconds later, your heart begins to beat faster, your hands sweat, and your breathing changes – in other words, the arousal response starts. It is then, James believed, that we feel the fear.

James went on to suggest that all human emotions actually come from our perceiving the physical condition that we are in. 'We do not weep because we feel sorrow; we feel sorrow because we weep.' He believed that the brain unconsciously monitors the body for changes, and then interprets those changes according to what the situation seems to demand.

Schachter and Singer's research

Over 60 years later, two psychologists named Schachter and Singer conducted an experiment to investigate this idea. Although it wasn't a very good experiment, because they didn't really control it very well, the experiment did give us some useful clues about how physical sensations and our own knowledge of the situation might be connected.

Schachter and Singer's study was really quite complex. They wanted to see what happened if people had the physical symptoms of arousal, and how they would feel in different situations. So some of their research participants were injected with adrenaline, producing the physical symptoms of arousal, while others were injected with just a neutral saline solution, which didn't have any effect.

Schachter and Singer then gave some of their research participants an 'explanation' for how they were feeling. Some of them were told accurately what was likely to happen – trembling hands, a pounding heart and feeling flushed. Others were misinformed, by being told that they might experience an itching sensation, a slight headache, or numbness. And a third group were not given any information at all, just told that the injection was mild and harmless and wouldn't have any side-effects.

What happened next was that the research participants were asked to sit in a waiting room for 20 minutes, supposedly to let the injection have its full effect. Each time, there was another person in the room with them who seemed to be another participant in the study. Really, though, the person was a stooge – an actor who was pretending to be a research participant but who was really acting the way the experimenters wanted.

Sometimes, during the 20-minute period, the stooge would act as if he was in a very happy mood: playing 'basketball' with pieces of paper, making paper aeroplanes, and playing with a hula hoop. Each time, he would invite the real research participant to join in, which many of them did. This was known as the 'euphoria' condition, designed to encourage the research participants to feel happy.

Other people experienced a different condition. They were introduced to the stooge and given a long questionnaire to fill in during the time. The stooge would begin to fill it in but would then become increasingly angry at how personal and insulting some of the questions were. Eventually, he would stamp out of the room in disgust. This was the 'anger' condition, designed to make people feel angry themselves (the questionnaire really was quite intrusive, too).

Schachter and Singer found that, by and large, the mood that people were in after the 20-minute period tended to reflect the mood that the stooge was expressing. In other words, whether they had an adrenaline injection or not, those who were in the 'euphoric' condition tended to be in quite a good mood at the end of the time, while those in the 'anger' condition tended to be irritable. Clearly, our moods can be influenced by social factors – by the other people around us.

However, Schachter and Singer also found that the degree of emotion that people experienced depended on the adrenaline, but only if they didn't know what effects it would have. People who had been kept ignorant or who had been misinformed about the effects of the adrenaline showed quite strong changes in moods. Their aroused state seemed to contribute to the way in which they interpreted the situation, so they felt more angry, or happier, than they might have done otherwise. You may have found a similar effect yourself, when you have been running for a bus but have just missed it. Running and anxiety both raise the adrenline levels in the bloodstream and people often find that they become much more angry at missing the bus than they normally would. It seems to exaggerate the reactions that we feel.

But Schachter and Singer found that this effect only happened when people didn't know what to expect from the adrenaline. In both the anger and euphoria conditions, people who were told what effects the adrenaline would have reacted in much the same way as people who hadn't had the adrenaline at all. In other words, they changed their mood a little, just from the social influences, but not a great deal.

The conclusion that they came to then, was that it is our awareness of the situation which produces the emotion that we actually feel. But it is our physical condition which influences how strongly we actually feel. As I said before, the study had flaws in terms of the way that the conditions were controlled – and of course it involved far too much manipulation for anything like that to be permitted today. However, most psychologists still believe that the study gave us some useful insights into emotion and how it works.

Describing emotions

There are other angles to the understanding of emotion. All human activities can be looked at from a number of different levels. And one useful level is to look at how an emotion is understood in different cultures and in different languages. In the English language, for example, we tend to use the word 'anger' as a general term to describe a particular emotion. However, that can sometimes lead to confusion because different kinds of anger may actually be quite different, both in their social meanings and in whether we judge the angry person as being fully responsible or not.

Lutz (1991) discussed how the Ifaluk people of Micronesia have five different words for anger, and each of these describes a different kind of emotion. For example, the anger which you might feel with relatives or friends who have not fulfilled their obligations is known as *nguch*. This is regarded as a different emotion from the irritability which people feel when they have been ill, and are convalescing, which is known as *tipmochmoch*.

A third kind of emotion is the anger we experience when we feel frustrated or helpless, or trapped into doing things that we don't want to do. The Ifaluk know this emotion as *tang*. And this is entirely different from the kind of anger which builds up gradually through lots of irritating little things going wrong, which is known as *lingeringer*. Finally, there is a sort of anger which society actually encourages: the kind of righteous anger or indignation which is to do with morality and justice, and making sure that things which happen are fair and equitable. That kind of anger is known as *song*.

When we look at these different words and their meanings, we can see that each of them reflects a kind of anger that Western people also feel sometimes. But the Ifaluk see them as quite different emotions, and so they find it easier to respond to them differently. An Ifaluk person would be much less likely to be disturbed or upset when a convalescent person was being snappy and unreasonable, for example, because, from the outset, they would be aware of where the emotion was coming from. We usually have to learn these things by experience, because our language doesn't sensitize us to them. We can learn something about human emotion from non-technological cultures like the Ifaluk, because people in such societies often have a much more sophisticated awareness of mental states than people in technological societies.

Anxiety and stress

If we have a fright, or if we become angry with someone, the emotion often passes. We calm down and get over it and, as we do, the physical symptoms of arousal disappear as well. But sometimes we can experience emotional arousal which doesn't go away. Being anxious about whether there will be enough money to pay the bills, for instance, is a continous worry, not a passing thing. This means that it is constantly producing physiological arousal, which doesn't go away.

Selye (1956) showed that long-term arousal such as this can have many harmful effects, including interfering with our physical health. We call it **stress**, and it is one of the most studied areas of psychology – mainly because it is such a big problem in modern society. Long-term stress suppresses the action of the body's immune system, making us much more vulnerable to colds, infections and more serious illnesses. In the long term it can make us more liable to contract heart disease. Long-term stress also makes us very jumpy and alert to potential threats – which means that quite often, we see something as a threat when it is really quite harmless. Because we over-react to what people say or do, we become more likely to quarrel with the people around us. And it interferes with judgement, so that we are less likely to make sensible decisions or to appraise what is going on realistically.

Obviously, this is not a psychologically healthy condition to be in, but there are ways of coping with long-term stress so that we do not suffer these effects. Many psychological researchers have investigated coping mechanisms: ways of minimizing or cancelling out the effects of long-term stress and making sure that we deal with it in a positive kind of way. Not all stress is bad, and we need to understand how it can be helpful as well as damaging if we are to use it positively. In order to do this, we need to understand how different levels of physiological arousal affect us.

Arousal

As I mentioned earlier, the 'fight or flight' response is an extreme state of physiological arousal. But there are less extreme forms of arousal, too. It is best to think of arousal in terms of a continuous scale, which has extreme relaxation at one end, and fight or flight at the other. In between are many different levels. A disagreement, an unpleasant interview, or even just a worrying thought are all things which can make us more aroused. Other influences, such as caffeine, exercise (while we are doing it, though not afterwards), or premenstrual tension, also raise our level of arousal.

The Yerkes-Dodson law

This isn't necessarily a bad thing, because a small amount of arousal is stimulating. Many people have a cup of coffee in the morning because the additional stimulation helps them to feel more alert. People do exercise for the same reason. In fact, up to a point, increased arousal helps us to do things better.

But only up to a point. If we become too aroused – say, by becoming very upset or very angry – then it can actually stop us doing things well. You might find, for instance, that you do better in an argument if you are annoyed by what the other person is saying. Your irritation helps you to find words and to argue more fluently. But if you become enraged by the other person's comments, so that your arousal level becomes too high, then you might find yourself speechless and unable to put what you want to say into words. Up to a point, the increased arousal brought on by irritation has improved your performance in the argument; but when the level of arousal went past that point, it interfered with it.

This principle is known as the Yerkes-Dodson Law of arousal (see Figure 4.1), and it can be applied to almost every task. Being angry or upset might mean that you do the washing up more quickly and efficiently – but if those feelings were too intense, you might break things or drop them. With a relatively simple such as like washing up, you can be much more aroused before you actually get to the point of breaking things, but in a complex situation, such as an argument or when doing something that you need to concentrate on, the optimal level of arousal for doing the job well is much lower. In other words, you can be put off more easily.

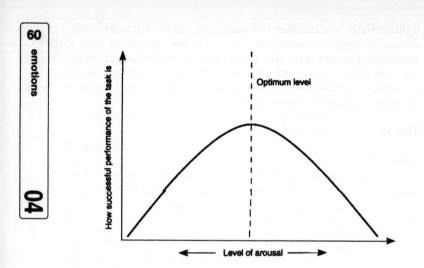

figure 4.1 the Yerkes-Dodson Law of Arousal

Coping strategies

Athletes, and other people who take part in highly stressful activities, need to be able to make sure that their levels of arousal will be enough to produce the best possible performance. So they often use **coping strategies**, which allow them to control the amount of arousal that they experience. Some of these strategies are physical ones which involve using the adrenaline constructively, to give additional energy when exercising. People who do a lot of sport often do better in exams than people of the same intellectual level who don't take regular exercise, and one possible reason for this is that they simply don't experience as much physical stress.

Some coping strategies though, are **cognitive** – they involve the person's thinking in some way. They include mental exercises, deliberate thinking strategies, and ways of using the imagination positively. By doing this, we can make sure that the thoughts we have are useful, and won't simply add to the amount of stress which we feel.

Visualization

For example, one of the most popular methods used in sports psychology is **visualization**. It is used for training, to help people to learn new techniques, as well as for stress management. When it is being used in this way, the person imagines him/herself going through the whole activity successfully – winning the race, or passing the exam, or whatever it is. By concentrating only on positive thoughts, and on systematically imagining the successful scene, the person leaves no mental room for the doubts and worries which would add to their level of stress.

Attributions

In everyday life, people often add to the stress they feel by thinking negatively: worrying about how dreadful things are, or might become. Since even a single worrying thought adds to our level of arousal, all thinking of this kind adds to the total arousal and stress which the person experiences. Sometimes, people even develop ways of thinking which are totally self-defeating. Abramson, Seligman and Teasdale (1985) found that chronically depressed people often have what they called a **depressive attributional style**, which makes their depression much worse.

Attributions are the reasons that we give for why things happen. Someone with a depressive attributional style will believe that anything which happens will only turn out for the worse, that it is always going to be that way, and that it can't be changed. These thoughts keep their depression going, partly by increasing the stress that they are under, and partly by making them feel that there isn't any pont in trying to do anything anyway. In other words, they feel helpless, and unable to control what happens in their lives.

Locus of control

People with different attributional styles, who see themselves as able to control events by hard work and effort, and who don't give up, tend to experience stress very differently. They are much less likely to become depressed, and much more likely to be able actually to do something about their situation, because they keep looking for ways to change it. These people have what is known as an internal **locus of control**. They believe that what happens to them is largely controlled by their own efforts. People with a depressive attributional style have an external locus of control, believing that they cannot influence what happens to them.

There is a great deal of psychological research which shows that having an internal locus of control is much healthier for a human being – both physically and mentally. Long-term stress can lower the body's resistance to disease and make us vulnerable to illness. But people with an internal locus of control experience less stress, even though their physical situation may be just as bad. This is because they channel their energies into looking for positive things to do, instead of just worrying. And because they are likely to gain at least a small success through trying so hard they experience positive emotions such as a sense of achievement, which people who are more passive don't feel.

Having an internal locus of control isn't something we are born with. We can learn to change our thought habits and behaviour, so that we shift from an internal to an external locus of control. **Cognitive therapy** is all about teaching people how to take control of their own lives, and how to avoid the self-defeating beliefs and attributions which have stopped them from doing so in the past. Almost anything which increases someone's self-confidence has the effect of giving them more of an internal locus of control over their own life. So there is a great deal that we can do to cope with stressful problems positively. Problems may be real, and not likely to go away, but we can make their effects worse or better, depending on how we go about it.

We can see, then, that the psychological study of emotions can give us a great many insights into this aspect of our lives. We have many more positive emotions than we sometimes realize, and these may be associated with quite small events as well as quite large ones. Studying fear and anger raises interesting questions about how our experiences relate to the physical states that we are feeling. And the psychological study of anxiety and stress has allowed us to identify a number of positive ways to cope with stress and other problems.

05 states of mind

In this chapter you will learn:
- to identify biological rhythms that affect us psychologically
- about the different effects that psychoactive drugs can have on the mind
- the cycles of sleep, dreaming and wakefulness.

In this chapter we will be looking at the psychology of consciousness. Consciousness is something that we often take for granted: we are aware of being awake, or of being drowsy, and don't usually think very much about it. But the alertness (or lack of it) that we feel at any given time in the day is the outcome of complex activity in the brain. Understanding something about that activity can tell us quite a lot about our own feelings and experiences.

Biological rhythms

Our state of consciousness changes all the time. We may be in a good mood and then something happens which puts us in a bad one. We may feel sleepy, but then an alarming experience brings us fully alert. We may be relaxed, but the sight of someone we really need to talk to can rouse us to an unexpected level of energy. All of these are changes in consciousness. Sometimes, we change our state of consciousness deliberately by using a drug, such as alcohol or caffeine. We will be looking at how these work later in this chapter. But a lot of the time our state of consciousness changes simply because of biological rhythms.

There are many biological rhythms in nature: daily rhythms, lunar rhythms, seasonal rhythms. Plants and animals all respond to these: birds begin courtship rituals when the lengthening days signal that it is spring; some plants open up during the day and close at night, and so on. And human beings, too, respond to natural rhythms.

Seasonal affective disorder

Poets and dramatists have long commented on the way that spring often results in young people thinking of love and romance. I am not aware of any psychological evidence which would either prove or disprove that, but we certainly seem to respond, physically, to increasing daylength. Many people experience a form of depression during the long winter months, which clears up completely when spring and summer come.

Seasonal affective disorder, as this kind of depression is called, appears to have a great deal to do with a lack of being in natural daylight. After all, for people who work indoors – which is most of us – it is possible to pass several months in the winter only seeing natural daylight at weekends. It is dark when we go out to work or college, and dark again when we return home.

Special lamps which mimic daylight have been quite successful in treating seasonal affective disorder.

But how can daylength have such a strong effect? The answer lies in a small gland in the brain, known as the pineal gland. This gland is situated deep in the brain, in a place which is roughly behind the centre of the forehead. The ancient Greeks regarded it as the location of the soul and, in other religions, too, this place often has a mystical significance. As far as psychology is concerned, we have recently become aware that the pineal gland seems to change its activity in direct response to daylength, stimulating the body to produce chemicals which lift our moods and make us feel more energetic.

Circadian rhythms

Human beings have rhythms, known as circadian rhythms, which are connected with the 24-hour cycle of the day. Through the course of the 24-hour cycle, we experience a regular increase and decrease of activity in several physiological systems, including body temperature, blood pressure, pulse rate, blood sugar level, and hormone levels. Moods, too, vary according to this cycle, as do our skills and abilities.

For example, between the hours of two and six in the morning, our blood sugar levels are low, body temperature is low, and so is blood pressure. If we are awake, we also experience quite a subdued mood; and if we are trying to do a demanding task of some kind, we are much more likely to make mistakes. But this isn't just from tiredness, because as soon as morning comes, we begin to feel better, and more alert, and our performance improves.

Siestas

As we progress through an ordinary day (not one where we have stayed up all night!) we find that there are particular 'low' points, where it is easy to become sleepy and to take a nap. Our biological rhythms are set to bring sleep twice a day: at night, but also in the early afternoon. In hot climates, a siesta is often an accepted cultural practice: everyone dozes or sleeps for a couple of hours, and then wakes up to resume work once the hottest part of the day is over. Even in colder climates, where a siesta is not the standard practice, many people take a nap after lunch if they have the opportunity, while others find they are inclined to daydream at that time.

There are other changes, too, during the course of the day. For example, many people experience another 'dip' around about 6 p.m., and then find that their energy levels gradually rise for the rest of the evening, until they drop again when it is time to go to bed. Figure 5.1 shows the highs and lows of body temperature rhythms during a 24-hour period. Psychological alertness often follows a similar cycle. In part, the cycles are maintained by what are known as **zeitgebers** – external signals, like daylight and night, which seem to trigger off these rhythms, But in part, they are also maintained by the body's own internal systems.

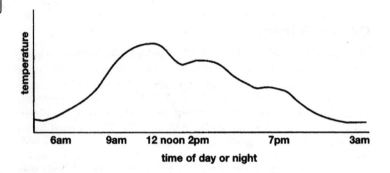

figure 5.1 body temperature throughout the 24-hour cycle

Shift work and jet lag

Sometimes, our body rhythms are disrupted so that we have to be alert at different times of the day or night. There are two common reasons for this: shift work and international travel. When we are doing shift work, we have to adjust our bodies to a different 24-hour rhythm, sleeping at different times of the day, and being awake at times when we would normally be asleep. When we are travelling across time zones, we also have to adjust to a different rhythm of activity.

Both cases produce the same type of problem, which we call **jet lag** when it is brought about by travel. At its worst, it can produce irritability, poor performance at work, and poor decision-making. But there are ways in which it can be minimized. For example, it seems to be easier for people to move forwards in time, rather than backwards. So a shift work cycle which progresses through the 24-hour period, with someone going from a night shift to an early one, then from an early shift to a late one, and then on to nights again, will be much easier for people to adjust to than a shift cycle in which someone goes from an afternoon shift to an early morning one. In international travel, too, shifting the 24-hour system forwards (for example, by staying awake for a longer period than you might do normally) can be helpful in minimizing jet lag.

Consciousness and the brain

Brain cells – in fact all nerve cells – work by generating tiny amounts of electricity and passing these on to one another. So some psychologists study brain activity, and how the brain works, by studying the electrical activity of the brain.

One way of doing this is by using **electro-encephalographs**, or EEGs for short. These are charts of the brain's electrical activity, which has been detected using small electrodes that are attached to the scalp. The changes detected by an electrode are recorded by a pen which rests on a moving sheet of paper and makes small movements whenever the electrical activity varies. Figure 5.2 shows an EEG chart. The diagram in the top left-hand corner shows where each electrode was placed on the person's head, and the lines show the electrical activity detected by the electrodes. There is a different line for each electrode, showing the electrical activity which is going on in different regions of the brain.

Of course, all of this is a bit like standing outside a factory and trying to guess what they are making by listening to the noises coming through the window. Studying the brain in this way doesn't tell us everything, by any means. But it can show us something.

Brain rhythms

One of the things it can show us is the general patterning of brain activity when we are in different states of consciousness. The type of EEG which is produced when we are awake and concentrating on something is very different from the pattern which is produced when we are awake but just lazily relaxed. When we are relaxed, an EEG trace shows quite large waves of electrical activity (large for the brain, that is). These are known as **alpha rhythms**. We produce them just before we drift off to sleep or when we are daydreaming or just relaxed and happy.

Female aged 15 yrs. Eyes closed - resting record. Subcortical seizure discharge

figure 5.2 an EEG chart

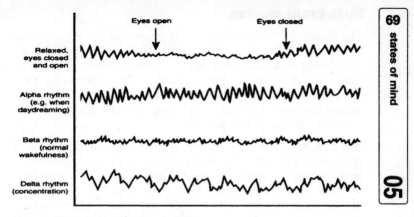

figure 5.3 EEG traces of consciousness

When we are concentrating hard, though, the EEG trace shows a different kind of activity. There are still detectible rhythms in its pattern, but they are smaller and closer together. These are known as **delta rhythms**. And when we are just generally awake, neither relaxing nor concentrating, the EEG trace doesn't show any regular rhythms at all. Instead, it shows continuous intensive activity with no particular pattern (see Figure 5.3). There are different EEG patterns produced when we are asleep, too, and we will be looking at these later in this chapter.

One method that some psychologists have used for investigating brain damage is to give a patient a particular stimulus, such as a flashing light or a particular sound, and observe the difference in their EEG. These differences are known as **evoked potentials**, and they can be useful because they will show if a particular area of the brain doesn't seem to be responding correctly.

Another method of investigating the brain while it is working is to use **brain scans**. One type of scan, known as a PET scan (short for positron emission tomography) involves looking at how much blood is being used by a particular part of the brain. Each time a nerve cell fires, it uses up some nutrients, and so it needs to replace them from the blood supply. So parts of the brain which are being active need a larger blood supply than those which aren't. The PET scan allows a psychologist or doctor to see which parts of the brain are using most blood, because the blood has been 'labelled' using a special radioactive chemical which can be detected by the scanner.

Split-brain studies

The illness epilepsy involves a sudden burst of electrical activity in the brain, when lots of brain cells all fire at once. There are many different kinds of epilepsy, and some of them are relatively localized – that is to say, the electrical activity happens only in a relatively small part of the brain. Even so, it can mean that the person becomes disoriented and forgetful, and it can interfere with their ability to concentrate.

A few particularly unfortunate people suffer from *grand mal* epilepsy, in which the electrical activity begins on one side of the brain but then spreads across it. This means that it interferes with the parts of the brain that co-ordinate body movement. The person falls down and has a 'fit', or seizure, as their muscles shake and spasm in response to the random messages being sent to them from the brain. When the seizure is over, they are usually very confused and can take some time to come back to reality.

In the 1960s, a pioneering operation was developed in an attempt to control epilepsy in a few patients who were experiencing *grand mal* seizures so often that they couldn't get on with their lives at all. The surgeons decided to cut through the brain cells which linked the right and left halves of the brain – known as the two **cerebral hemispheres**. By doing this, they reasoned, the seizure would only affect one side of the brain, because it couldn't be passed over to the other side. That way, even if the patient had a *grand mal* seizure, at least they would be able to keep control of one side of the body.

The two halves of the brain

In fact, carrying out the operation seemed to reduce the fits much more than that. But what was even more interesting was what psychologists found when they came to study these 'split-brain' people. By conducting a whole series of different tests, they found that the two halves of the brain seemed to be able to act quite independently, as if each were a separate brain in its own right.

One patient, for example, reported how she would sometimes decide to wear a particular dress and would go to her wardrobe to take it out with her right hand, only to find that her left hand would pick out something entirely different for her to wear. Since the right side of the brain controls the left side of the body, and the left side of the brain controls the right side of the body, the action implied that the two halves of the brain had different ideas about what she ought to be wearing that day!

The psychologist Sperry also found that the two halves of the brain seemed to act in different ways. It has been known for a long time that our ability to use language comes from a few areas on the left side of the brain. By using a special screen (Figure 5.4), Sperry showed that split-brain people could easily name an object that was shown to the left eye, because that meant that the image was interpreted by the left side of the brain. However, when the right eye was shown something, the person couldn't say what it was.

That didn't mean, though, that they couldn't recognize it. They could point to a picture of it, using the left hand (controlled by the right side of the brain). And they could pick it out by touch from a tray of other objects. They just couldn't name it, because the image had been passed to the right side of the brain, and the right side of the brain does not control language.

figure 5.4 a split-brain study

Hemisphere differences

By doing more tests of this kind, Sperry found that the two cerebral hemispheres seemed to have different abilities. As we have seen, the left side of the brain handles language and it also seems to be concerned with mathematical problems and arithmetic. The right side of the brain, though, is better at geometric or spatial puzzles, and seems to be particularly good at interpreting drawings. We understand speech with the left side of the brain, but most of us (apart from trained musicians) understand music with the right side.

These findings are interesting, but it is important to realize that we are talking only about how some kinds of information are processed. Some mystics have claimed that the right side of the brain contains all of the creative and spiritual side of being, while the left side is purely logical and mechanistic. But really there isn't actually any psychological evidence to support this.

In fact, each side does have the basic rudiments of the other side's abilities, even though they aren't very highly developed. The right hemisphere can sometimes cope with very simple language, while the left hemisphere can deal with simple drawings. And if a child under 12 suffers some kind of serious brain damage, the other side usually takes over the damaged side's functions as well as its own. Similarly, learning and experience has an effect: trained musicians perceive music with their left hemispheres as well as their right, because they are able to analyse the music, and analytical skills are located mainly on the left. But this has been something they have learned – it isn't some magical ability, inborn from birth.

Alertness and attention

Actually, when we talk about the 'brain' in terms of split-brain research, we don't really mean the whole of the human brain. The whole brain is a highly complex structure, consisting of a lot of different parts. EEGs, scans, and split-brain studies have been concerned with the largest part of the human brain, which is the two structures known as the cerebral hemispheres. These are so big that they cover all the other parts of the brain, and are the parts of the brain that we think with.

But there are other parts of the brain involved in consciousness too. For example, if something unexpected catches our attention, we become instantly alert. This involves a set of reactions which are very similar to the arousal which we looked at in the last chapter, although not quite as extreme. For example, the blood pressure goes up slightly and our heart rate increases. We also turn towards the source of the unexpected stimulus, keeping muscle movement to a minimum so that we can catch any slight sounds, and keeping our eyes open so that we can see anything there is to see. All this is known as the **orientation response** and it is partly controlled by a part of the brain known as the reticular formation.

The reticular formation is located above the top of the spine, just above the part of the brain that controls basic, essential activities like breathing and digestion. It seems to act as a general switching mechanism for the cerebral hemispheres, switching them on if we need to be awake, nudging them into greater activity if we need to pay attention to an unexpected stimulus, and damping them down when it is time to sleep.

In a set of studies reported in 1957, French showed how gentle electrical stimulation to a particular part of the reticular formation would rouse a sleeping cat. The cat would wake up in the same way as it did naturally, which suggested that electrical activity in this part of the brain might be the normal way that mammals – including humans – change from sleep to wakefulness. French also found that cats who had the reticular formation removed would sink into a deep coma, from which they could not be woken up. It seems likely that coma in human beings, too, may sometimes happen as a result of damage to the reticular formation.

Drugs and consciousness

As human beings, we don't just experience the different states of consciousness involved in waking, concentrating, relaxing and sleeping. We also deliberately change our consciousness by using drugs. Every human society uses some drugs to change people's state of awareness in some way. In our society, the main drugs are alcohol, nicotine and caffeine, while in Peru chewing coca leaves (which are used to produce cocaine) is an everyday activity, and in some middle Eastern countries smoking hasheesh or opium is legal while alcohol is banned. Drugs which influence our state of consciousness are known as **psychoactive drugs**. But how do they work?

Caffeine

Caffeine is a very common drug in Western society, but it is much more powerful than many people realize. All psychoactive drugs affect the nervous system in some way, but they have different effects by influencing different parts of it. For example, as I mentioned in the last chapter, the drug caffeine, which we take in coffee or cola drinks, acts on the autonomic nervous system to produce a state of arousal in the body. It also acts on the reticular formation of the brain, as a stimulant. So it isn't surprising that it helps people to wake up in the morning! It also isn't surprising that, while a little caffeine may pep you up, too much of it can make you irritable and edgy.

Caffeine is also physically addictive, and many people who give it up find that they can experience unpleasant withdrawal symptoms, including blinding headaches, nausea and stomach upsets. This addiction comes as a surprise to many people because caffeine is so readily accepted in society that people assume that it must be innocuous. However, being addictive doesn't necessarily mean that it is damaging – most people live perfectly healthy lives with a daily dose of caffeine, with no problem that we can detect arising from that. The main problem with caffeine is that, when people take it in large amounts, it can add seriously to day-to-day stress. So reducing your caffeine intake is quite a constructive thing to do if you are feeling under pressure.

Alcohol

Alcohol works in almost entirely the opposite way, that is as a sedative which calms down the autonomic nervous system and relaxes the muscles. That's why people often slur their words, or even fall asleep, if they are very drunk. In small doses, though, the influence of alcohol can often be quite stimulating because it relaxes the everyday tension that most of us feel and allows us to feel more at ease with other people. So we find it easy to talk and to join in things which are going on. It isn't really a stimulant, in a physical sense, but in small doses it can be a sociable drug.

The biggest problems with alcohol though, come from its other psychological effects. Alcohol can severely interfere with memory, which is why people often drink too much when they have serious problems. Once in a while that doesn't matter, but people who drink heavily over a period of years can lose their ability to store new memories altogether, which is much more serious. This condition is known as Korsakoff's syndrome and it can be very disturbing. Sacks (1985) described the case of a 60-year old man with Korsakoff's syndrome who could only remember his life up to his mid-twenties. When he looked in a mirror he became extremely upset because he didn't recognize the old man he had become. Since he couldn't remember anything from day to day, the distress was just as strong every time.

The other psychological effect which alcohol has is to impair our ability to make a balanced judgement. People who have been drinking – even quite small amounts – make far more mistakes on physical co-ordination tasks than people who haven't. But perhaps because they feel relaxed by the drug, they usually shrug off these mistakes, or don't even notice them at all. This is why so many people believe that they can drive well even if they have been drinking. It's not that they really can. It's that they don't notice any of their mistakes, so they think they are driving safely when really they are quite dangerous.

Nicotine

Many people who smoke believe that nicotine helps them to relax. But what it really does is to make their muscles more sluggish, so that they are harder to move. It also damps down the activity of the autonomic nervous system, so that they are less likely to become aroused. In the same way that alcohol can give us the illusion of being a stimulant when it isn't really, so nicotine gives us the illusion of being relaxed when really we are just feeling more inactive.

To understand how this happens, we need to take a look at how our nerve cells work. When we want to move – say, to lift an arm – the brain sends a small electrical message along our nerve cells (which are very long and stretched out) to the muscles. When the message reaches the end of the nerve cell, it stops, but it then causes a special chemical, called a neurotransmitter, to spill out of the ends of the nerve cell. The neurotransmitter spills out just next to a special place on the muscle, known as a receptor site. The molecules of that chemical fit into the receptor site like a key fitting into a lock. When that happens, the muscle receives a message to contract. If it happens with enough receptor sites, then the whole muscle will move, and the arm will be lifted.

What nicotine does, is to nip into the receptor site and block out the real neurotransmitter. Nicotine molecules have nearly the same shape as those of the neurotransmitter, so they can be picked up at the receptor site very easily. But they don't pass the message on, as the real chemical would have done, so only about half of the message from the brain actually gets through. The person can still lift their arm, but not as easily – it takes more effort.

This, of course, explains why people often feel fidgety when they are first giving up cigarettes. The brain has become so used to the nicotine that it is also used to sending very strong messages to generate each movement. But if there is no nicotine in the system, then the whole message gets through and the muscles respond easily, and that can sometimes feel as if we have too much energy.

Because a similar thing happens in the autonomic nervous system, we also feel our emotions much more freely. People often comment on how they become more irritable when they have stopped smoking, and that is true. But what they often don't notice, is that they also become happier, or more easily pleased. In fact, all of our emotions become more intense, not just the negative ones.

Morphine and heroin

It is difficult to be quite so precise about the actions of some of the illegal drugs which people use to change their state of consciousness, mainly because, for obvious reasons, there has been less research into them. Nevertheless, we understand the effects of some of them fairly well. For example, we know that the highly addictive narcotic drugs such as heroin and morphine have their effects because they have a chemical structure which is very similar to naturally occurring painkillers which the body makes by itself.

If you are doing something very demanding, it is possible to ignore injury or hurt while you are actually doing it – indeed, sometimes you might not even notice it at all. In both war and peacetime, there have been many instances of people who have been completely unaware of serious wounds or injuries while they struggled to save someone else's life. In a situation like that, the brain suppresses our own pain until the emergency is over. It does this by releasing special brain chemicals, called endorphins and enkephalins, which act to deaden feeling and sensation in the body.

Morphine and heroin both have very similar chemical structures. So they can slip into the receptor sites in the brain which are normally reserved for endorphins and enkephalins, producing similar results. People who take the drug report that it makes them feel euphoric, as though they are not quite in touch with reality, and good because there is no physical discomfort or fatigue at all. But the problem is, of course, that when it wears off it feels very unpleasant, so it is extremely easy to become both physically and mentally addicted to these drugs.

Endorphins and enkephalins are also released through vigorous exercise, so that is a much better way of getting the same sort of effect. When people talk about 'feeling good' after a strenuous physical work-out, they are talking about much the same effect that taking these illegal drugs produces, but they have managed to get it in a much safer and more natural way. And it also doesn't have the unpleasant after-effects when it wears off, either.

Both morphine and heroin are sometimes used medically because they are such powerful painkillers, so medical researchers have been able to investigate how they work in some detail. However, because of the difficulty of conducting systematic research into illegal drugs, we are much less certain about the effects of marijuana.

Marijuana

We do know that marijuana was widely used as a tranquillizer in the nineteenth century, and for over 2,000 years in the Far East. We also know that it acts as a mild depressant, damping down the actions of the autonomic nervous system and producing muscular relaxation. Perhaps because of this, some users report a sense of time passing very slowly, and an increased sensitivity to sensory stimulation such as music or art.

We are a long way yet from understanding exactly how marijuana works, chemically, in the brain. But one important clue occurred when researchers in Israel discovered a chemical, anandamide, which seems to be a natural substance that has the same effect in the brain as THC (tetrahydrocannabinol, the active ingredient of marijuana). Not long afterwards, American researchers discovered that there may be specific receptors for anandamide in brain cells, which implies that these would also respond to THC. But these findings are relatively tentative (Mestel, 1993). It needs a great deal more research before we can be sure of these processes, but for social and political reasons, it is difficult for scientists to get research funding to investigate this particular drug.

Ecstasy

We understand the actions of some other psychoactive drugs much better, though. We saw earlier how the brain chemicals known as neurotransmitters are used to pass information from one nerve cell to another, or from one nerve cell to a muscle fibre. There are several different chemicals which act in this way, and some researchers have been able to trace 'pathways' of nerve cells in the brain, which use a particular chemical. Some psychoactive drugs have their effects by acting directly on these pathways.

One of these is the drug MDMA, which is also known as ecstasy or just 'E'. MDMA (which is short for 3,4 methlyenedioxymethamphetamine) is a highly **prosocial** drug. In other words, it makes people feel social and pleasant towards one another, as opposed to feeling aggressive and irritable. It also enhances awareness of music and colour. MDMA was first discovered in 1914, and used to be used in marriage guidance counselling, to ease the tensions between people so that they could talk over their problems more effectively. In the 1970s, however, it became popular as a recreational drug, and has now been made illegal.

MDMA appears to work by acting directly on a particular neurotransmitter pathway in the brain. This pathway involves nerve cells which use the chemical serotonin. Normally, when a neurotransmitter chemical is spilled out by the nerve cell, it only remains around for a few seconds, because it is then recycled by the cell that it came from. But MDMA prevents this recycling, so the spilled serotonin stays where it is, and continues to work on the next nerve cell. It does this all through the serotonin pathways of the brain, and this seems to be what produces such a strong effect on the person's moods.

Amphetamines

The stimulant drugs known as amphetamines or 'speed' also sometimes appear to have a prosocial effect, at least in small doses. People find that they can talk to others more easily, and may seem to be in a better mood – although often they may feel slightly edgy or tense. But in large or regular doses, amphetamines can lead to severe mental illness – a disorder which is known as **amphetamine psychosis**. This involves a distortion of reality, with the person becoming extremely paranoid and disturbed. Since amphetamines are also highly addictive drugs, it is all too easy for people who enjoy the effects which they have in small doses to slip into taking larger and larger ones, often with tragic results.

Where MDMA increases the level of serotonin in the brain, amphetamines work by increasing the level of two other brain chemicals, known as dopamine and noradrenaline. We know that the dopamine pathways in the brain are associated with willpower, or motivation. The illness known as Parkinson's disease comes from a shortage of dopamine in the brain, and it leaves people unable to make deliberate actions. Noradrenaline is associated with active and aroused states of the body, such as anger.

It seems as though it is the combination of these two brain chemicals which produces the psychological effects of amphetamine. In the short term, it increases motivation and arousal, so people find it easy to be sociable even when they are tired. But in the long term, and in high doses, it makes people more likely to become agitated and suspicious. This is made worse, too, by the fact that amphetamines act as appetite suppressants, so people who take them frequently usually suffer physical debilitation as a result.

LSD

Another well-known psychoactive drug is known as LSD, or sometimes just acid. LSD, which is short for lysergic acid diethylamide, is a **hallucinogen**, and taking it gives people some very interesting psychological affects. It can produce distortions of reality, so that sounds and colours become extremely exaggerated. People who take it can also experience hallucinations, seeing things which are not actually there.

Sometimes, these experiences can become extremely disturbing, and possibly cause long-term psychological distress. Leary (1965), in research conducted while the drug was still legal, stressed that LSD should not be taken casually, but only when what he called **set** and **setting** were right. Set refers to the person's mental state, since fears or anxieties can produce disturbing effects; while setting refers to the physical situation, which needs to be relaxed and friendly, since being in a strange or threatening place could bring about disturbing experiences.

Like MDMA, LSD involves the serotonin pathways of the brain, but it doesn't work in the same way. The molecules of LSD are a very similar shape to the molecules of serotonin, so they can fit into serotonin receptor sites. They produce their effects by mimicking the effect of the drug, but the chemical isn't identical. So where the normal effects of serotonin seem to be to produce a sociable, highly aware mood, the effects of LSD in serotonin receptors seems to be to produce a kind of hyper-awareness, which can easily turn into hallucination.

This discussion of how drugs work may have been a little bit technical, but it shows us how closely consciousness and the chemicals in the brain are linked. We can change the chemical balance in the brain, and we do, each time we have an alcoholic drink or a cup of coffee – or even a glass of milk, which contains mild, naturally occurring morphine-like substances (which is why it can help us to feel calmer). Both natural and synthetic drugs can change our moods, our state of awareness, and our perceptions of reality.

Sleep and dreaming

For many years, psychologists regarded sleeping as a time when nothing much happened, except for the occasional dream. But in the late 1930s, people began to use EEGs to record brain activity. When EEGs were taken of people during the whole of a night's sleep, researchers found that actually the brain is extremely active, even if the body seems to be quiet.

In fact, we seem to have at least four different phases of brain activity which take place while we sleep. These are shown in Figure 5.5. As we can see from the diagram, level 1 involves very rapid and irregular activity of the brain, with very low voltages. Level 2 sleep still shows rapid and irregular activity, but with greater changes in the voltage becoming apparent from the peaks and troughs on the chart. Also during this level of sleep, patterns known as spindles begin to appear, which are very rapid, changeable bursts of activity.

By level 3, the frequency of the electrical activity has become a little slower, and the peaks and troughs (the amplitude) on the graphs are higher, meaning that the changes in voltage have become larger than they were in the first and second levels. This trend continues with level 4, which shows very large changes in voltage, and a much slower rate of change.

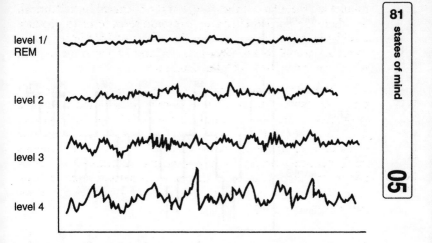

level 1/REM

level 2

level 3

level 4

figure 5.5 EEG traces during sleep

Sleep cycles

These patterns of sleep, like so many other aspects of consciousness, happen in regular cycles through the night. We begin sleeping at level 1, and spend maybe ten minutes in it. Then our sleep pattern changes to level 2, and stays there for ten or 15 minutes before changing again to level 3. During the first part of the night, it will shift down to level 4 for about 20 minutes or so, and then come back up to level 3, then to level 2, and then back to level 1 (see Figure 5.6). A complete cycle, from level 1 to level 4 and back again, usually takes about an hour and a half.

Interestingly, the levels of sleep as shown on an EEG chart also reflect how deeply asleep we feel. When researchers wake people up from level 4 sleep, they are very hard to rouse, whereas people in level 2 sleep wake up much more easily. At least, that's the case for levels 2, 3 and 4. Level 1, though, is a bit special, because that is the part of our sleep when we dream.

When we are in level 1 sleep, our eyes are continually making very quick movements. For this reason, level 1 sleep is often called **REM sleep**, which is short for rapid eye movements. If people are woken up from this sort of sleep, they report dreaming. We all dream four or five times during the course of

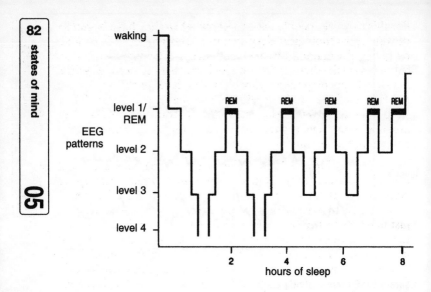

figure 5.6 cycles of sleep

an average night, although some people remember dreaming while others don't. That seems to depend on whether you have woken up from REM sleep (in which case you remember the dream you were just having) or whether you have woken up from level 2 sleep, which feels dreamless.

Dreaming

Although we seem to be 'switched off' while we are asleep and dreaming, we aren't totally unaware of our surroundings. Dement and Wolpert (1958) sprinkled people lightly with water while they were in REM sleep. Then, a little later, they woke them up and asked what they had been dreaming about. Some people had dreamed about being under waterfalls, some about swimming, and some about being out in the rain. Most of them dreamed about water in some way. In other words, they had managed to incorporate the outside stimulation of the water into their dreams.

In fact, we may have far more control over our dreams than we realize. Most of us have occasionally had dreams in which we knew we were dreaming, but the dream carried on anyway. These are known as **lucid dreams**. Recently, psychologists have discovered that it is possible to learn how to make a dream into a lucid dream, and then for the person having the dream to control what happens.

For this to work, people need to know when they have begun to dream. In psychological sleep research laboratories, this is done by giving dreamers a pre-arranged signal. The signal won't be enough to wake them up, just enough for them to become aware that it is happening, like a tiny electrical tickle to the wrist, or a red light flashing on the eyelids. When the person begins REM sleep, they are given the signal, so they become aware that they are dreaming. Once they know this, they can make things happen in the dream.

According to Hearne (1981) the secret of controlling a lucid dream successfully is to make sure that what happens is believable – as far as the dream is concerned. For example, if you wanted to dream about a particular person, you couldn't just make them appear from nowhere. But you could dream that there was a door nearby, and make the person come in through it. Some people dream about flying, and so they would be able to make themselves fly, in the dream. Other people don't, so it would be impracticable for them to try it in a lucid dream. Green and McCreery (1994) discussed how training in lucid dreams can be used therapeutically, for example, in counteracting nightmares.

Functions of dreaming

But what is dreaming for? In the early days of psychology, the psychoanalysts, led by Sigmund Freud, believed that dreams come from the unconscious mind telling us about our innermost secret wishes and desires. These are disguised by the brain, using symbols to stand for the real meaning. The books about dream interpretation that you sometimes see on railway and airport bookstalls are following this idea, but most psychologists do not believe that dream symbolism is quite as extreme as Freud maintained, even though they may accept that it has some part to play.

Some medical researchers believe that dreams come from random brain activity, which happens as nerve cells restore and reorganize themselves while we are asleep. The experience of the dream is simply imposed by our mind, as it tries to make sense of these haphazard bursts of nerve cell activity – in the same way that we can sometimes 'see' castles or animals in cloud shapes. According to this view, then, dreaming is just an accidental by-product of the physiological activity of the brain, and has no real significance.

Most psychologists, though, do believe that there is a psychological function to dreaming as well as a physiological one. We see dreaming as playing an important part in how we organize our psychological experience. Throughout each day, we are bombarded with a massive amount of sensory information and experiences. At some time, the mind needs to make sense of it all: to store information in its proper place so that it connects with similar things that we know; to identify patterns in our experiences, and to filter through things that have happened to us to identify particularly meaningful events. It does this while we are dreaming.

This explains, too, why sleeping on a problem is so often helpful. Before we go to bed, we may be perplexed, upset, or completely at a loss as to how to deal with something. But when we wake up, it often all seems clear. This is because we have been working on the problem unconsciously while we sleep. The brain activity which takes place while we dream has allowed us to knit loose ends together, and to put things, mentally, into their proper place. So when we wake up it is much easier to decide what to do.

In this chapter we have looked at several aspects of consciousness, and how consciousness can be changed, influenced, or affected in different ways. The human state of consciousness is constantly changing, so understanding something about how that happens can help us in our attempt to understand the human being.

06

motivation

In this chapter you will learn:
- to identify at least two ways in which human beings can be motivated
- three examples of 'defence mechanisms'
- how social motivation can help reduce racism.

In this chapter, we will be looking at motivation – why we do what we do, and why we bother to do anything at all. If we want to understand human beings, we need to look at what makes people 'tick' – what moves us to act, or at least to action. And, as with every other aspect of psychology, there isn't a single simple answer to this question. Human motives are complex, ranging from simple physiological ones to complex issues of social respect and identity. We usually have more than one reason for doing things, and bearing this in mind it is worth trying to sort out the different kinds of motives which contribute to our actions.

Physical and behavioural motives

Sometimes what we do is motivated by very basic needs: if you go to the kitchen and fetch a glass of water, it's a fair bet that you do it because you are thirsty. The level of fluid in your body has dropped below its ideal level, and this sets off a complex range of physiological mechanisms in the body. Messages about your fluid level are passed from your body to a particular part of the brain, known as the hypothalamus. This sends messages to the cerebral cortex, which is the part of the brain that you think with, so you realize that you feel thirsty and go to get a drink of water.

Homeostasis

Psychologists investigating such physiological motives have found that these mechanisms are all concerned with getting the right balance in the body. As long as everything is at the right kind of level, we don't feel the motivation. But if something becomes imbalanced, for instance, if our blood sugar level gets too low or if we don't have a high enough level of fluid in the body, then we take action to put it right. This is known as maintaining **homeostasis** – maintaining the appropriate balance in the body so that we can function well, physically.

Of course, maintaining homeostasis also means that the brain has to have some idea of what the appropriate balance is, so that it can be maintained. Psychologists researching into hunger have found that the body has a kind of **set weight**, which it seems to try to maintain. In studies with animals, they would eat until they had consumed enough food to reach their set weight, and then stop eating. Even if they went on a restricted diet for a while, so they lost weight, as soon as the restrictions were off they would eat enough to return to the set weight.

It seems likely that human beings, too, have this kind of body mechanism, which might explain why so many people have problems with dieting. They are trying to achieve a weight that is lower than the physiological set weight which their body functioning is based on. So even if they diet and get their weight down for a short while, they will find it very difficult to maintain that weight.

Physiological motivation, though, doesn't really have all that much to do with how we act in other ways. Even eating and drinking, in human beings, are affected by other kinds of motives: dieting, for instance, has more to do with social approval than it does with physiological needs, and people often drink even non-alcoholic drinks to be sociable rather than because they are actually thirsty. So we need to look at other levels of explanation as well, if we are really to understand human motivation

Behavioural motives

Sometimes, what we do comes about as much because of habit as anything else. Habits are behaviours or feelings that are associated with particular settings or situations. We learn how to act in certain places, or with certain people, and these come back to us if we find ourselves in that situation again. At such times, we can surprise ourselves with how we react.

It is interesting, for example, how powerfully an examination room can affect us, even if we are not actually taking the exam. Exam rooms are something we usually only encounter at school, and under quite tense conditions. People are usually worried and anxious when they go into an exam room to take an exam. Because we don't usually have anything to do with them at other times, those feelings of worry and anxiety often come flooding back when we go into an exam room – even years later. So we act nervously, and not like our usual selves at all.

What has happened here is that the behaviours and feelings associated with a particular situation have been brought back, simply by being in that situation again. You might habitually buy a certain brand of tights, simply because that is the kind you have bought in the past, in that particular shop. Sometimes we do this even though we meant to try something else, purely because the association of that particular action with that particular situation is so strong.

The same thing can happen, too, with interpersonal relationships. For example, if you meet someone that you haven't seen for a while, you can find yourself slipping back into ways of behaving with them that aren't typical of the way that you behave with other people. As a child, I used to argue continually and very vehemently with my cousin and, even now, when I am with my cousin we tend to do the same thing – though I don't argue in that way with anyone else. Being with that person brings back old habits, and it is sometimes hard to break out of them.

Changing habits

Habits can be broken, though – we're not stuck with them for ever. For instance, teachers who have to invigilate exams as part of their job don't feel anxious when they go into these rooms – at least not once they have had a couple of years' experience. You can deliberately decide to try a new brand of tights, and remember to choose them when you are in the shop. And even my cousin and I are gradually learning to communicate more reasonably with one another! Breaking a habit involves replacing the actions or feelings which are triggered off by that situation, with some other actions or feelings. It is hard at first, but the more often you succeed, the weaker the original habit becomes. We will be looking at this more closely when we look at association learning, in Chapter 7.

Cognitive motives

The way that we think also sometimes motivates us into action. Cognitive motives are motives which come from our thoughts, beliefs and ideas. They are to do with how we understand what is happening to us, and the way that we understand a situation can make all the difference to what we decide to do about it.

Personal constructs

Each of us has had our own personal experiences, and we have learned from them. In particular, we have learned about other people. We have formed our own personal theories about what other people are like from the way that people have interacted with us in the past. These theories are called **personal constructs** and we use them when we meet new people.

Personal constructs take the form of a two-ended kind of classification, such as like 'kind – cruel' or 'hot-tempered –

calm', or 'interesting – dull'. Table 6.1 gives an interesting exercise which you might like to try out. If you do it, it will help you discover some of your own main constructs. As a general rule, we tend to use about eight or ten main personal constructs most often, but we have several less important ones as well. Whenever we meet someone new, we weigh them up on the basis of our own personal construct system. Then we use those judgements to decide whether we like them or not.

All this is a bit like saying that our decisions about whether we like new people or not depend on whether they remind us of someone else that we once knew. And that's true, to some extent. But the new person doesn't have to be exactly like the person that we knew before – they just may have one or two qualities in common, which we can recognize as being similar. Using personal constructs, we can identify a particular set of human qualities, which different people may have more or less of.

---

table 6.1 exploring personal constructs

This is an exercise which you can do to find out the main personal constructs that you use. Begin by naming eight people who are important in your life:

A............................   E..............................
B............................   F..............................
C............................   G..............................
D............................   H..............................

Then think about these people in groups of three at a time. You will be able to think of a way that two of them are similar, and different from the other one. Write these down in the form given below:

(A,B,C) .... and .... are ...., but .... is ....
(D,E,F) .... and .... are ...., but .... is ....
(A,F,G) .... and .... are ...., but .... is ....
(B,D,H) .... and .... are ...., but .... is ....
(C,E,G) .... and .... are ...., but .... is ....
(H,B,F) .... and .... are ...., but .... is ....
(A,E,H) .... and .... are ...., but .... is ....
(D,G,C) .... and .... are ...., but .... is ....

The words you have used to describe the similarities and differences indicate the personal constructs that you habitually use. Try comparing your results to those of a friend.

Individual explanations

Since each of us has led a different life, our experiences of other people have varied, and our personal constructs are also unique. They represent our own distinctive way of looking at the world, and that can be entirely different from someone else's. Two people could meet a third person for the first time, and even though they were together and had the same objective experience, they might come to very different conclusions. One, for example, might see the new person as being friendly and outgoing, whereas the other might see them as ingratiating and manipulative. Just because we are in the same situation doesn't mean that we see things the same way.

And that, of course, can motivate our behaviour. If we see someone as manipulative and ingratiating, for example, we behave very differently towards them than we would if we saw them as friendly and outgoing. If we used the first type of personal constructs, we would be likely to avoid them, and be suspicious of any approach that they made towards us. If we used the second, we would be likely to be welcoming and to treat them as a friend.

Social expectations

This type of thing can become circular, of course. As we saw in Chapter 2, the expectations other people have of us can influence our behaviour quite a lot. They can even become **self-fulfilling prophecies**, so that we live up to what people expect of us. If you have a set of personal constructs which mean that you treat anyone new as if they were not really friendly but had some ulterior motive for pretending to be so, then they will react to how you are behaving towards them, and avoid you. You would take that as 'proof' that they weren't really being friendly, not realizing that it was your own behaviour which had produced that effect.

A self-fulfilling set of personal constructs such as this can easily mean that someone becomes very isolated from other people, and deeply unhappy. It is good to be cautious, of course, but it is not good to suspect everyone you meet, automatically. Many psychologists use personal construct theory to help people whose belief systems have become stuck like this. They use techniques that will help people to develop a new set of personal constructs, which will be more helpful to them in the long run.

Defence mechanisms

There are other ways, too, that our minds can motivate us. Many psychologists are deeply sceptical about the ideas of Sigmund Freud, the psychoanalyst, who developed a theory about the unconscious mind during the last century. But Freud did identify some important mental processes which the mind uses to protect itself against threats. These are called **defence mechanisms**. Other psychologists, too, have found the idea of defence mechanisms to be a useful one, although they don't necessarily share Freud's views about other aspects of the working of the human mind.

Denial

Defence mechanisms are unconscious, but they can be very powerful. They are all to do with how we protect our own self-image. For example, if we are faced with an awkward or uncomfortable fact about ourselves, our first impulse may be simply to deny that it is true. Sometimes, we will be able to get beyond that first impulse and see that the idea does, perhaps, have some justification. At other times, though, the implications of the idea may be too much for us to cope with. So we stick to our **denial**, even though it may be quite irrational, simply because we are protecting ourselves from having to re-think all our beliefs and ideas. In this situation, denial is acting as a defence mechanism, protecting us from a threat to how we see ourselves.

Repression

There are other kinds of defence mechanisms, too. One of them is **repression**. We often repress memories which are personally distressing, or which would seriously challenge our beliefs about ourselves. When a memory is repressed, we forget it – but it is different from normal forgetting because we become very agitated or upset if something comes close to reminding us of it again. The mind has repressed that particular memory or knowledge because it is too emotionally demanding to cope with.

Reaction-formation

Sometimes, something can be repressed so hard that it turns into its opposite. For example, if someone has a very strong desire or need which they feel is wrong and needs to be suppressed, they may try very hard never to let it come to their awareness (remember that a defence mechanism is unconscious – we don't know we are doing it unless someone else intervenes and shows us what is happening). Because their unconscious mind is trying so hard, they become very hostile to any hint of that particular desire or need in other people, and react aggressively to it. This is known as a **reaction-formation**.

The classic example of a reaction-formation, of course, is **homophobia**. Most people, whether they are homosexual or heterosexual, are unaffected by other people's sexual choices. But some people become very upset and agitated when they encounter any mention of homosexuality. These people can end up reacting quite irrationally – and sometimes very aggressively – towards homosexuals. We refer to these people as homophobic. Their homophobia often comes from their own unconscious homosexual desires, which have been repressed so hard that they have become a reaction-formation.

Self-efficacy and learned helplessness

Another way that our cognitions can motivate us to action is to do with our **self-efficacy beliefs**. These are our beliefs about how effective we are at doing things – how capable, or how skilled, we are. And these are very important, because they affect how hard we try. Bandura (1989) showed how it is generally a good thing if people have high self-efficacy beliefs because it makes them more self-confident, and more likely to succeed. It's even a good thing to have higher self-efficacy beliefs than the evidence would really warrant – in other words, to believe that you are better at things than you actually are – because that way, you will take on more challenges and improve your abilities as you deal with them!

The effects of high self-efficacy beliefs

In one study which Bandura described, a psychologist looked at how having high or low self-efficacy beliefs affected children's work in school. The children in the study had different abilities: some were good at maths, while others weren't very good at all, but they also had different self-efficacy beliefs. Some of the children believed that they would be able to do it if they made an effort; while others believed that they wouldn't be successful no matter how much they tried.

The psychologist found that the children with high self-efficacy beliefs did much better than the other children, regardless of their level of ability. In other words, even if they really weren't very good at maths, children with high self-efficacy beliefs did better. They solved more maths problems in the time that they were given, they spotted where they had gone wrong more quickly, and they were more prepared to go over problems which they had got wrong. The children with low self-efficacy beliefs, on the other hand, would make a single try at the maths problems, and then give up.

It's not hard to see why having high self-efficacy beliefs helps you to do well. Obviously, if you are prepared to put effort into learning, and to keep trying and learning from your mistakes, then you will eventually get somewhere – even if you are working at something that doesn't come easily to you. Many psychologists nowadays believe that bringing up children and training adults to believe in their own ability to take effective action is one of the most important things of all.

Learned helplessness

There's another side to this, as well. Some people go through a seres of demoralizing or unpleasant experiences, which they can't do anything about, and then they just give up trying altogether. So when they are in a situation which they could actually change if they made an effort, they don't bother. This is known as **learned helplessness** – they have learned to be passive and helpless, rather than trying to influence what happens to them.

In 1978, Abramson, Seligman and Teasdale argued that learned helplessness has a lot to do with why people suffer from depression. When people are living for a long time in demoralizing situations which they can't do much about, they often slip into a 'victim mentality' which encourages them to feel helpless and passive. They develop an **attributional style,** or a way of thinking, which suggests that things happen because of global, large-scale reasons which are always likely to be there, and can't be controlled. So whenever they encounter a new problem, they see it in this way and don't realize when it is actually something they could do something about.

Locus of control and self-efficacy

As we saw in Chapter 4, it is important for people to feel that they have some control over what happens to them. To feel that you are helpless is very stressful, which just makes things worse. So one way that psychologists try to help these people is to set up situations which will help them to raise their self-efficacy beliefs, such as encouraging them to tackle an entirely new activity, or to trying a different approach in dealing with a problem. By doing this competently, the person comes to realize that they can be effective – that they can actually do something about their situation.

We can see, then, that self-efficacy beliefs are closely linked to the idea of **locus of control,** which we looked at in Chapter 4. They are all about seeing yourself as someone who can be in control of what happens to you, and who can take effective action when it is necessary. If we are to understand human motivation, we need to understand about these beliefs, because they can make all the difference to whether someone tries to influence what is happening to them, or not.

Social motives

What we do is motivated by social influences, as well as cognitive ones. We are surrounded by other people, and how they see us can be a powerful influence on whether we do something or not. We are also influenced by shared social understandings and, as we have already seen, by the expectations which people have of us. So a great deal of our motivation is social in its origins.

Social respect

One of the most important social motives of all is for respect from other people. We all feel a deep need to avoid looking foolish, and sometimes, if we feel that we have made ourselves look stupid in front of the wrong people, even the memory of it can continue to embarrass us for a long time.

Harré identified the need for social respect as a very fundamental social motive. A great deal of what we do, Harré argued, is aimed to ensure that people will take us seriously, or will at least notice us, and acknowledge us as worthwhile people. We hate it if other people just dismiss us or, worse still, ignore our existence.

We can see how deeply rooted this need is by looking at children in a playground, when there is an adult present. Most of the children will be clamouring for attention in some way, looking to 'show off' something that they can do. Although this is often dismissed as attention-seeking, it is really a way of looking for social respect. A child who has learned to stand on her hands, or to do a long-jump, wants an adult to acknowledge that skill and to say 'well done'. Quite rightly, children want to be noticed for their achievements.

Adults need that kind of acknowledgement, too. Most of us work better if our efforts are recognized by other people – especially on those occasions when we have made a special effort. We like to know that we have been noticed. In fact, being ignored is one of the worst thing that can happen to use – we feel it as a deep social insult – and we can go to great lengths to get over it by proving that those people are less important than we are, or by making sure that they are forced to acknowledge us on a future occasion. This need for social respect is quite often the motivation underpinning human ambition and achievement – although not always.

Conflicting personal images

Sometimes, the need for social respect can work in our own minds, as well. Because we are always aware of how our behaviour is likely to come across to other people, we need to make sure that our own behaviour appears reasonable, even to ourselves. One consequence of this is that we don't like to appear inconsistent. Yet each of us acts differently when we are with different people, so sometimes we can get into difficulties when we are trying to balance the two.

The musical *Grease*, for instance, was based entirely around this problem. A young couple meet during the hoidays, as individuals, and fall in love; but when they meet again at school, the boy is with his friends and feels he has to appear casual and uncaring, which hurts her. Even though he is still in love with the girl, to show it would be inconsistent with his public image, and might lose him social respect. It is the way in which the two resolve this dilemma which forms the plot of the musical.

Cognitive dissonance

Sometimes we resolve dilemmas like this by changing our attitudes or beliefs. In a very famous study conducted in 1956, Festinger, Riecken and Schachter joined in with a religious cult, who believed that their city – and the rest of the world – was about to be destroyed by a great flood. On a special day, the cult members sold all their possessions and spent the night praying, on a hill outside of the city. Festinger, Riecken and Schachter were there too. They interviewed the cult members and found that they believed that the flood would happen, and only they would be saved.

The psychologists wanted to know what the cult members would say when the world didn't come to an end at the appointed time. So the next day, when no flood had materialized, they interviewed as many cult members as they could. Interestingly, they found that the cult members had adapted their beliefs, so that they didn't have to face up to the fact that their actions had been a waste of time. They now believed that it was the fact that they had spent the night praying which had actually saved the world. The flood would have come as scheduled, but God had repented at the last minute and so everything – thanks to them – was all right.

Festinger, Riecken and Schachter interpreted this in terms of what they called **cognitive dissonance**. We all like to believe that we are consistent, and not irrational. So if things happen which could make us appear irrational, we change our beliefs to make them seem consistent again. Festinger believed that cognitive dissonance is one of the main reasons why people change their beliefs: we don't like to seem foolish to anyone, not even ourselves.

Festinger gave some less dramatic examples of cognitive dissonance, as well. In one study, people were asked to do an extremely boring task for a long time. Then they were asked to go out and tell someone who was waiting outside that the task was interesting. They were paid either $1 or $20 for doing this. Then the psychologists asked the research participants to describe how interesting the task had really been. They found that the people who had been paid $20 to do the experiment said what they expected – that the task was really boring. However, the people who had been paid only $1 said that, actually, they had found it moderately interesting.

Nobody in their right mind could really have found the task interesting. Part of it involved giving each of 48 pegs in a peg-board a quarter-turn, one after the other, for half an hour! But what seemed to have happened was that the research participants needed to justify why they had lied to the person in the waiting room. It was OK for those who had been paid $20, because they could say they did it for the money. But being paid only $1 wasn't enough, so they needed a better reason for their lying. As a result, they convinced themselves that the task hadn't really been all that bad.

Cognitive dissonance, then, might be something which goes on in our minds, but it is another aspect of our need for respect. We need to avoid looking silly, even to ourselves. So avoiding cognitive dissonance, and seeming to be consistent in our beliefs and actions can be an important motive for acting in a particular way.

Aggression and scapegoating

Sometimes, one of the ways that we avoid cognitive dissonance is by blaming other people for what happens to us. This is known as **scapegoating**, and is a significant mechanism which underlies social aggression such as racism. Scapegoating seems to be a mechanism which can bring out the very worst in human nature. As things get difficult, people become frustrated and angry and they take that anger out on the nearest clearly identifiable target.

Racism and economic recession

It is noticeable, for example, that violent racist incidents increase when the economy is in recession. Recent events in Europe are an example of this, as is the massive increase of racism in Germany and elsewhere during the 1930s' depression – an increase which made the concentration camps possible. In the United States, too, Hovland and Sears (1940) showed that the number of lynchings of black people in the Southern States was closely linked to the price of cotton. The lower the price, the more lynchings.

The key to understanding this side of human nature lies in looking at where all that aggression comes from. For the most part, people tend to live co-operatively with one another. As we will see in Chapter 8, our first social impulse is to go along with other people, not to confront them aggressively. But sometimes, human beings show that they are capable of brutal inhumanity towards one another. How does that happen?

Frustration and aggression

There have been a number of studies that have shown how aggressive behaviour in human beings is particularly likely when we feel frustrated or helpless. This idea was first put forward by Dollard and others in 1939, although at the time they phrased it in a rather limited way. They suggested that people would always react aggressively if they were frustrated in achieving their personal goals. Nowadays, we recognize that people react differently – not everyone becomes aggressive in such situations. However, for the most part, being prevented from doing something that we feel we should be able to do (even if it is only getting on with our own lives in peace) is something which makes us very tense. And some people express that tension in aggression and violent action.

But why should that tension become displaced onto ethnic minority groups? The reason for this lies in two other important motivators for human behaviour. As we saw earlier, and in Chapter 3, it is stressful for a human being to feel that they are helpless. Yet economic recessions are something that few of us can do anything about: we all feel helpless as we hear about jobs disappearing and companies collapsing. Many of us, too, are personally threatened by these situations, yet there is little that we can do.

Social representations
One very striking characteristic of people, though, is that we look for explanations for what is happening to us. Some people seek those explanations in ideas such as luck, or mystical concepts like astrology; some look for them, as we are doing here, by looking to the human sciences; while others look for them in the social beliefs and explanations which are shared by the people around them. These explanations are known as **social representations**, and they are an important key to understanding how economic frustration becomes displaced onto the people who are usually suffering the most from it.

Social representations, as we saw in Chapter 2, are shared beliefs, which are held by groups of people in society. Each of us adopts our own set of social representations, by talking with other people, picking ideas up from the mass media, and fitting these into our own personal construct system. They give us ways of explaining what is happening in our everyday experience. In some ways, they are a bit like the personal constructs which we looked at earlier in this chapter, but they are shared by other people too.

Among racists, a common social representation is the idea that they are somehow in competition with members of ethnic minorities for the benefits of society. So when those benefits become fewer, they blame the members of the ethnic groups because they think they are taking an unfair share of what is available. (In fact it is generally the members of ethnic minority groups who suffer most economic deprivation in these situations, but racists are not noted for logical thinking.) While most people will put the blame where it belongs – with the government or economic forces – racists blame ethnic minority groups, and express their own personal frustration through violent action towards them.

Social identifications

Why should they seize on members of a particular group, rather than on particular individuals? The answer to this question lies in the mechanism of social identification, which we looked at in Chapter 2. As we saw there, it is a very basic tendency for human beings to see the world in terms of 'them' and 'us' groups. We are aware of the social groups and categories that we belong to, and we are also aware of other groups in society.

Stereotyping

Because we tend to know the people in our own groups best, and we only see members of other groups from the outside, we become much more aware of the differences between people in our own group than we are of differences among others. So it is very easy for us to slip into the idea that 'we' are all different, whereas 'they' are all the same. One of the first steps in breaking down any sort of social prejudice is to recognize that any group of people is made up of individuals, with their own different ideas and opinions – that 'they' are not, in fact, all the same.

These are psychological tendencies that all people have to some extent. We all tend to stereotype groups of people if we don't know them that well. The stereotyping isn't necessarily about ethnic groups: we also stereotype businessmen, doctors, schoolteachers, Americans, and other groups of people. It is partly a way of making sense of the mass of information that we have to deal with; but it can also be dangerous, when it leads us to ignore individual differences.

Social comparison

Another aspect of social identity theory is that we tend to make comparisons with people in groups which are close to us, socially and economically, because that way it helps us to feel good about belonging to our own group. Those racists who engage in violent action tend to be relatively less educated and to undertake unskilled work when they are employed. So, rather than place the blame for their unemployment on those in charge of the economy, who are socially very distant from them, they prefer to blame people who are in a similar economic position, but belong to a different social group.

We can see, then, how looking at why violent racism often rises at times of economic recession reveals a number of motivating mechanisms in human behaviour. One of these is that frustration and discomfort often produce aggressive reactions in people, partly as a way of getting rid of the tension produced by feeling helpless. Another is the tendency to use shared beliefs, or social representations, as a way of explaining what is happening. And a third is to seize on a visible group who represent a clearly identifiable target, who are close by, and who are in a weaker position, both economically and socially.

Counteracting racism

One thing which has become apparent, though, is that this kind of consequence to economic recession doesn't seem to be inevitable. In a population which is highly sensitized to issues of racism and multiculturalism, the efforts of racists to stir people up into violent action are much less effective. As people become more aware of individual differences within different ethnic groups, and of how political and economic factors influence recessions, they become less likely to produce such simplistic, and tragic, responses. We may have a long way to go, but understanding the psychological mechanisms which underly the phenomenon can give us some useful hints as to which direction we should take.

As we know, human beings can act in some astoundingly vicious ways. But it is important to keep this in perspective. For the most part, people tend to co-operate with one another, rather than compete – in fact, some psychologists believe that this is the baseline for human interaction, and that it takes some kind of disruption, like frustration or illness, before people begin to interact in more unpleasant ways. There are individual differences, of course, and there are also questions of social learning, as we model our behaviour on other people around us, including characters on TV and in films. But still, in their everyday lives, most people are not aggressive most of the time.

Hierarchies and levels

One of the most famous psychological theories of human motivation was put forward by Maslow, in 1954. Maslow was trying to understand why it is that people never seem to be satisfied with what they've got. We often find that we are dissatisfied with our situation, and want something more; but if we get what we want, then it doesn't take long before we want something else.

Maslow's hierarchy of needs

Maslow suggested that it is useful to think of human motivation in terms of a hierarchy of needs (Figure 6.1). We have some needs which are absolutely basic – our physiological survival needs – and if these are not satisfied, they will motivate our behaviour almost completely. Our actions will be aimed towards getting food, drink, shelter from the elements, and so on, and we will have little time for anything else. But once those needs are satisfied, a different layer in the hierarchy begins to become important. It becomes important to us that we should feel safe and secure. Once that has been achieved, according to Maslow, social needs become paramount, and what we do will be geared towards fulfilling our need to belong with other people and to be accepted. Each time one level of needs is satisfied, the next level becomes important as a motivator.

At the top of the hierarchy, Maslow argued, is **self-actualization** – realizing our talents and abilities to the full. We have met this idea before, when we looked at Rogers's work, in Chapter 2. But Rogers saw self-actualization as a fundamental human need, whereas Maslow saw it as an ultimate achievement, managed by only a relatively few remarkable people. Effectively, Rogers saw it as an ongoing process in our personal development, whereas Maslow saw it as a goal to be reached.

Problems with Maslow's theory

The difference between how the two psychologists saw self-actualization also points up one of the weaknesses in Maslow's theory. It may be OK as a general tendency, but there are numerous examples of people acting in ways which are quite different from that which would be predicted by Maslow. What Maslow described as 'higher' needs are often extremely important to people – so much so that whether their basic needs have been satisfied sometimes doesn't come into it.

The classic example, of course, is the dedicated poet or artist, who denies security and sometimes even goes hungry in the quest to fulfil needs for beauty or symmetry. Another example is the person who gives up the safety and security of a salaried

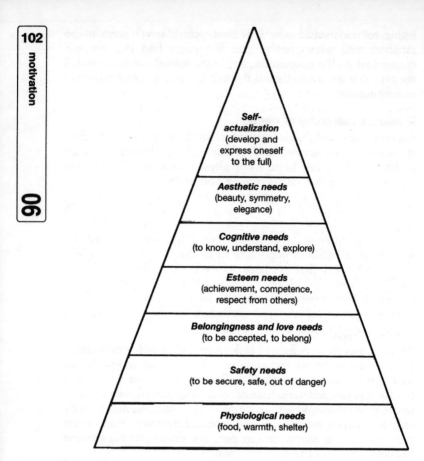

figure 6.1 Maslow's hierarchy of needs

job in order to do voluntary work overseas, or to take on something which is less regularly paid, but much more challenging. It may not be what most people do, but such people are less rare than Maslow's theory might predict.

Another great weakness in Maslow's way of looking at motivation is that it is very specific to Western cultures. It assumes that people are motivated by a need for individual achievement, and that things like social needs are somehow optional, at least by comparison with the satisfaction of physical ones. While this may, at least partly, represent how things are in America and other parts of the Western world, it isn't by any means a good description of what human beings are like elsewhere.

For example, in many parts of the world, the kind of upward ambition and striving represented by Maslow's approach simply doesn't apply. To take one example: in Balinese culture people see their identity as firmly located within their village's community, and the idea of accumulating personal wealth is an alien one. If it does happen, the money is usually spent on a particularly elaborate funeral celebration, or something equally transient. While Balinese people would like to be less poor than they are, naturally, the idea of achieving this through personal ambition and saving up personal wealth is not one which comes naturally to members of that particular culture.

There are other ways in which Balinese culture is different from many others. For example, the idea of 'art' as a separate entity doesn't exist, either. Although Balinese culture is full of what we would call art, in dance, carving, weaving, and many other ways, there is no separate word for 'art' in the Balinese language. It is simply a part of day-to-day living. So seeing it as a separate set of motives, which we adopt once other needs are satisfied simply can't explain what is going on.

Levels of explanation

This is only one example, but there are many others. It is perhaps more useful, if we are trying to understand human motivation, to take an approach which looks at it in terms of **levels of explanation**, than to try to explain it as a hierarchy of needs. We all operate on different levels at the same time. We may do something because it is approved of by our social group, but also because we want to do it personally and because we believe it will be good for us.

By looking at the many different kinds of motives which people have for their behaviour, we can identify some of the influences which might be working in any one example of human behaviour at a given time. It isn't a simple way of explaining things, like the hierarchical model, but then human beings aren't all that simple, either. It does, though, seem to be more useful in explaining why human beings act as they do.

7

cognition

In this chapter you will learn:
- to distinguish between 'concepts' and 'schemas'
- about the Gestalt principles of perception
- why information that you are interested in is easier to remember than information which does not interest you.

This chapter is all about cognition – about how we think, how we take in new information, and how we remember. In other words, it is about how the mind works. Psychology began as the study of the mind, so the study of cognition goes back to its very earliest history. But psychology's emphasis changed during the first half of the twentieth century as a result of the influence of behaviourism. The behaviourists thought that studying the mind was impossible, since we can't see it, or analyse it directly. So although some psychologists did continue to study the mind, they had only a limited influence on psychology until the last few decades of the twentieth century.

From the 1950s onwards though, psychologists began to develop ways of studying the mind in a more objective manner. They found that it was possible to do controlled experiments which would show how the mind was working and, doing this, they identified some surprising things about how we think and remember. Most of all, they discovered that the human mind is not just a passive recording and analysing machine. It has its own influence on what we perceive and remember, and on how we think.

Thinking

When we think, we draw on our experience, and that means that the mind has to have its memory readily available, to draw on. But thinking involves plans, possibilities and ideas, not memory alone. For example, one of the things which makes human beings very special is that we can imagine things which haven't happened – and which might actually never happen. And sometimes, as science fiction and other books which train the imagination show, those imaginings can seem almost as real to us as the world that we're actually living in.

Somehow, therefore, the brain contains all this information, and all of these possibilities and plans and ideas. However, it needs to contain them in a way that allows us to use them all, and to draw on it when we need to. In order to do that, the mind has to organize all this material in a way that makes sense, and which allows things to be brought to mind when they become relevant to what we are doing, or thinking.

Concepts

One of the ideas which psychologists use to understand how the mind is organized is **concept**. Concepts are ways of grouping together or classifying information, so that we can see which types of things belong together. For example, we automatically realize that a chair, a table and a bed all have something in common, and are different from, say, a frog. We classify chairs, tables and beds as part of the same concept – as items of furniture. A frog, on the other hand, belongs to a different concept – that of animals, or perhaps amphibians.

By grouping things together like this, we are able to make much more sense out of the world that we live in. If we weren't able to classify things, and to use concepts, then we would have to treat everything that we came across as if we had never encountered anything like it before, and that would mean that we spent an enormous amount of time trying to work things out from first principles. But if we recognize something as belonging to a particular concept, we can treat it in much the same way as we treat other examples of that concept.

How we store concepts

I mentioned earlier that psychologists began to study the mind again partly because they developed ways of investigating how it works experimentally. One of the most famous studies of how we store concepts is a good example of this. Collins and Quillian (1972) asked people to say whether a set of statements were true or not. In order to answer, they had to think about the concept, and the psychologists timed, very exactly, how long it took them to find the answers.

People were asked questions like 'Is a robin a bird?', 'Does a shark have gills?' or 'Does a goldfish have wings?' Collins and Quillian found that some questions took longer to answer than others. For example, it took longer to answer the question 'Is a blue jay an animal?' than it did to answer the question 'Is a blue jay a bird?' By comparing the different times which the answers needed, Collins and Quillian were able to deduce something about how concepts were stored.

Their most important finding was that concepts are stored hierarchically. In other words, we begin with large-scale general concepts, like 'animal' or 'plant', and then we have a number of smaller concepts nested within the large one. The general concept of 'animal', for example, contains within it lots of smaller categories, such as 'bird', 'fish' or 'mammal'. Each of these has other kinds of concepts within it, like 'shark' or 'goldfish' (see Figure 7.1).

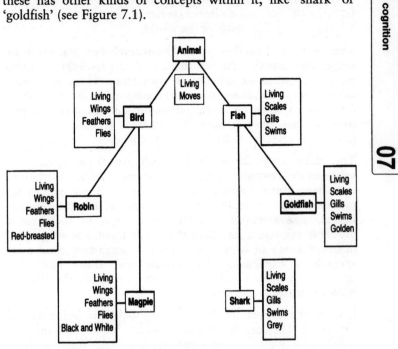

figure 7.1 hierarchical organization of concepts

In the Collins and Quillian study, people could give the answers to the questions quickly if they involved only a single step in the hierarchy. So they knew very rapidly that a blue jay is a bird, because that involved only one step. However, when more than one step was involved, they needed to think about it more – to know that a blue jay was an animal involved more than one step, and that meant that it took longer. Even though the time difference was only in fractions of a second, it was possible for the psychologists to use it to tell them something about how the person's mind was organized.

Levels of concepts

Another psychologist, Rosch (1973), also looked at the different levels of concepts, and how they were stored. Rosch came to the conclusion that there are really three levels of concepts. There are high level, **superordinate concepts**, which are general classifications about types of things, such as 'furniture' or 'animal'. These help us to group together some of the main features of our day-to-day experience, so they are vital in helping us to make sense of the world.

Then there are what Rosch called **basic level concepts**, which are things like 'chairs' or 'horses'. Basic concepts are linked together because of what we actually do with them. There are lots of different types of chair: some have arms or backs, some have cushions and some don't, and so on, but they all have one thing in common – we sit on them. It is what we do with them which links them together to form the basic concept.

The third type of concept which Rosch identified are **subordinate concepts**. These are a more detailed ways of classifying things, which we might use only for specialized purposes. For example, there are many different breeds of horses, and someone who was interested in them could probably tell you a lot about them. For them, knowing about different kinds of horses is a way of organizing their more specialized experience. For people who don't have that specialized experience, the subordinate concept of the different kinds of horses is less necessary.

Basic level concepts are the main level which we use in day-to-day living. They are the concepts about what we do – the ones which link with our personal actions. And there is some suggestion that these basic level concepts may have a very old history, because researchers have shown that some animals, too, seem to use basic level concepts.

Animal concepts

Seyfarth, Cheyney and Marler (1980) were observing the behaviour of vervet monkeys in Africa, and looking at how wild monkeys responded to threats. They found that vervet monkeys have three different types of alarm call which they give when they see one of the three different types of things which can threaten their lives. Whenever they hear an alarm call, the monkeys make the appropriate actions to avoid the threat – but those actions are different, depending on what type of threat the call describes.

One of the calls is given when there is a rock python about. When other monkeys hear this, they look around at the ground to identify the threat. A different call means that there is a martial eagle around. Martial eagles can swoop down and carry off young monkeys, and when they hear this call the monkeys look up at the sky. The third type of call is given when a monkey sights a leopard, and when they hear this, the other monkeys look into the trees.

So the calls which the monkeys give represent different types of threat. But what is even more interesting is the way that the young monkeys learn to give alarm calls themselves. Although they often give the call at the wrong time – giving the leopard alarm when they see a warthog, or an eagle alarm when they see another large bird -they never get the categories wrong. Always, the call is of the right kind to indicate a bird, a mammal, or a snake, even if the animal they have been alarmed by isn't actually the dangerous variety.

Natural categories

Marler (1982) discussed how this is also similar to the way in which some birds use different calls, and suggested that there are **natural categories**, which both animals and human beings are predisposed to learn. These natural categories are based on the idea of different kinds of action, and Marler suggested that we, and other animals, are particularly ready to learn them, because they help the species to adapt and survive.

Natural categories are all about actions – with things that we do and movements that we make. So in that way, they are closely linked with Rosch's idea of basic level concepts. Each species, Marler argued, is particularly ready to learn to organize its experience in some ways rather than others. In human beings, this seems to be what basic level concepts are all about, and may explain why a young child, for instance, learns about 'chairs' and 'doggies' much more easily and quickly than it learns about furniture and animals.

We can see, then, that this way of looking at concepts means that they are much more than just ways of categorizing information. They also include ideas about what we do with those things – with the way that we ourselves take action. This links concepts with another important idea in our attempt to understand how the human mind works: the idea of the schema.

Schemas

A **schema** is a bit like a concept in some ways, but it is much broader. Schemas contain ideas, plans, memories of actions and possibilities for future actions, as well as straightforward information. Schemas are what we use to guide and direct our behaviour when we are dealing with the world. So a schema is a very active kind of thing, not just a passive way of recording information.

For example, you will probably have a schema to do with using public transport. This will contain your memories of buses or train journeys, but it will also contain your knowledge of what to do about paying the fare and how to signal that you want to get off a bus, and many other aspects of using buses. If you were in a new town and had to get somewhere, you wouldn't be completely uncertain of what to do. Instead, you would begin by using your 'bus-catching' schema to guide your actions.

Developing schemas

As we learn more about the world, our schemas become more sophisticated, and sometimes even change completely. The first schema of all is probably the **body schema**, as a young infant gradually develops the sense that the world consists of some parts which are 'me' and some parts which are 'not-me'. As the infant's experience grows, it learns more about its body and the rest of the world. The schema becomes broader as it assimilates more information. But the schema also adapts and changes as it accommodates itself to new information. It may even divide into several entirely different schemas. The infant gradually learns that the part of the world which is 'not-me' actually seems to have two different parts: a part which is other people, who smile and interact with the infant (and to which it responds very easily, as we saw in Chapter 2), and a part which is more static, like the infant's cot or chair. The more we learn, the more our schemas adapt and change – all through life.

Applying schemas

We use our schemas when we are thinking or reasoning about problems. In the 1960s and 1970s, a number of psychologists investigated how human beings go about solving problems, and found that, often, we don't seem to do it particularly logically. This is mainly because we focus on the meaning of the statement, and not on its strict logical form, the way a computer would.

For example: If I were to tell a computer 'If it is raining on Sunday I shall go to the cinema', then the computer would take that as a logical statement. However, if I said that to a human being, they would listen to the meaning of what I had said, which wouldn't necessarily be the same thing. The computer and the human being would draw different conclusions if they found me at the cinema on Sunday. The human being would conclude that I was there because it was raining outside. But the computer wouldn't. As far as the computer was concerned, it could just as well be sunshine outside, because all I actually said was that I would go if it was raining. I didn't actually say anything at all about what I would do if it wasn't raining. The computer works from strict logic, and what I said didn't, logically, mean that it was possible to draw that conclusion.

A human being, though, would apply their well-developed schemas about what we usually mean when we say things in conversation. So they would know what I really meant – that I would go to the pictures only if it was raining. They would also see the sense in it – since a cinema is a dry place, and seeing a film is a good thing to do on a wet afternoon. They would see it as having a rational meaning, even though it might not be a strictly logical one. We apply a lot of this type of social knowledge in understanding each other, and it is why human thinking doesn't fit very easily into computer models.

Mental set

There are other ways that our existing knowledge influences our thinking. One of the most important of these is when we have expectations about what we are likely to find, and these affect how we go about doing something. Expectations can mean that we develop what is known as a **mental set**, which is a state of being especially ready to think in certain ways.

There are lots of examples of mental set because it is such a powerful mental mechanism. One of the first demonstrations was by Luchins, in 1932, who asked people to solve problems which involved water jars which would hold different amounts of water. People were asked to work out how they would get an exact amount of water by pouring water from one jar into another. The first few problems could be solved by pouring water from large to small jars in a particular order and, as people worked through the problems, they got used to this way of doing things. Then Luchins gave them problems with a much simpler solution. But because they had become used to the other way of doing it, they didn't see the easy answer at all. Instead, they solved the problem using the method they had been using before, which was much more complicated than it need have been.

What had happened was that they had developed a mental set – a readiness to see one particular way of solving the problem – and that meant that they simply didn't see the other possibilities. The mental set in Luchins's study was developed by their experience with other examples of the problem; but sometimes, we draw on our existing mental sets rather than creating one specially. The nine-dot problem shown in Figure 7.2 is hard to do only if we assume that the solution has to fit within the boundaries of the dots. However, because of our previous experience of such puzzles we would normally expect this. It is the mental set arising from our previous experience which makes it difficult.

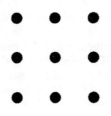

figure 7.2 the nine-dot problem
Join the dots without taking your pen off the paper or going over the same line twice.

Perception

Mental sets also make a difference to how we perceive what is around us. We are often particularly ready to notice certain kinds of things rather than others, and this can make a considerable difference to how we make sense of what we see. Perception is all about interpreting the information that the mind receives from the outside world, and working out what it means. So the psychological study of perception involves looking at how the mind acts on the information it receives through the senses, to give us our perceptual experience.

Most psychological research into perception has concentrated on visual perception because vision is the most important sense for human beings. But there are other kinds of perception too. We make sense out of what we hear, what we touch, what we smell and what we taste. Party games which involve touching different objects while blindfolded show us how strongly we interpret what we receive through our sense of touch. Sometimes, a particular smell can bring back a whole flood of memories. And we saw in Chapter 4 how the way we interpret our physical state can influence the emotions that we feel. So perception really involves all of our senses, even though it is vision that we know most about.

Organizing perception

One of the first things we need to explain when we are looking at visual perception is how we can distinguish things, rather than simply seeing a whole mass of disconnected colours and patches of light and dark. The retina of our eyes, which receives the information from the outside world, is simply composed of a whole array of light-sensitive cells, so what we actually receive is a bit like the dots which make up the TV screen. But automatically, it seems, we organize our perception so that we perceive whole objects and shapes, set against backgrounds. The way that we do this is very interesting.

Principles of perception

One of the ways that we do it is that we apply a set of perceptual 'rules' to what we are seeing. These rules tell us how to group different bits of information together into whole units. They are known as the **Gestalt principles of perception**, after the Gestalt psychologists who discovered them during the first half of the twentieth century. There are four of them altogether, and together they show how our perceptual system automatically tries to make complete, meaningful units out of the information which it receives.

The first Gestalt principle is the principle of **similarity**. In the absence of any other cues, we group together items or stimuli which are like one another (as shown in Figure 7.3a). The second principle, though, overrides the first one. It is known as the principle of **proximity**, and is the way that we tend to group things together if they are close to one another, even if they aren't very similar (see Figure 7.3b).

The principle of **closure**, the third of the Gestalt principles, overrides the other two (Figure 7.3c). If a group of stimuli hint at a closed or complete figure, the mind automatically groups them together and fills in the gaps. This tendency is so strong that if people are asked to draw an incomplete figure that they

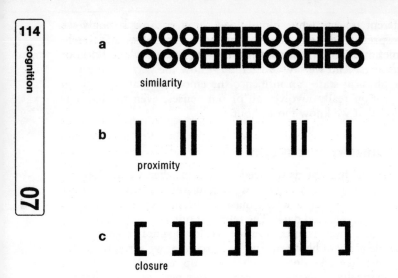

a

similarity

b

proximity

c

closure

figure 7.3 three Gestalt principles of perception

have seen, they will often fill in the gaps automatically, because they didn't notice that they were there. And the fourth principle is that we tend to look for figures which have **good Gestalt**, or whole, complete shapes, rather than figures which seem to be 'bitty' or disconnected. Together, the Gestalt principles of perception mean that we can organize the information we receive through our eyes into meaningful units – objects against backgrounds.

Brain cells and perception

There is some suggestion, too, that our tendency to see objects and shapes against backgrounds – which is known as **figure-ground perception** – may be hard-wired into our nervous system. In 1979, Hubel and Wiesel showed that there are special cells in the visual cortex (the part of the brain which interprets visual information) and in the thalamus (the part of the brain which channels information from the eyes to the visual cortex) which help us to identify patterns and shapes.

One type of cell, known as a simple cell, fires when it detects a single type of stimulus, such as a line at a particular angle in a particular part of our vision. A second type of cell, known as a complex cell, receives information from lots of simple cells, so that type of cell fires when it detects a line at that particular angle anywhere in our vision. And a third type of cell, known as a hypercomplex cell, receives information from lots of different complex cells. These cells fire when they detect simple shapes, such as a triangle or a square.

Although we are only just beginning to understand how visual cells in the brain combine information, what we do know does suggest that seeing shapes and objects may be something that our cells do automatically, from the way that they are connected up. The psychologists Marr and Nisihara (1982) showed how connecting information about edges and surfaces, detected by simple and complex cells, and then applying computational rules like the Gestalt principles of perception, allows us to identify whole, real objects like people, trees, or animals. The process is complicated, involving several stages including one where the image which is detected is almost like a stick figure. But by the time it is completed, we can make sense of it as a three-dimensional object.

Marr's computational approach tells us something about how we perceive the physical world, as does work by many other psychologists too. But we don't just spend our time looking at objects and trees. Often, the things we are looking at are more complex than that, and have special meanings. When we are making sense of these, we use our schemas and our existing knowledge, as well as processing the physical image that we receive through our eyes.

Perceptual set

In the same way that experience gives us mental sets which influence how we think when we are solving problems, so expectation or mood, or other social influences, can give us **perceptual sets**, which influence what we perceive. In one famous study, Bruner and Minturn (1955) showed people sets of letters or numbers. Each time they saw a letter or a number, they were asked to say what it was out loud. Then they were shown an ambiguous figure, which could be seen as either the figure 13 or the letter B. People who had previously been looking at letters said that it was a 'B', while people who had previously seen numbers said that it was a 13. Their prior experience had given them a perceptual set, which had affected their perception.

First impressions

Perceptual sets can be set up in other ways, too. Jones *et al.* (1968) asked people to watch as a student tried to solve a set of difficult multiple-choice problems. Each time, the student got 15 out of the 30 problems right. However, when some people watched, most of the correct answers came near the beginning, so that their first impression was that the student was very good at them. Other people saw the student get more wrong answers at the beginning, and more correct towards the end. When they were asked to estimate how many questions the student had got right in the end, the two groups of people made entirely different estimates. Those who had seen more correct answers at the beginning estimated that the student had got around 20 out of the 30 questions right, compared to estimates of only 12 out of 30 by those who had seen more wrong answers at the beginning. So our perception can be influenced quite powerfully by first impressions – something you need to bear in mind if you are going for an interview, or something else where first impressions might be influential.

Motivation and perception

Perception can also be influenced by our physical or motivational state. In 1952, Gilchrist and Nesburg asked people to look at pictures and to rate how brightly coloured they were. Some pictures were of neutral stimuli, such as landscapes, while others were of food and drink. If the research participants had gone without food or drink for four hours or more, they saw pictures of food and drink as more brightly coloured than the other pictures. Their motivational state – hunger – had affected how they perceived the pictures.

The perceptual cycle

All this sounds as though we only see what we want or expect to see. That's partly true, but it isn't the whole story. We can also be surprised by what we see, so it's obvious that our expectations don't entirely determine our perception. Neisser (1976) described perception as taking place in a continuously active cycle. We begin with schemas that we use to make sense of the world. Those schemas help us to anticipate what we are likely to encounter, so Neisser referred to them as **anticipatory schemas**.

Our schemas direct what sorts of things we notice as we explore the perceptual world. We don't take in everything around us – if we did, we would soon become overloaded. We wouldn't know when to take notice of the shadow of a leaf, or the texture of the tarmac on a road, or anything else. So what we do is sample the relevant information. If we want to cross the road, we notice the speed of the car that is approaching, the width of the road and other bits of information which might be relevant to what we want to do, and we ignore the rest. We sample the perceptual world through our perceptual exploration and that in turn has been shaped by our anticipatory schemas (Figure 7.4).

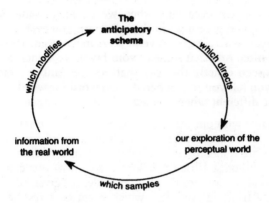

figure 7.4 Neisser's perceptual cycle

Once we have sampled that information, it feeds back to the anticipatory schema, and modifies it. You may have been about to step into the road because your anticipatory schema has to do with being on the other side, but your perceptual exploration led you to focus on approaching cars, and the information available told you that there was one coming up fast. So you modify your anticipatory schema, waiting until it has gone past. The modified schema in turn directs a new set of perceptual exploration (looking further down the road to see how many more cars are coming), and so on.

In Neisser's model, then, perception is a continuous, active cycle, not just a passive snapshot of what is there. What we anticipate or expect to happen affects what we perceive; but what is actually there affects what we anticipate. So our expectations are continually changing and adjusting themselves as we take in new information and revise our schemas accordingly.

Memory

Memory, too, is an active mental process rather than a simple tape-recording of what has happened. In many ways, this is quite a hard concept to grasp, because we always feel as though we are remembering exactly what happened. But it's true, nonetheless. The trouble, though, is that we don't often have a separate, objective record of what actually did happen, so we can't compare our memories with the real thing.

Active remembering

There are a few occasions when we do have some objective evidence to compare it with, though. Have you ever been to see a film twice, with a gap of several years in between? If you have, you will often find that some of your favourite scenes in the film don't happen exactly the way that you remember them. Even though you felt you remembered them word for word, they turn out to be different when you actually see them again.

It's the same with our other memories, too. Very often, we think that we are remembering a conversation word for word, but really we are remembering a slightly different version of it. The great psychologist Ulrich Neisser showed how this can happen in an analysis of some of the evidence given during the Watergate trials in America, which eventually resulted in the impeachment of President Nixon.

John Deane's memory

One of the important witnesses in these trials was John Deane, a man who was considered by many to have an astoundingly accurate memory. During the trials, he related a number of very specific conversations which had taken place between the President and other people in the White House. Dean was convinced – as were the other people involved – that he had recounted them accurately. However, later on in the trials, a number of tape-recordings of the same conversations were discovered. So in this case, it was possible for Neisser to compare the testimony given by John Deane, including word-for-word descriptions of conversations, with an objective record of what had actually been said.

The results were fascinating. In almost every conversation, John Deane's recollection of what had actually been said was wrong.

Different words were used, topics were mentioned in a different order, and sometimes particularly memorable phrases hadn't actually been said at all. And yet, even though the details were all wrong, the social meaning of what had gone on was perfectly correct. Deane didn't remember the details accurately, even though he thought he did, but he did remember what had happened. It was the meaning of the events which he actually remembered, and his knowledge of what it all meant influenced his recall of the details.

Stories and schemas

This actually reflects a very powerful feature of our memory, which has been known to psychologists for a very long time. Bartlett, in 1932, showed how when people are asked to remember a story, they make sense of the story in their own way. We fit new information into our existing thought structures – into the **schemas** that we use for understanding the world. This often means that we unconsciously adjust the information so that it will fit.

Bartlett found this out by telling people a story which wasn't the sort of story that they were used to hearing. He used an American Indian legend, called 'War of the Ghosts'. This story tends to be confusing to European and white American listeners, because it includes the involvement of the spirit world, in ways that seem illogical to Westerners. When people wrote down what they remembered of the story, Bartlett found that they made systematic changes as they tried to make sense out of it. The more often the story was reproduced, the more it changed until eventually it was nothing like its original.

Bartlett identified seven types of changes, which are listed in Table 7.1. These changes can be detected when we are remembering other types of information, too, and that can sometimes be very important. A lot of courtroom evidence, for example, is based on the idea that people can remember things accurately. So we need to be aware that someone's memory for what happened is likely to have been influenced by their own expectations and social assumptions, no matter how accurate they try to be, or believe they are being.

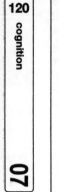

table 7.1 how memories change

1 **Changes in importance** – People tend to focus on one part of the story and see that as most important, even if it isn't really.

2 **Changes to the emotional impact** – People adjust the story so that it fits with their own reactions and emotions.

3 **Drifting** – The more often the story is told, the more its meaning gradually changes.

4 **Shortening** – The story becomes shorter and less detailed, as things which the person doesn't understand are left out.

5 **Coherence** – Bits are added to the story, or its sequence is changed around, so that it seems to make better sense.

6 **Conventionality** – Well-known ideas and themes are introduced, so that the story becomes more like other stories which are known in that culture.

7 **Losing names and numbers** – These get lost as the story is repeated, or sometimes change into more familiar forms.

Words and memory

Memories can be influenced by all sorts of subtle factors. In a study described by Loftus and Loftus in 1975, people were shown a film of a traffic accident. They were then asked questions about it. Among the questions there was one about the speed of the cars, and this was phrased very carefully. Half of the people were asked 'How fast were the cars going when they hit one another?', while the other half were asked 'How fast were the cars going when they smashed into one another?' All the other questions were the same.

A week later, the same people were asked to remember the film they had seen. Among other things, they were asked whether there had been any broken glass in the film. There hadn't been any, and those who had been asked about the cars hitting one another remembered that. But those who had been asked about the cars smashing into one another distinctly remembered broken glass strewn around the road, and were surprised to find that it wasn't there when they saw the film again. The words which were used when they were asked about the accident had directly influenced what they remembered – to the point of introducing details which hadn't been there originally.

This is an important finding, particularly for people who have to ask questions to witnesses for court. People can pick up subtle hints and suggestions from the words that are used, and are often entirely unaware that they are doing it. In some American states, the police experimented with helping witnesses to remember what happened by using hypnosis, because they believed it would help people to recall events. But when people are hypnotized, they are even more easily influenced, and they are also trying very hard to be co-operative. Because of this, they often adjust their memories without knowing it, to fit what they think the questioner wants to know.

As a result of this, Gibson (1982) argued that the use of hypnotism on witnesses in police investigations should be regarded as being equivalent to tampering with evidence. Memory doesn't work like a tape-recording. It can be changed and adjusted even some time after the event, without the person even knowing. And once that has happened, there is no way at all of telling the difference between a constructed memory and a 'real' one.

Coding memories

Memories may be affected by social influences, but this doesn't mean that everything we remember is wrong. And we do store a tremendous amount of information, which means that we have to have a way of retaining information in the mind, and bringing it back to awareness again when we need it. So a part of the research into the psychology of memory has been concerned with studying **representation** – how information is represented in the brain, as it is stored.

Modes of representation

The kinds of memories that we are most aware of using in everyday life generally involve one of four different modes of representation. One of these is when information is stored in complete meaningful units, such as concepts and schemas, and we have learned something about these throughout this chapter. The other three are also interesting, partly because we can see how they develop as we grow older, and partly because of the implications that they have for studying and using our memory for tests or exams.

When an infant is first born it has a lot to learn, and a great deal of that learning is to do with the body. A baby needs to learn how to move its arms, legs, eyes and head when it wants to, and it needs to make sense of the different sensations and feelings it experiences. Since actions and feelings are the central part of the child's interaction with its world, its memories tend to be stored as impressions of actions – as 'muscle memories'. This is known as **enactive representation**.

It is possible to see babies using this enactive representation as they repeat actions that have produced an effect – such as moving a hand as if they were hitting a rattle, even though the rattle isn't there. You, too, are likely to have some memories stored using enactive representation. Imagine the feel of a Waltzer, or a roller-coaster, and the chances are you will get an impression of how it felt on the muscles of your body. That's enactive representation. Adults can use it too, but they have other ways of storing information as well.

One of the other ways is known as **iconic representation**. This involves storing information as images, like pictures, or images of sounds. Iconic representation first develops as the young child's world begins to expand, and they encounter some kinds of information which can't really be stored using muscle memories. When you are reading a book, for instance, or watching television, the muscle actions which you use are much the same. But the information you are receiving can be quite different. So the brain needs to develop additional ways of storing information.

Children tend to use iconic imagery a great deal. They remember what things looked like, very clearly and, sometimes, even photographically. About one in ten children have **eidetic imagery** – visual memories that are so clear that they are almost photographic. But this usually disappears with puberty, and the number of adults with eidetic memory is estimated to be less than one in 10,000.

One of the reasons why it seems to disappear is because iconic memory is much less flexible and adaptable than other ways of remembering. Bruner and Kenney (1966) showed that children who used iconic imagery could remember a particular pattern of glasses, arranged on a grid in ascending size and order (Figure 7.5) quite accurately. But if they were asked to describe what the grid would look like if the order was reversed, they couldn't do it.

Children who used **symbolic representation**, though, could do it quite easily. Symbolic representation involves remembering things by using symbols to represent the information in the

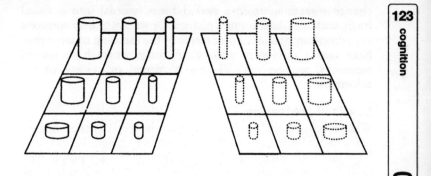

figure 7.5 Bruner and Kenney's experiment

mind. We actually learn this from a very early age – numbers, for instance, are symbols, and we use those to remember many different kinds of information. But as we approach adulthood, symbolic representation becomes more important because it is so much more flexible and adaptable than iconic imagery. It also lets us remember abstract information, which can't be visualized very easily.

So by the time we are approaching adulthood, we have a number of ways of remembering which are available to us. We can use enactive representation, iconic representation, symbolic representation, or schemas, as well as some more specific modes which we don't have space to look at here. We draw on each of these as we need to, because each of them works best with remembering different types of information.

What makes a good memory?

There are times when the type of representation which we choose to use makes a great deal of difference to whether we remember things or not. You may have wondered what makes a good memory and why some people seem to have good memories while others don't. A very large part of that answer is to do with how we go about storing the information in the first place.

Whenever we store information, we process it in some way. At the very least, we are changing it from an external stimulus in the outside world to an internal, mental form and, sometimes, we change it a great deal more than that. We might, for instance, change something from a verbal form (words) into a visual form, such as a diagram or a picture. Or we might hear someone say something and store it in terms of the meaning of what they have said – linking it with other things which have similar meanings, and so on. All this is **mental processing** of the information.

Levels of processing

What is particularly interesting, is that the level of processing we carry out affects how well we remember things. People who have bad memories – or who think they have – are people who tend to try to remember things passively, accepting the information but not trying to process it mentally. People who have good memories are people who process the information that they receive. They think about it, work out what it means and examine how it links with other things that they already know. By the time they've done that, they know it, and can remember it.

In fact, all of us have extremely good memories – for things that we are interested in! Even someone who thinks they have a bad memory has no problem remembering their social life, and what has been happening lately among their friends – because they are interested in it. But usually they find it difficult to remember schoolwork and other information because they aren't all that interested in it, and so they don't process it much.

And this, of course, becomes circular, because schoolwork can only become interesting when you do think about it and link it with other things that you have learned. People who are 'good at school' do this automatically. People who aren't are generally people who haven't learned the trick of making themselves interested. It can change, though – a lot of people learn how to make themselves interested by following up details and thinking about implications. When they do this, they find that the subject is much more interesting than they thought it was.

Interest and motivation

Being interested in something can make a dramatic difference to how well you remember it. In one classic study, Morris *et al.* (1981) asked people to remember a list of words and numbers – a single number attached to each word – which was read out to them. They had two groups of people participating in their study. One group was not particularly interested in what they were doing, but tried to remember the list anyway. The other group was really, deeply interested in it. When they were tested to see how many items from the list they could remember, the interested group remembered far more than the disinterested group.

The reason why they were so interested was because they were very keen football supporters, and this was Saturday afternoon. They had agreed to come along to the researcher's laboratory, and were hearing the results of that day's matches read out on the radio. So as they listened, they were thinking about each result, about how it fitted into the overall picture, and what difference it would make to that team's league position. In other words, they were processing the information. The others, who were not particularly keen on football, just listened and tried to remember, but they didn't process the information as much, which is why they didn't remember as well.

The researchers made sure that the two groups were just as good at remembering things by giving them another set of scores to remember, which had been made up. In this case, the football supporters were just as bad at remembering as the others. It was because they knew that these were real results that they put the effort into processing the information.

So, if you want to try to improve your memory, there's the answer. Don't just try to remember things passively: process them. Change the form of the information in some way: use iconic imagery to change it into pictures, or change it into symbolic form. Fit it into your schemas and concepts, by working out what it means and why it matters. You'll be surprised how much you can remember when you do that.

In this chapter, we have taken a brief look at some of cognitive psychology. There is much more which could be said: psychologists have been studying memory for over 100 years now and we know a great deal about it. But in a book like this, all we can really do is look at some of the psychological findings which are most helpful in understanding human beings in their everyday lives. In the next chapter, we'll go on to look at how people learn things, and at what we mean by the idea of intelligence.

08

genetics and evolution

In this chapter you will learn:

- the difference between 'phenotype' and 'genotype'
- about the evolutionary process of natural selection
- what is meant by the term 'critical period' in the case of imprinting.

Up to now, we have looked at psychology as the study of human beings. As we've seen, there are many different approaches to understanding people, and each contributes to the overall picture. However, there is another level of explanation which is also important in psychology, and that is the biological level: the level of explanation which says that since human beings are animals, evolutionarily and physically speaking, looking at other animals may help us to understand what we are like.

This branch of psychology is known as **comparative psychology**, because it is all about comparing different species to identify underlying mechanisms of behaviour and development. Comparative psychology isn't just concerned with comparing animals with human beings: it's also about comparing one species of animal with another, in an attempt to understand how and why different types of animals act as they do. For example, in a comparative exploration of dolphin cognitive abilities, Schusterman, Thomas and Wood (1986) drew on studies of the behaviour of many different species, including parrots, elephants and chimpanzees. By comparing what is known about, say, learning in one species with learning in another very different type of animal, it is sometimes possible to identify general laws or principles about learning which will apply to all animals, including us.

We will begin this chapter by looking at how evolution happens, since that is why animals are different from one another, and also why human beings are different from other animals. As part of that, we will be looking briefly at genetics, and how we inherit characteristics from our ancestors – even if we have not been brought up by our biological parents. Then we will go on to look at some of the characteristics of animal learning which can help us to understand something about human learning as well.

Evolution

Comparative psychology is firmly based on the idea that all animals, including human beings, have evolved from primitive common ancestors. Essentially, the theory of **evolution**, as put forward by Charles Darwin in 1859, proposes that there has been a continuous process by which different animal species have changed and developed. Evolution happens as the species gradually adapts to the demands of its environment, through small genetic changes. It may need a little bit of explanation, and since it is so important to psychology in general, as well as to comparative psychology, it is worth going into here.

The genetic basis of evolution

Inside the nucleus of each of our body's cells, there is a complex substance known as **DNA** (deoxyribonucleic acid, to give it its full name). DNA is made up of long strands of molecules, with two strands running side by side, arranged so that the molecules on the two strands are linked together in pairs, a bit like a zip fastener. These strands are twisted so that they form a spiral-like shape known as a helix. Because there are two strands, the end result is a double helix – like a very twisted ladder (Figure 8.1).

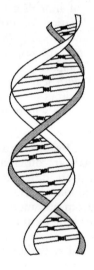

figure 8.1 a double helix

Genes and chromosomes

There are four kinds of DNA molecules, and different combinations of the four occur all the way along each double helix. Together, they spell out what is known as the **genetic code** – a tremendously complicated set of information, which gives instructions to the cells in the body so that they develop in certain ways. As a result of these complex instructions, we grow specialized liver cells, heart cells, hair cells, skin cells, and all the other different types of cells which make up a body. Sections of

DNA – known as **genes** – also give instructions about when different types of cells should develop, and whereabouts in the body they should be.

The strands of DNA in our cell nuclei are grouped together into larger units, known as **chromosomes**. These, too, are arranged in pairs and for the most part, each pair of chromosomes is very similar. The genes on each chromosome all have a matching gene, known as an allele, on the other one, except for one special pair of chromosomes known as the X and Y chromosomes, where the Y chromosome is much shorter and so doesn't have a full matching set. These particular chromosomes are the ones which determine which gender we will have.

When we, or any other living things, reproduce ourselves sexually – that is, by combining sperm from one parent with ova from another – we do it by producing special cells which only have half of the chromosomes: one of each pair. These combine with other cells from the other parent to form a complete set, which can then develop into a new individual. In this way, the new individual inherits some characteristics from each of its parents.

Mitochondrial DNA

It used to be thought that the genes and chromosomes in the cell nucleus were the only sources of DNA – and therefore the only set of instructions which the body uses to develop. But we now know that there is also DNA in other parts of the cell – in the mitochondria, which are small structures in the cell body which seem to have a number of different functions. It seems that mitochondrial DNA also gives instructions about the body's development, and this can happen as a foetus develops in the womb. So it isn't just the DNA which we inherit through sexual reproduction which matters in our development. The DNA which we acquire from our biological mothers during the gestation period also has an influence in our development.

This is quite a new idea, and geneticists are not quite sure how it works yet. But it challenges quite a lot of generally accepted assumptions. It used to be thought, for example, that it would be possible to grow an identical copy of an animal simply by using the DNA from the cell nucleus – a process known as **cloning**. But experiments with cloning, such as the famous one that produced Dolly the sheep, have shown that the new animal also absorbs mitochondrial DNA from the host mother – that is, from the animal which provides the womb for the cloned embryo to develop in. Although the clone is almost identical to its genetic parent, it isn't completely so because of the difference in mitochondrial DNA.

Genotype and phenotype

The genetic code, as we've seen, provides instructions for how the body should develop. But that doesn't mean that the body automatically develops them, no matter what. From the moment that the embryo begins to develop – in other words, from the moment of conception – there is a continual interaction between the two types of DNA and the environment in which the individual is developing. Factors such as the amount of oxygen or nutrients available, the presence of stress hormones or drugs, and the amount of activity of the mother all have an influence on the embryo's development; and these environmental factors continue and become even more significant throughout the whole of an individual's development.

What this tells us is that inheriting characteristics from our ancestors is only part of the story. How we develop them depends on our experiences, and how they affect us. The total set of genetic characteristics that we inherit is known as the **genotype** – but nobody ever sees a genotype in real life. What we actually see, in any animal, plant or human being, is the **phenotype** – what has actually developed as a result of the interaction between the genes and the environment.

That's an important thing to know, because it tells us that genetic influences are not fixed and inevitable. Genetic influences work alongside environmental influences, and having the right environment can make a tremendous difference. Take heart disease, for instance. Some people have inherited a tendency towards heart disease, which means that with certain kinds of environmental stressors, they are likely to develop it. But if they know that they carry the gene, then they can develop a lifestyle which will help them to avoid the illness – by keeping to a healthy diet, taking regular exercise, and so on. Having a genetic tendency to something doesn't make it inevitable. It just means we are more vulnerable and so we need to take precautions.

Individual differences and mutations

The combination of genotype and environment, then, produces the individual. The genotype occurs as a result of a combination of characteristics from the biological parents. Sometimes this combination is particularly beneficial: the individual may have inherited the very best from each parent and so (given the right environment) may be stronger, or healthier, than others of its kind. Each of us is individual, and different from other people, and the same applies in other species as well as humans.

Sometimes, too, there are small errors in copying the DNA when the special reproductive cells are made, which result in the new individual becoming different in some way. These differences are known as **genetic mutations**. Large-scale genetic mutations are quite rare, although they do happen occasionally. Most of the time, mutations are just tiny changes in the DNA, which may or may not make a difference to the individual's development. The process of evolution, though, is based on these small mutations.

Any individual, whether it is a plant or an animal, exists in the world and needs to survive in it. That means that it needs to obtain enough nutrients and whatever living space or other conditions it needs to keep it alive. It also needs to have some way of combining reproductive cells with another member of the same species, if it is to reproduce by sexual means. And in doing all this, it will often be in competition with other animals or plants, which are also trying to survive.

So anything which helps an organism to get an advantage over the competition will be useful. And slight physical changes, such as the ones which can be produced by genetic mutations, can sometimes give an organism just the edge it needs. If a mutation helps the animal to become better adapted to its environment, it will be more likely to survive than other members of its species. And it will also be more likely to reproduce successfully, so its beneficial mutation can be passed on to future generations.

Natural selection

One of the 'classic' examples of evolution is that of the finches on the Galapagos islands. When Darwin reached these islands, on the voyage made by the famous ship *HMS Beagle*, each island had a slightly different kind of finch living on it. However, when he examined the different finches, it was apparent that, at some time in the past, they had all developed from just one species of finch. That species had originally colonized all the islands. But because each island presented a slightly different environment, natural selection meant that the birds had gradually adapted to their particular island. In the process, they had become different from the finches on the other islands.

Imagine, for example, an island in which the main source of food was seeds, with thick, strong shells. If a finch inherited the genes for a slightly thicker, stronger beak – perhaps as the result of a genetic mutation – then it would have an edge over the competition. It would be able to get to its food more easily, using less energy than the other birds. So it would be likely to grow to be strong and healthy. When it mated, some of its offspring would also inherit the gene for a thick strong beak and they, too, would become stronger and healthier than the others.

Survival of the fittest

So if something happened which made the food supply scarce – perhaps a drought, or some other natural change – these would be the birds which survived. They would be less likely to die of starvation because they were healthier and better fed in the first place. And they would be more likely to be able to get at particularly tough seeds which the other birds couldn't manage, so they could make the most of whatever was available. As a result, more of them would be likely to survive the drought or famine than the ones with smaller beaks. In the end, over thousands of years, it would be their descendants which occupied the island.

On an island where the main food supply was insects which hid under stones or tree bark, a thick strong beak wouldn't be much help. Adaptation to that particular environment would benefit birds with thinner, longer beaks which could poke into crevices. They would be the ones who would become better fed and stronger, and so they would be more likely to survive the hard seasons. Natural selection is all about the **survival of the fittest** – and the fittest animal is the one which is best adapted to its environment.

Human evolution

This continuous process of adaptation and development has produced a vast diversity of living organisms, ranging from plants and yeasts to mammals and birds. Each species has evolved its different characteristics through natural selection, and when we look at different species, we can sometimes use those comparisons to detect part of their evolution, or of the evolution of some particular structure or ability. For example, Figure 8.2 tells us something about the evolution of the largest part of our brain, the cerebrum, and how it has developed in different animals.

Human beings are primates, which is a group of animals that includes monkeys, lemurs and apes, as well as human beings. Primates have a number of distinctive characteristics, but the one which is being illustrated in Figure 8.2 is the large cerebrum. Having a large brain helps an animal to learn and therefore to adapt to new environments quickly. As we can see, the human cerebrum is particularly large, which may give us the key to the way that human beings seem to be able to adapt to so many different environments.

Although it's quite common, it's a mistake to think of evolution as a straight-line development leading up to the human being. Human evolution is only one out of many different branches of evolution. There are lots of different groups of animals, each of which has adapted to its environment in different ways. We often think of a shark's brain as being quite primitive, for instance: it isn't really up to much in the way of learning or intelligence. But a shark is superbly adapted to its environment and in many ways represents a triumph of evolution. It would be hard to design a more efficient and better adapted animal to fill the ecological role which the shark plays. In a sense, every animal which is alive nowadays is the outcome of a battle for survival which has been going on for millions of years, so none of them can really be regarded as inferior or inefficient.

The most important part of the whole evolutionary process is the fact that the animal is able to pass its genes on to its offspring. Evolution has meant that this has been achieved in a vast number of different ways. For the most part, natural selection favours an animal that can make sure that its offspring will survive. A species might do this, as frogs do, by having hundreds of offspring, so that at least a few will avoid being eaten by predators and grow up to become mature frogs. Alternatively, members of a species might have just one or two young, but nurture them carefully in family groups until they are old enough to look after themselves.

When we actually look at what plants and animals do, we find a tremendous range of different behaviours and options. The

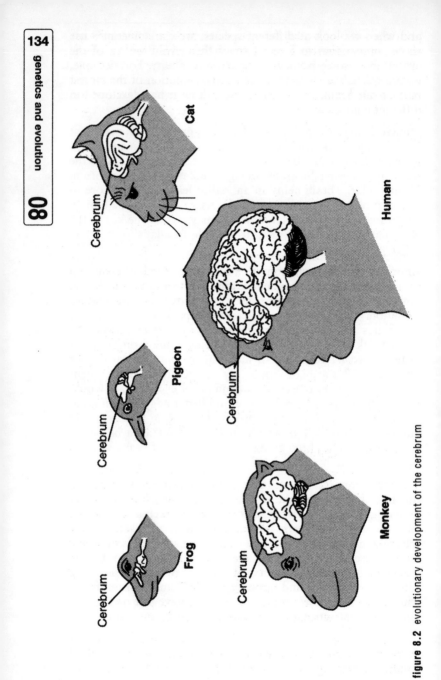

figure 8.2 evolutionary development of the cerebrum

principle of **biodiversity** means that there are examples of almost every different kind of activity that we could think of, somewhere in the animal kingdom. In many species, for instance, it is the fathers which rear the young rather than the mothers – after all, they too have invested their genes in their offspring. In some species, males hold territories; in others, females do. The more we look, the less there seem to be general rules about what is an optimal strategy for survival.

Sociobiology

Sometimes, even, we find that an animal helps its genes to survive by laying down its own life. The sociobiologist E.O. Wilson (1975), from his studies of ants, showed how it was often an evolutionary advantage for a single animal to die to protect its relatives, since they too shared the same genes. Moreover, it was also sometimes an advantage for an individual animal not to have offspring directly, but instead to devote its life to taking care of siblings or cousins, which again shared the same genes. In this way, ultimately, that animal's own genes would survive and be perpetuated.

Wilson used this argument to explain how ant societies, and similar insect communities in which very few individuals reproduce directly, could have evolved. In these societies, altruism, or self-sacrificing behaviour could sometimes become an evolutionary advantage. Survival of the fittest didn't necessarily mean the biggest and strongest, but the one which was best able to make sure that its genes were perpetuated.

Evolutionary psychology

Wilson, and also Dawkins (1976), then went on to draw a number of parallels between the sociobiological processes which he had observed in ant societies, and things which happened in human societies. This way of thinking eventually became the basis for a school of thought known as **evolutionary psychology**, which is extremely controversial. Although almost all psychologists accept the idea of human evolution, the argument that what human beings do – in terms of things like aggression, prejudice, mate attraction and other such phenomena – is a direct outcome of our evolutionary history is one which is nowhere near as widely accepted.

This is partly because human beings use a rather more direct method of controlling their behaviour: by caring for their children, teaching them, and helping them to survive to maturity. So simplistic parallels between what human beings do and what animal societies do are often very misleading. They may appear attractive on the surface, but don't really stand up to scientific scrutiny. And evolutionary psychologists also ignore the massive behavioural diversity of the animal kingdom, which produces a huge range of behaviours and possibilities.

The main objection to the sociobiological version of evolution as applied to human beings isn't really the ideas themselves, but the evolutionary psychologists' claim that human behaviour is essentially determined by these biological mechanisms. As we've seen throughout this book, what human beings do needs to be understood on a number of different levels, including cultural, social and interpersonal ones. We may be influenced by our evolution – indeed, I have often remarked on how our evolution as social animals has made us particularly ready to learn from other people. But that's not at all the same thing; because what we learn can be different in each generation and each cultural group. We human beings are not determined by our evolutionary history. There are any number of other factors which influence what we do, and all of them make a difference.

Coevolution

Furthermore, evolution isn't just a one-way process. Animals don't just adapt to their environments, they also change those environments – just by living in them. Even an amoeba, which has only one body cell, secretes chemicals into the water that it swims in, and so changes that water. And more complex animals often exert quite a strong influence over their environments, so that the environments also evolve with the animals.

This process is known as **coevolution** and it is something which is often overlooked when people talk about evolutionary processes. The usual assumption is that the relationship between animals and their environment is just a one-way thing: that animals use their environment to live in, but don't really affect it, except to use up its resources. But that isn't really the case, and a number of large-scale ecological problems have arisen from this rather simplistic view of the world.

When the first white settlers arrived on the American prairies, for instance, they found it teeming with buffalo, as well as the small animals known as prairie dogs. When they exterminated the buffalo and introduced cattle, they also systematically wiped out the prairie dogs. Since these ate grass, they reasoned, they would be in competition with the cattle. More recently – and almost too late because the prairie dog was nearly extinct – biologists have found that the prairie dogs' activities didn't use up the grass at all. Rather, they enriched it, so that it grew more lushly and provided more foodstuffs for the buffalo and everything else.

Similarly, Trevor (1992) reported on a 30-year old experiment in Tsavo National Park, in Kenya. In other national parks, the elephant population was culled when it seemed to be growing too large for the park's resources; but in Tsavo they decided to let nature take its course and to see what would happen if the elephants were allowed to multiply unrestrictedly. Although this led to some heartbreaking scenes in the short-term, by producing a country virtually stripped of vegetation and the deaths of a large number of elephants through starvation, in the longer term the country became richer and more lushly vegetated than before. The elephants' activities had spread the vegetation more widely, they had scraped out new water-holes during the drought, and all the other species had benefited too, over the 30-year period.

These examples of coevolution show how animals and their environments interact – and there are some similar examples with human societies, too. The Native Australians, for instance, managed the Australian bush by using fire, systematically, for many thousands of years. They lived from the land, but also managed it, and the plants and animals also adapted to this management. And this process meant that the environment changed, as well. Australian plants burn easily, but their seeds and roots are well protected, and they regenerate from fire very quickly indeed.

In some sanctuaries in Australia which have been set up by white people, and protected from fire for many decades, the native plants often develop serious diseases. They haven't evolved natural resistance to plant disease, as European and American plants have, because they didn't need it. Under the Native Australians' management, regular fires wiped out the diseased plants and sterilized the soils so that the new plants grew up more healthily than before.

Coevolution, then, is a significant part of the evolutionary process, for people as well as for animals and plants. We have all evolved in order to be well adapted to our environments. But animals don't just adapt to their environments, environments also adapt to their animals. It is this two-way relationship which we need to bear in mind when we are looking at what the study of animals can tell us about animal or human psychological processes.

Animal learning

In the next chapter we will be looking at some of the main types of learning, and much of that research was undertaken with animals. Comparative psychologists in the first half of this century studied association learning, and the way that animals can learn new behaviours and complex tasks by using different kinds of reinforcements or rewards. This is the kind of training we use to teach tricks to pets, or to train performing animals – although there has always been a certain amount of debate as to whether the animals are really responding as mechanically as all that, or whether they are simply going along with their trainer because they enjoy it!

Some comparative psychologists, though, are concerned with investigating animal behaviour in the natural environment. This approach is known as **ethology**, and psychologists using this approach have identified a number of other interesting aspects of animal learning, some of which is relevant to human learning too.

Imprinting

Some mechanisms became apparent as a result of research into **imprinting**. Imprinting is how young farmyard birds become attached to their mothers. Anyone who has seen young ducklings following their mothers around, or young chicks with a mother hen, will probably have been struck by how close the young birds stay to her, and how they scurry to catch up if they have been left behind.

Researchers exploring this attachment found that these young birds engage in a special, very rapid form of learning not long after they are born. This learning begins by the young animal following around the first large moving object that they see. After they have followed the object – which is normally their mother, of course – for a few minutes, the young birds become firmly attached to it, and will become distressed if they are separated from it. They are showing a particularly rapid form of learning known as imprinting.

Because imprinting is a special kind of learning, this means that young birds can sometimes become attached to animals which are not their mothers. People living on farms have known this for centuries: ducklings which have lost their mother while still unhatched have been 'fostered' very successfully with hens, and people who have hand-reared ducklings or chicks have found that for the next couple of months they would be constantly followed by a little procession of young birds. Imprinting is particularly interesting to psychologists, partly because of how it happens, partly because of why it happens, and partly because of when it happens.

How imprinting happens

Unlike, say, the way that a young kitten learns to hunt, imprinting happens very quickly indeed. There is a kind of inherited 'readiness' to learn the attachment. Moreover, as soon as imprinting has happened, the young bird avoids other large moving objects – as if the inherited 'readiness' has switched itself off.

It appears that the young animal inherits genetic instructions which make it ready to learn at the proper time, and which end as soon as the learning has taken place. It doesn't inherit an image of its parent. Instead, it is born ready to learn at a time which makes it most likely that it will imprint on its parent and nobody else. And in order to strengthen the probability that it really will imprint on its parent, and not something else, the duckling is also influenced by what it hears while it is still in its shell.

By hiding microphones in nest boxes, Hess (1972) found that the mother clucks gently to her eggs as she is sitting on them. When they hatch out and have become strong enough to leave the nest box, the mother takes up a position outside and clucks to the chicks, which go towards the familiar sound (Figure 8.3). By calling gently to a set of unhatched eggs, Hess showed that the sound of his voice could become a similar attraction to a group of young ducklings when they hatched out.

Imprinting is interesting, then, because it shows us how genetic instructions can work to 'shape' the kind of learning that we are most likely to do. Human beings, too, seem to be genetically prepared for certain kinds of learning. As we will see in Chapter 9, we learn very quickly to avoid any food which has made us sick, and we often continue to avoid that food for the rest of our lives. Like imprinting, it's a rapid form of learning which has evolved because it helps us to survive.

figure 8.3 imprinting

Why imprinting happens

For a long time, psychologists believed that all attachments between parents and young happened by imprinting, and some went on to develop dire theories about the damage that could happen if a young infant wasn't with its mother all the time. But as we saw in Chapter 2, it gradually became apparent that young human infants develop their attachments in a rather different way – they develop them gradually, through the social interactions that take place between the infant and older people.

So why would a rapid, powerful form of attachment like imprinting evolve? As with anything else, it evolved because it helps members of the species to survive and adapt to their environments. When we compare attachment mechanisms in animals of different species, we find that the ones which form an imprinted bond – a rapid, powerful attachment soon after birth – are the ones that have **precocial** young. Precocial animals are ones that can move about freely soon after they are born. Young horses, for example, can run around about an hour after birth, and so can lambs and goats. They, too, imprint rapidly on their parents.

So imprinting is nature's way of making sure that a young animal which is capable of getting around freely doesn't just run off and get lost, or eaten by the first predator that it meets. By developing a strong, rapid attachment to its mother, it stays close to her until it has learned a bit more about its world and how to survive in it. Human beings are much more helpless for some time after they are born and don't need to develop an imprinted bond with their caretakers. Instead, they have time to develop a relationship more gradually, through interaction with other people.

When imprinting happens

The other thing which is particularly interesting about imprinting is when it happens. There is a particular period – between about 5 and 25 hours after birth, for ducklings – when imprinting is most likely to take place. At first, researchers investigating imprinting believed that this was the only time it happened, and so they called it a **critical period**. A critical period is a time when a particular kind of learning absolutely must take place, or it will never happen.

Comparative psychologists soon found that critical periods also occurred with other kinds of development. Marler and Tamura found that young white-crowned sparrows had a critical period for learning to sing a full adult song, complete with the regional 'accents' that all these sparrows have. This period occurred when the birds were very young – long before they were old enough to sing themselves. But they had to hear an adult bird singing at that time. If they didn't, then when they grew up, they would sing only a very basic version of the song, without any of the full trills and embellishments that wild birds produce.

With imprinting, though, it became apparent after a while that the period when it usually happened wasn't absolutely critical – although it was undoubedly the strongest period for that type of learning. If a young duckling was kept in isolation, away from any other kinds of moving objects, even small ones, then it was possible for it to imprint even once the normal learning period was over. So researchers came to regard it as a **sensitive period** – a period when development was most likely to happen – rather than an absolutely critical one.

Critical and sensitive periods are also interesting because they suggest that there can be times when genetic influences make us more ready to learn things than we are at other times. Lenneberg (1967) suggested that childhood is a critical period when human children have to learn to speak, and which ends at puberty. If children don't learn by then, Lenneberg argued, they never will.

Fromkin and others (1974) challenged this view, by describing a case study of a girl called Genie, who had been brought up in virtual isolation and not discovered until after puberty. Although she was unable to speak when she was discovered, because she had never heard human language before, Genie did eventually learn to talk. But she learned a little bit differently from ordinary children, and the researchers concluded that childhood probably is a sensitive period for learning language, even if it isn't a critical one.

The idea of childhood as a critical period for language learning led to a number of experiments with teaching children foreign languages. In the early 1970s, for instance, a project was set up which involved teaching French in state primary schools in Britain. The project was eventually abandoned by government decree, on the grounds that the children concerned didn't seem to be doing much better in secondary school French than those who hadn't learned it. More recently, though, there is some evidence that those children – who, of course, are now adult – are much more likely to speak conversational French when travelling in Europe than most other British people, which implies that the project may have been on the right track after all.

So even though, on the surface, it might seem as though there isn't all that much that the study of the ducklings can tell us about human beings, when we look at the underlying mechanisms more closely, we can find quite a few insights which may help us to understand ourselves a bit better. But that doesn't mean that what human beings do and what ducklings do is exactly the same, by any stretch of the imagination. As we saw, human beings develop their attachments in a quite different way from ducklings. But discovering the underlying mechanisms for that kind of learning can be useful.

Learning by instinct

Both human beings and animals can have an inherited predisposition to learn some things very quickly indeed. Avoiding foods that have made you sick in the past isn't confined to humans – it's something that most animals will do. And it's a good survival mechanism, because food that makes you sick is quite likely to be poisonous if you carry on eating it. Avoidance learning seems to be shaped so that we are more ready to do it with some types of stimulus than others. Which makes us particularly ready for learning which will help us to survive.

Learning for survival

For example, in one study in 1966, Garcia and Koelling looked at how rats respond to different unpleasant experiences. They began by showing how the animals quickly learned to avoid salty water, if they had been given an injection to make them sick soon after drinking it. But rats who drank salty water and were then given an electric shock didn't learn to avoid the water. They didn't learn to connect the two stimuli at all. But they did learn to connect the electric shock with a light or a clicking sound.

In other words, the rats had been ready to learn some connections, but not others. They could associate shocks with lights or sounds, but not with tastes. They could associate sickness with tastes, but not other unpleasant happenings. It's easy to see, I think, how this type of learning fits with the idea of evolutionary adaptation. In real life, you would be likely to be able to hear or see something which was about to cause you pain; but you would taste something which was about to poison you. So it makes sense for any animal to be ready to learn those kinds of associations.

Pretty well all animals, it seems, are more ready to learn some things than others. Honey bees, for instance, find it very easy to learn to recognize particular smells. If a bee is fed with food that has been scented with a distinctive smell, such as lavender, then it begins to select lavender scents, and to go to those for food even if other food is available. They make the association between smell and food very readily.

But they don't associate other stimuli with food as easily. Menzel and Erber (1978) showed that a honey bee can learn to link smell and food 90 per cent of the time, after just one learning session, as long as it is a flower scent that is being used. They take longer to learn smells which are not from flowers, and they take even longer to learn stimuli which aren't smells at all. For instance, although they will learn to go to a particular colour for food, it takes then three or four learning sessions, not just one. And it takes them five or six learning sessions to go to a particular shape. They can learn it in the end, but they are not nearly as quick to learn as they are with smells.

There are some stimuli, too, which bees simply will not learn at all. For instance, they don't learn to associate light with food, no matter how many learning sessions they are given. It simply doesn't form an association. Yet bees are very sensitive to light:

they detect polarized light and use it in navigation. Evidently, as far as bees are concerned, foraging for food and finding your way home are two entirely unconnected skills!

What we find, then, when we look at this kind of animal learning is that it isn't simply a matter of random associations between stimuli. Evolutionary pressures have 'shaped' both animals and humans to be particularly ready to learn certain things rather than others. We've seen a human application of this principle already, when we looked at how strongly the human infant is pre-programmed for social interaction with other people, and how readily human children will learn by imitating others. Gould and Marler (1987) discussed how this evolutionary 'shaping' of the capacity to learn applies across many different species, and seems to be a fundamental feature of learning.

Novelty and curiosity

The examples we've looked at here have been about readiness for very specific kinds of learning: imprinting on a parent, being sociable with one's caretakers, or seeking out or avoiding food. But some animals have inherited a predisposition for a more general kind of learning. They will explore places, or be curious about new objects. And sometimes, too, they seem to be ready to learn entirely new forms of behaviour.

Rats and monkeys, for example, will generally explore new situations and investigate strange objects that they come across – unless there is some good reason to avoid them. And this exploration, too, can be an evolutionary advantage. In one study, Blanchard, Fukanaga and Blanchard (1976) put experimental rats in a box with a cat – separating them by a clear screen. If the rats had been in the box before, and so had explored it, they crouched down and remained immobile to avoid attracting the cat's attention. But if they hadn't had a chance to explore the box, they ran around looking for a way to escape.

In other words, rats use the knowledge that they obtain from their natural tendency to explore new places, to tell them what to do in the case of a potential threat. If you know that you are in a place with no escape, then the best thing to do is to try not to attract a predator's attention. If you don't know, then the best thing to do is to try to find a way out. But it is better to know, so exploring new places is a good way of surviving.

Learning and brain development

As we saw in Figure 8.2, the cerebrum of the brain is much larger and more highly developed in some species than it is in others. This is the part of the brain which we use for learning and thinking, and those animals which have the largest and most highly developed cerebrum also seem to be those animals which are most able to take advantage of opportunities for learning. As far as land animals are concerned, human beings have the most highly developed cerebrum of all. And we are also capable of learning more than any other land animals.

A dolphin's cerebrum is even larger and more convoluted than a human being's, but we don't really know what that implies, since a dolphin's experience is so very different from ours. Almost from the first time that human beings can co-ordinate their muscles, we are manipulating objects, changing them and shaping our environments. Although dolphins play with objects, too, their experience is much more to do with living in and experiencing their environment: they don't manipulate it as much. That's very different and it's not at all clear whether we actually have any common ground for understanding dolphin intelligence.

It is apparent to anyone who works with dolphins that they are intelligent, but it is unlikely that intelligence means the same thing in a dolphin as it does in human being. What we do know, though, is that dolphins are very ready to learn all sorts of things, including entirely novel kinds of behaviour. Moreover, they give every sign of enjoying doing so. Pryor, Haag and O'Reilly (1969) trained a dolphin to perform a new type of action each day, by giving her a reward when she did something she hadn't done before. By the end of the study, the dolphin was producing many entirely new actions, including tail-walking and back flips, and some actions which were so elaborate that the researchers found it hard to describe them!

We can see, then, that when we are talking about animal learning being shaped by the demands of adaptation to the environment, we are not just talking about learning simple responses. If an environment is constantly changing, it makes evolutionary sense to be prepared for novel kinds of learning. A species which can live in different environments may need to be able to learn very different behaviours to survive. Human beings live in all kinds of conditions, from arctic wastes to tropical forests, so it would be inappropriate for us to be genetically prepared to deal with a particular physical environment.

Instead, we are genetically prepared to interact with and learn from other human beings, and that's what allows us to survive.

There is, of course, a great deal more to comparative psychology than we have been able to look at here, and much of it is extremely fascinating. There is a great deal of research, for instance, into animal communication, and into whether animals can be taught language, as well as research into animal social behaviour and territoriality. It's a rich and complex area, and looking for simple answers is as inadequate in comparative psychology as it is in any other area. As with every other branch of psychology, we find that we need to look at things using several different levels of explanation, in order to make sense of what is going on. But the process of doing so is always interesting.

09

learning and intelligence

In this chapter you will learn:
- to identify at least five different ways in which we can learn
- about the possible uses of intelligence testing
- why it is misleading to describe anyone as 'intelligent'.

Human beings learn all the time. Indeed, our capacity to learn seems to be one of the main things which distinguishes us from other animals. Not the fact that we can learn at all – as we've seen, other animals can also learn, and those which are closest to us in evolutionary terms can learn a tremendous amount. But human beings seem to have a greater capacity for learning than any of these other animals.

Infant learning

From its very earliest days, a young infant is learning to handle its world. At first, that consists mainly of learning to control its body movements, and to make sense of the information which it is receiving through its senses. But as the infant continues to develop, it continues to learn. Its knowledge of its world becomes more sophisticated, and its competence in handling it develops throughout childhood. This applies both to social skills and to the physical and co-ordination skills which are the basis of effective human action.

Adaptation

Human infants are born particularly prepared to learn. Moreover, there are some significant features of the ways that we respond to what is around us that encourage this. We have already looked at some of these earlier in this book. One of the most important ones, which we looked at in Chapter 2, is that of a readiness to respond to other people. The young child's **sociability** means that human beings are a major factor in the child's early learning.

This links with another very fundamental ability which the human infant has – that of **adaptation**. A human infant is able to adapt to a tremendous range of physical environments, child-rearing practices and diet. As long as it has a good quality of social interaction, and adequate physical care, an infant is able to adapt and develop. And as a result of this, human beings are found living successfully in nearly every part of the world.

Transactions and contingencies

Part of what enables the infant to adapt so well is its ability to learn. Infants are strongly predisposed to learn – indeed, that is what the large human brain is all about. Some scientists argue that the reason our babies are so helpless by comparison with other animals is because they are born prematurely, to allow the brain to continue growing outside the womb. It wouldn't be possible for the brain to reach a comparable level of maturity as other animals before birth, because that would make the brain much too large for the birth process.

Whatever the reason, part of the infant's predisposition to learn involves responding very strongly to certain types of events. One such type of event is to do with **transactions**. Transactions are social exchanges with other people, and babies are particularly fascinated by turn-taking and activities which allow them to create exchanges with people. Transactions are a very important way that the young infant learns about its social world, and acquires the basis for social interaction in later life.

Another very special mechanism of learning for the infant is learning about **contingencies**. Contingencies are events which happen after a particular action has been made. For example, making a car move along a road is contingent on starting the engine; winning the jackpot on a fruit machine is contingent on putting in money and pulling the handle. In the same way that infants are particularly interested in other people, so they are also particularly responsive to things which are contingent on their own actions. If they can make something happen by, say, hitting it, they will do so over and over again.

This is the reason why babies like rattles and other things they can do to produce a noise. When the baby discovers that waving its hand around causes a rattle to make a sound, it explores that effect and continues to practise it over and over again. In this way, it gradually gains control over the situation. Infants become fascinated when they find that they can do something which makes something else happen – and this interest means that they continue to try to master the skill. In other words, human beings are strongly predisposed to learn from contingencies: it is an important basis for skill learning.

Discrepancy

Another aspect of the young child's learning is that infants also become very interested when things are different from what they expect. Not if everything is totally new, of course – then they are simply bewildered. But moderate amounts of **discrepancy** between what they expect and what actually happens is something that interests them a great deal. This, too, is the foundation for further learning, since learning about the world also involves learning what to expect under different circumstances. As the infant continues to develop, its environment will broaden and so will its range of experience, and we all learn most when the results of something are not quite the same as they have been in the past.

Of course, it is only moderate discrepancies which are helpful to the child's learning. If everything suddenly changes, then all the child's carefully acquired competence in dealing with its environment has been lost, which doesn't help it much. But some discrepancy is very good, even for relatively young children. For example, if an infant is staying with a grandparent or other relative, many aspects of its daily routine will be the same, but some will be different. Those differences allow the child to explore new contingencies and transactions and so help it to broaden its understanding of the world.

Schemas

One of the reasons discrepancies are important is because they help the child to build up its store of knowledge. The child psychologist Jean Piaget argued that knowledge development in children happens through the formation of **schemas** – cognitive structures which store information. This isn't just information about the outside world. It also includes information about plans, intentions, and what is the right thing to do in certain situations. Adults use schemas too, and we will come back to look at how they develop later in this chapter.

The very first schema that an infant develops, Piaget believed, is the body schema – the idea that some parts of the world are 'me' while others are 'not-me'. This distinction, he believed, is originally enough to encompass everything that is important about the young infant's experience. But gradually, as the infant becomes more aware of its world, its experience becomes more differentiated, and its 'not-me' schema begans to expand and divide into different areas. One of the first of these is the differentiation between the physical environment and other people – we have already seen how the young infant responds differently to other people than it does to the things around it, and this suggests that it may be using different schemas.

Developing competence

All of these mechanisms work together to help the young infant, and later child, to develop **competence** in its dealings with the world. Perhaps the most important principle of child-rearing, in psychological terms, is that child development should be a continuous process of developing competence and effectiveness, in dealing with whatever happens. We have already seen how feeling helpless is stressful to human beings. Feeling competent is the opposite: when we feel that we can deal with our world adequately, we thrive, both mentally and physically.

As we saw in Chapter 6, when we feel competent we are more likely to cope with problems, to make efforts to overcome difficulties, and to be successful in the end. So a child who has been brought up to interact competently in its world – who has experienced appropriate transactions and contingencies, and enough discrepancy to keep stimulating its interest in learning more – is a child who is better equipped to deal with the problems and disappointments which it may encounter in later life than one who has not had those experiences.

Many of the damaging effects of the experience of refugee children, those who have suffered abuse from adults whom they trusted, and others with traumatic experiences, arise from the sense of helplessness and futility as the child's safe, secure world is torn apart. Not all of it, of course, as there are other sources of psychological damage in those situations as well. But it takes a great deal of love, safety and help before the child, or adult for that matter, is likely to feel secure and competent enough to begin a personal and emotional recovery.

We can see, then, what sort of situations stimulate an infant to learn. But how, exactly, do we go about learning things? As we've seen, human beings are complex and operate on a number of different levels. Learning, too, can take place on several different levels. As human beings, we have several different kinds of learning available to us, and each kind is appropriate for different aspects of our experience. In the rest of this chapter, we will look at several different aspects of how people learn, before going on to look at how modern psychologists see the general abilities and knowledge which we think of as intelligence.

Forms of learning

One of the most basic forms of learning of all, and one which is shared by other animals too, is known as association learning. Association learning is sometimes called **conditioning**, on the grounds that it is all about producing a particular response under particular conditions. It isn't really a 'thinking' type of learning at all. Instead, it is where we have learned to make an automatic response to some outside event or stimulus. This response is even controlled by the lower parts of the brain, and sometimes directly by the spinal cord, rather than by the cerebral cortex, which is the part of the brain concerned with thinking and decisions.

Classical conditioning

There are two main types of conditioning, known as classical conditioning and operant conditioning. **Classical conditioning** is the purest form of association learning and also seems to be the most primitive kind of learning of all. Even an animal as simple as a flatworm can learn to turn left rather than right at a junction if it is trained using classical conditioning – and a flatworm doesn't even have a brain, just a kind of grid of nerve cells running through its body.

The most famous examples of classical conditioning were reported by Pavlov, in 1927. Pavlov observed that the dogs he was studying would begin to produce saliva when they saw the lab assistant bringing their food to them. This interested him because salivation is a reflex – a response controlled by the lower part of the brain which occurs automatically in response to an appropriate stimulus. Reflexes are basic survival responses – jerking your hand away from a hot object is also a reflex – but they have nothing to do with thinking or recognition. So the fact that the dogs salivated when they saw the lab assistant was interesting, because it suggested that they had learned to make a connection between the sight of the assistant and dinner.

Pavlov reasoned that the dogs must have learned by **association**; in which case, they would be able to associate a different stimulus with salivation, too. He experimented by sounding a bell each time food was placed in front of the dogs. After a while, the dogs would produce saliva whenever they heard the bell, even if there wasn't any food nearby. The dogs had become conditioned to salivate when they heard the bell.

Conditioning human beings

Classical conditioning works in human beings, too. One of the best examples of this was a study conducted by Menzies, in 1937 concerning the reflex which we call vasoconstriction. This is something which the body does automatically when it is cold. In order to retain heat, the blood vessels near the surface of the skin shrink, while those in the middle of the body enlarge. This is why your skin will go paler when you are cold. It is an automatic reflex and one which we can't control deliberately.

Menzies asked research participants to plunge their arms into a bucket of ice-cold water, and each time they did so, a buzzer sounded. As you might expect, the cold water produced vasoconstriction. What was even more interesting, though, was that after a few trials, the vasoconstriction was also produced when the people heard the buzzer. It had become conditioned to the sound of the buzzer.

We can see, then, that classical conditioning can work even on responses which we don't consciously control. Vasoconstriction is an autonomic response – in other words, it is controlled by the autonomic nervous system. As we saw in Chapter 4, many of our emotional reactions are also controlled by the autonomic nervous system, and this may be why we sometimes find that emotional reactions can be triggered off suddenly by an unexpected event or situation.

Treating phobias

Certainly phobias – extreme fears which interfere with a person going about their ordinary life – seem to have a lot to do with classical conditioning. They are often formed by a learned connections between the object and a fear response in the past. Many people become frightened of spiders or wasps, for instance, because as small children they see adults responding in a frightened kind of way, which also frightens the child.

Phobias are often kept alive and strengthened by the person imagining the feared object, and frightening themselves at the thought. Each time someone does this, they are strengthening the association between fear and the object. But classical conditioning can also be used to break a phobia, if it is deliberately used to make new associations with the object. One method for doing this is called **systematic desensitization**. In this method, the person gradually learns to relax in the presence of the object. They begin with something very indirect and non-threatening, like, say, a picture of the object, and learn to relax while looking at it. Once they can do this, they move to a slightly closer stimulus, like a realistic photograph of the object, and learn to relax again. Since you can't relax and feel frightened at the same time, what this method does is to replace the conditioned fear response with a learned relaxation response and, by doing this, the phobia disappears.

Another approach is much more direct. As we saw in Chapter 4, the fear response is all about getting as much energy available as possible. So it is very demanding of the body's resources, and hard for us to keep it up for long. After a while, the physiological fear reaction dies away and we calm down, even if we are still in the presence of the thing that we are frightened of. So another approach to treating phobias, known as **implosion therapy**, is simply for the person to be placed in a room with the thing that they are frightened of until the fear subsides. It may sound unpleasant, but it works – and it is much quicker than desensitization methods!

One-trial learning

Classical conditioning, as we have seen, is often to do with survival. This applies particularly to a very strong kind of classical conditioning which you have probably experienced at one time or another. If you have ever eaten something which made you sick, the chances are you won't want to eat that thing again – even several years later. This is a particularly powerful kind of classical conditioning, known as **one-trial learning**.

It's actually a very old survival response. After all, if something makes you sick, the odds are that it is poisonous. Being sick is your body's way of trying to get rid of things which are dangerous. So avoiding things which have made you sick would help you to survive, particularly if you were living by foraging in the wild. One-trial learning isn't unique to human beings: most mammals seem to have it. It's a survival trait for other animals, too.

Operant conditioning

The other main type of association learning is known as **operant conditioning**. In this type of conditioning, we learn something because it is immediately followed by a pleasant effect. That pleasant effect is sometimes a direct reward. For example, a squirrel will learn to climb a washing pole to reach a bird feeding tray and gain the food. Sometimes, though, the pleasant effect comes from the removal of something unpleasant. An animal might learn to press a lever in order to avoid receiving an electric shock; or a schoolgirl might do her homework purely in order to avoid getting into trouble the next day.

Reinforcement

These two types of pleasant effect are both known as reinforcement – because they reinforce, or strengthen, the behaviour that we have learned. The kind where we receive a reward is called **positive reinforcement**, whereas the kind where we escape from, or avoid, something unpleasant is known as **negative reinforcement**. Both positive and negative reinforcement have to happen immediately after the particular action which is being learned. Conditioning doesn't work if they happen later – if we do learn from delayed rewards, it is a different type of learning.

Sometimes people confuse negative reinforcement and punishment, but the two are really quite different. Both positive and negative reinforcement are about training a person or animal to do something – they encourage a particular kind of behaviour. But punishment is about stopping the person or animal from doing something, not about encouraging them to do something else. It's a bit confusing, because the threat of punishment can sometimes act as negative reinforcement, but the punishment itself never does.

The psychologist who became known as the 'father' of operant conditioning, B. F. Skinner, insisted that punishment was a very bad way of training children – or animals, for that matter – because all it did was to try to stop them from doing something, but it didn't give them any idea of what they ought to be doing instead. Skinner believed it was better to train children using operant conditioning, because that way they were encouraged to act correctly.

Training autistic children

Operant conditioning has been used in a number of different ways, including training severely autistic children to talk by rewarding them for making noises, and then words, using rewards of pieces of fruit. Many of these methods used the principle of **behaviour shaping**, which allows us to use operant conditioning to produce entirely new types of actions. In behaviour shaping, a new action is trained by gradually changing what needs to be done to earn the reward.

For example, at the beginning of training, if an autistic child who is normally silent makes a noise, that would be enough to earn a reward. After a while, the child makes noises more often. Once the child is making noises, the psychologist or parent rewards them only when they make noises which sound a little like words. Once they have learned that, then they are rewarded only for making proper words. Eventually, the rewards 'shape' the child's behaviour until it is saying proper words, even though at first it was unable to speak.

Of course, we don't have to produce a reward every time. In fact, learning is generally stronger if the reward comes only now and again. This is known as **partial reinforcement**. People who play fruit machines are a classic example of how human behaviour can be manipulated by partial reinforcement: they will often play for hours (if they can afford it), only receiving a reward now and again. Playstations and other video games don't give money rewards, but they do give a strong sense of achievement when we get a bit further each time. It is carefully calculated to make sure that we get enough rewards to continue playing with the machine.

Conditioning and society

In 1972, Skinner went on to argue that society as a whole should develop systematic ways of conditioning people into behaving appropriately. People are always conditioned by the reinforcements around them, he argued, but these reinforcements act in a random, haphazard manner. If society were to take control of these reinforcements, it would be better than the random, unplanned approach, because then people would be trained to meet society's needs, and wouldn't act in anti-social ways.

As you might imagine, this caused a considerable amount of debate. The real core of the argument was that Skinner, along with many of the other behaviourists, believed that *all* human learning and personality came from conditioning. So there was no such thing as 'freedom' or 'dignity' – they were just an illusion. Even language, Skinner argued, was only 'verbal behaviour', and had developed simply through conditioning and association.

Other psychologists, and people from other professions too, disagreed. They argued that people do have free will and are able to make real choices. Conditioning, they argued, is only one part of what it is to be human. As we've seen in the other chapters of this book, there are other sources of personality and personal growth. Being human is much more than just being manipulated by reinforcements.

Other forms of learning

Like almost everything else that human beings do, learning can be understood as having several different levels. Classical conditioning is probably the most basic level of all types of learning, with operant conditioning coming next. But there are other levels too. Some of these are to do with learning ways of behaving, while others are to do with understanding the world around us.

Imitation and modelling

One of the psychologists exploring alternatives to conditioning was Albert Bandura. Bandura was particularly interested in how we learn by imitating others. Imitation is an important form of learning because it is a kind of short-cut. If we learned everything through operant and classical conditioning, we would have to do everything by trial and error – doing it, and seeing what the consequences are. But life is too short for that. Using imitation we can learn much more quickly.

Bandura performed a number of studies showing how people learn through imitation, and whom they are most likely to imitate. In one well-known study by Bandura and Walters (1963), young children saw someone in a playroom with a lot of toys. The person was acting aggressively towards a bobo doll – a kind of doll which rocks backwards and forwards when it is hit. Some of the children saw the scene in real life, some saw it on film, and some saw a cartoon version. After they had seen this, they were then let into the same playroom and left to play with the toys.

After a while, the experimenters came in and removed the toys that the children were playing with. This was to make the children feel aggrieved and frustrated, so that they would be more likely to act aggressively. Then they observed how the children acted. Table 9.1 shows the average number of aggressive actions towards the bobo doll which children made during the next 20 minutes. As you can see, those children who hadn't seen anyone acting aggressively didn't make as many aggressive acts as those who had seen aggression being modelled.

When the children's actions were analysed more carefully, so that the researchers could tell which actions were specific copies of what the model had done, Bandura and Walters found that it

table 9.1 aggressive acts performed towards a bobo doll

Situation	Average number of aggressive acts
Real-life model	83
Filmed model	92
Cartoon model	99
Model playing unaggressively with toys	54

(adapted from Bandura and Walters, 1963)

was the real-life model which was copied most closely. In other studies, Bandura found that children were most likely to imitate models like themselves – other children in preference to adults, people of the same gender, and so on. They also were more likely to imitate people that they admired.

Latent learning

The most important finding of all, at least as far as psychology was concerned, was that what the children had learned from the model didn't necessarily show up straight away. It remained latent, until it was needed. A child could see someone acting aggressively, and not seem to copy it at all. But later, if the child was in a situation where acting aggressively looked as though it would be useful, the child would act out the behaviour it had learned. Children store what they have learned, and only use it when the time seems right.

This is an important finding for two reasons. The first, of course, is what it suggests to us about the influence of violence on television, and we will be looking at that a bit more closely in Chapter 13. But it is also important in terms of our general understanding of how learning happens. Skinner and the other behaviourists saw learning as an immediate change in behaviour. But Bandura showed that we can learn things even if we don't change our behaviour straight away. We can store our experience and use it later.

Cognitive learning

In fact, Bandura wasn't the only person to have shown how we store our experience for later use. As early as 1932, Tolman had shown how experimental animals can develop **cognitive maps**, so that they have a mental image of what a maze looks like.

Tolman gave a set of rats the opportunity to explore a complicated maze. If they were just put in the maze, they would just wander around. But then, if they were put in the maze and given a reward for getting out of it quickly, they would make their way straight to the exit point. This showed that they could use what they had learned from their explorations.

Human beings use cognitive maps too. Learning our way around somewhere new is often a matter of joining up apparently disconnected places, until we have a mental map which makes sense to us. We organize our cognitive maps in terms of landmarks, such as special buildings that we have particularly noticed. Often, too, we have only a vague idea of the distances between these landmarks. Briggs (1971) found that we underestimate familiar distances, so they seem shorter. But we overestimate distances that we don't know very well. This is why, when you go somewhere new, distances often seem very large; but they shrink as you get to know the place.

Insight learning

Imitation and cognitive maps are both cognitive forms of learning, in that they involve remembering and thinking rather than just linking a stimulus with a response. There are other types of cognitive learning too. One of these is known as **insight learning**. In this, we learn something new by suddenly understanding its underlying principles. We might solve a maths problem, for instance, by getting a sudden insight into how we should reach the solution – why the problem is like it is.

Animals can show insight learning too. In 1925, Köhler reported a study with a number of different chimpanzees. One of them, Sultan, was particularly good at insight learning. He would be given problems to solve, such as reaching a piece of fruit hanging high above his head out of reach. A number of boxes would be scattered about in his cage. In one typical trial, Sultan dragged a box under the fruit and tried to reach it but it was still out of reach. After a few unsuccessful jumps, he would seem to give up. But then, suddenly, he would go to the other boxes and begin to pile them up until they were high enough for him to reach the fruit. He had solved the problem by getting an insight into what he needed to do.

Learning sets

Some researchers argued that the chimpanzees in Köhler's study weren't actually thinking at all. Rather, they had simply learned from a lot of experience with trial and error learning. Harlow

(1949) showed that monkeys could develop what he called **learning sets** – a readiness to solve a particular type of problem, rather than just learn a single answer. By rewarding a monkey with a raisin or a peanut each time it solved an odd-one-out problem, Harlow showed that the monkey could learn to look for the odd one, instead of just choosing the object which had hidden the reward on the last occasion.

Harlow took this as evidence that simple trial-and-error learning was all that an animal really needed to produce what seemed to be insight. But it can just as well be taken as evidence that animals, too, can develop concepts. It would be very difficult to draw a clear line between a learning set and the type of stored experience which is contained in the concepts and schemas that we looked at in the last chapter.

Schemas

As we saw earlier in this chapter, schemas, too, are an important way that human beings learn. We fit new experiences into what we already know and try to make sense of it that way. Sometimes, we are successful, and the new experience fits into our existing schemas without anything needing to change much. That learning process is known as **assimilation** – where an existing schema is applied to a new situation.

Sometimes, though, our new experience doesn't fit into our previous schemas very well. When this happens, the schema has to change, as it adjusts itself to the new information. This is known as **accommodation**. Some psychologists and educationalists see accommodation as being the basis of all cognitive learning: we develop our understanding by extending and adjusting our existing ideas.

Skill learning

Not all types of learning are to do with absorbing new information. A great deal of the learning that we do is concerned with learning skills – both physical skills and mental ones. And one of the main features of skill learning is that if we are skilled at doing something, we don't think about it.

Whether we think about what we are doing or not is what distinguishes experts from learners. A skilled skater doesn't think about balancing his body, but someone new to skating thinks about it all the time. A fluent reader doesn't have to look at each word in a sentence: instead, she usually looks directly only at one or two words in the middle of the sentence, and recognizes the others instantly by their shape. Someone who isn't very good at reading, though, has to read every single word. A skilled driver doesn't have to think what to do when changing gears to turn a corner, but a learner tries to remember everything at once, and often gets very flustered as a result.

Automatizing actions

All of these skills are different, but they all have one thing in common. That is, that the individual units of the skill have become **automatized**. The person does them automatically, without thinking about it. Because they don't have to think about specific actions, this leaves the person free to concentrate on other aspects of what they are doing – such as thinking about their complete performance in a skating exhibition, or the meaning of the story they are reading, or the best route to take.

An action which has been automatized is actually controlled by a different part of the brain than an action which we have to think about. The **cerebrum** is the part of the brain which we think with. It also has areas which receive information from our senses, including the body; and it has an area which is used for deliberate movement – when we consciously decide to move a particular part of the body. This area is known as the **motor area** and, as you can see from Figure 9.1, it is on the top of the brain, next to the **sensory area** which receives bodily feelings.

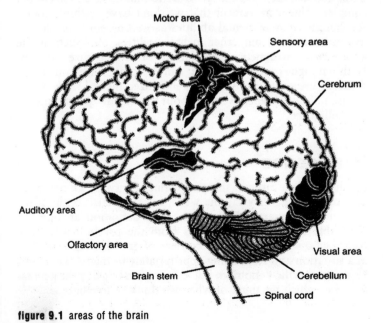

figure 9.1 areas of the brain

But the area of the brain which co-ordinates skilled movements isn't in the cerebrum at all. Instead, it is an entirely separate part of the brain, known as the **cerebellum**. The cerebellum is still concerned with deliberate movements, but it co-ordinates all the little actions which are involved so that they happen smoothly. If you decide to take a drink from a cup, for example, you don't think about reaching out, closing your fingers around the cup, and so on. All you think, if you think about it at all, is that you'd like a drink. The cerebellum co-ordinates all the actions needed to make that happen.

When a set of actions becomes automatized, control moves from the cerebrum to the cerebellum. A learner driver coming up to a corner has to think about the actions needed for signalling, braking, changing gear, turning the wheel and looking out for other traffic all at the same time, because these actions are all single, conscious ones being controlled by the cerebrum. We become flustered because it's a lot to think about all at once. But as we get more practised, the physical actions gradually weld themselves into a fluent unit, which is controlled by the cerebellum. This leaves the cerebrum free, so it can concentrate on looking out for other traffic, and can be alert for anything unexpected that might happen.

Skills become automatized through practice. The more we do a set of actions, the more likely we are to link those actions into a complete, fluent movement that we don't have to think about. We can automatize mental abilities as well as physical actions: not only reading, but other mental abilities, too, such as the ability to do arithmetical calculations or to recognize patterns. With enough practice, people can become fluent in many different mental skills. And it is generalized mental skills which we are talking of when we talk about the human quality known as intelligence.

Intelligence

Intelligence is a difficult thing to define. Everyone knows what they mean when they say the word, but it is hard to pin down that meaning exactly. Perhaps the best definition anyone has been able to come up with was from the psychologist, Alice Heim, who said: 'Intelligence consists of grasping the essentials in a situation and responding appropriately to them.' It may not be a very specific definition, but it does seem to carry the general meaning which we think of when we think of intelligence.

Psychologists were studying intelligence throughout the twentieth century, although for the first 50 years that research was seriously distorted by political and social influences. These distortions occurred mainly because of some influential psychologists who believed in **eugenics**: the idea that people who were genetically inferior should not be allowed to reproduce, because they would weaken the species.

It was an old-fashioned idea, stemming partly from a limited view of evolutionary theory, but mainly from the nineteenth-century belief that people inherited their abilities and characters – and also their position in society – and that these could not, and should not, be changed. But it was a vicious idea too. It formed the ideological basis of several political atrocities, including the Nazi concentration camps, restricted immigration for certain groups of people, and compulsory sterilization laws for those who did not achieve a certain IQ level in some American states.

Temperament and potential

Nowadays, most psychologists take a much more positive view of the human being. We are aware that inheritance provides us with potential – for example, that each infant has a different temperament – but we are also aware that the potential is shaped and guided by our subsequent experience. A child who is born with a physically active, fidgety temperament can develop in many different ways, depending on social factors. For example, much will depend whether the family sees its temperament as a positive thing, so that the child is encouraged to develop physical skills, or whether they see it as a nuisance, and try to make the child learn to be quiet and restrained.

In other words, the same temperament can develop into very different personality traits depending on how people respond to it. Also, as we have seen, people continue to grow and develop psychologically throughout life. So to speak of genetic influence as if it were a fixed thing, setting some kind of top limit to our potential, is an idea which has become increasingly implausible as we have discovered more about the mechanisms by which people adapt and develop, thoughout adulthood as well as in childhood.

Intelligence tests

Psychologists do, however, use intelligence tests sometimes. Not because they measure the limit of our intelligence (you can get better at intelligence tests if you practise them) but because they can help us to know a bit more about that person. Intelligence tests may not tell us exactly how intelligent someone is, but they do tell us how well-developed certain of their skills are. Some skills – such as the ability to comprehend words quickly and accurately – are skills which we often need to do a particular type of job.

There are two kinds of intelligence tests: group tests and individual tests. Group tests are usually pencil and paper tests, which consist of several different problems that the person has to solve as quickly as possible. Because they are carried out in conditions a bit like an exam, it is possible for several people to be tested at once, and they are often used for selection to courses or career opportunities, such as the civil service.

Individual tests, though, involve a psychologist seeing just one person and presenting each part of the test to them separately. They consist of lots of varied tasks, each of which assesses different mental skills, and so they are often useful for helping to understand people who are having specific difficulties, perhaps with learning, or sometimes in coping with their day-to-day lives.

But no psychologist nowadays would see an intelligence test, on its own, as giving enough information to make a decision about whether somebody was suitable for a job or a course. Intelligence tests, like other psychometric tests, have to be used along with interviews and records of achievement: they are not accurate enough to be the basis for decision-making all on their own.

Theories of intelligence

We actually use the word intelligent to mean a lot of different things. Sometimes, we are talking about someone who is very quick to grasp things and make decisions. Sometimes, though, we are talking about someone who is a 'deep thinker', and can see into problems more deeply than the rest of us. And sometimes, we are talking about someone who can be quick-witted and humorous in conversation. Each of these are examples of what we would think of as intelligence, but they are actually very different.

Intelligence as multiple abilities

There are two significant ways of looking at intelligence in modern psychology. One of them is to look at intelligence as consisting of a number of different abilities. Gardner (1986) proposed that there isn't a single thing called intelligence, but that what we are actually referring to is a set of seven entirely different intelligences. The seven types of intelligence are listed in Table 9.2.

table 9.2 Gardner's seven intelligences

1 **Linguistic intelligence** – to do with language and how we use it.
2 **Musical intelligence** – to do with musical appreciation as well as performing and composing music.
3 **Mathematical-logical intelligence** – to do with calculation and logical reasoning.
4 **Spatial intelligence** – to do with art and design, as well as finding your way around.
5 **Bodily kinaesthetic intelligence** – to do with physical skills, like sport, dancing and other aspects of movement.
6 **Interpersonal intelligence** – to do with interacting with people socially and sensitively.
7 **Intrapersonal intelligence** – to do with understanding your own personal self and abilities.

Each of these types, according to Gardner, is completely separate. Most people that we would call 'intelligent' have a combination of these different abilities, but some are particularly good at only one or two, and not at the others. A musical genius, for instance, will have one type of intelligence very highly developed, but might be quite ordinary in other respects. What we call an 'idiot savant' is someone who is well below average intelligence in most respects, but has one outstanding ability – to remember, or to calculate. Gardner's idea of separate intelligences shows how this may be possible.

One problem with Gardner's approach, though, is that it tends to treat these separate intelligences as if they just developed within the person, and have nothing to do with social influences. Although he drew much of his evidence from the biographies of high-achieving people, Gardner ignored the social influences on them. But people who achieve outstanding ability in any area have usually had at least one person who believed in them and encouraged them. Some psychologists believe that this influence may be more important than we realize.

The triarchic theory of intelligence

The other way of looking at intelligence is to see it as nested very firmly within its social and cultural context. Sternberg (1986) developed what became known as the **triarchic theory of intelligence**. He identified three different aspects of intelligence, each of which contributes to how intelligently we interact with other people.

The first facet of intelligence is **contextual intelligence**. Any intelligent act or ability, Sternberg said, takes place within a context. It happens in a society and a culture, and that makes all the difference to how the act or ability is regarded. For instance, imagine someone who is particularly quick at responding to something that has been said to them. In one culture, this might be regarded as a sign of intelligence; but in another culture, it might be seen as a sign of impulsiveness and lack of thought. A slower, more thoughtful way of responding would be seen as being more intelligent. So one part of intelligence is to do with how the person responds to the demands and expectations of their culture.

The second facet of intelligence which Sternberg identified is **experiential intelligence**. In the last chapter, we saw how experiences and expectations affect the way that we think, perceive and remember. We also learn from our experiences, and all this forms a significant part of our intelligence. Experience can influence intelligence in two ways: firstly, because of the automatized skills which we have developed and, secondly, because of the way that it helps us to recognize the demands of a situation, and what would be the best thing to do.

The third facet of intelligence is the one which is usually assessed by intelligence tests – or at least, by modern intelligence tests. Some of the early ones were very culturally biased, assuming that anyone who was not familiar with the practices of white American or English culture was automatically mentally inferior. But modern tests are much better at assessing what Sternberg called **componential intelligence**. Componential intelligence consists of three parts: firstly, our ability to learn and acquire knowledge; secondly, how well we actually carry out a task, such as problem-solving or calculation; and thirdly, higher mental abilities such as our ability to plan and make decisions.

So each part of componential intelligence contributes to how well we think and process information. But how we do it is also influenced strongly by our own personal experience, and by the cultural and social setting in which we find ourselves. Intelligence isn't something which just happens in a social vacuum: it is part of social living. And different societies value different intellectual skills, which means that what we consider to be 'intelligent' behaviour also varies.

An adjective, not a noun

Rose, Kamin and Lewontin argue that part of the reason why people find so much difficulty defining what intelligence actually is, is because it is an adjective, not a noun. When we talk of someone being intelligent, what we really mean is that they are able to do something intelligently. They do things in a certain way, which is distinctive. These researchers question whether intelligence as a separate 'thing' actually exists at all. It is more a question of how we go about things, than a separate ability that we actually have. It is probably more useful if we think of intelligence in this way, because this means that we are much more likely to see intelligent actions in their context.

We have seen, then, that human beings can learn in some very different ways. As with all of the other aspects of psychology in this book, we have only been able to skim over some of the main areas – there are other forms of learning, too, and much more psychological research into these areas than we have been able to look at here. What is important, though, is to remember that as human beings, we don't just use one way of learning. We can learn in a number of different ways, and sometimes even on several levels at once.

10

childhood and adolescence

In this chapter you will learn:
- why 'playing' is so important for human infant development
- to identy five different types of play
- the four approaches to understanding adolescence.

In the next two chapters, we will be looking at developmental psychology. Developmental psychology used to be almost synonymous with child psychology because for many years the entire focus of interest was on the way in which children developed. More recently, though, we have come to recognize that we continue to develop throughout our lives. As ten-year-olds, we are obviously very different than we are as 20-year-olds; but we are also different at age 20 than we are at age 30; and different again at 40, and so on. People continue to develop and change right through their lifespan, so developmental psychology covers the whole lifespan too.

Having said that, it is still the case that most developmental research tends to focus on infancy and childhood. The period during which an infant becomes a child is a period of rapid, almost visible change; and development is almost as intense in the years that follow, taking many different forms. The child grows physically, cognitively, socially, morally, and temperamentally during this time, and psychologists have investigated aspects of all of these types of development. Obviously, there is not enough space here to look at every area of developmental psychology, but in this chapter, we will take a brief look at some of the ways in which psychologists have investigated childhood and adolescence.

Childhood

We have, in fact, already looked at several different aspects of child development during the course of this book. In Chapter 2, we looked at how the young infant is primed to be sociable, almost from the first moment that it is born; and in Chapter 9, we saw how children learn through interacting with other people and building up their schemas about the world around them. These are fundamental aspects of the child's social and personal development which form the foundation for later, more complex forms of social learning during childhood.

We have also explored several different aspects of the young child's cognitive development. In Chapter 6, we saw how children develop different kinds of mental representations as they grow older and their worlds become more complex; in Chapter 7 we saw how important self-efficacy beliefs are in the young child's learning, and this also connects with the influence of parents' and teachers' expectations during the child's school experience, which we will be looking at in Chapter 11. These aren't the only examples of child psychology which have come up throughout the book, but they are some of the main ones.

Play

Because we have already looked at child development in some detail, we will not go into it at length here. But we will look at one special aspect of child development, which is very important to the child's psychological development – play. There are several different kinds of play, and the main ones are listed in Table 10.1.

---

table 10.1 types of play

Physical play – e.g. running, jumping about, spinning etc.

Pretend play – e.g. imagining situations, characters, scenes etc.

Play with words – e.g. puns, rhymes, riddles.

Play with objects – e.g. playing with toy cars, dolls, household objects.

Social play – e.g. ring o' roses, competitive games, role play.

Physical play

Each of these types of play serves its own function. Physical play, of course, helps the child to develop a strong body through exercise, and improves the child's general physical health. It also encourages the child to develop a clear body schema, so that it becomes aware of physical capabilities and develops better co-ordination. Physical confidence isn't everything, of course, but it can be quite an important source of self-efficacy beliefs, and we have seen how important those are. Although it's often overlooked in modern Western societies, or relegated to the limited arena of school sports, physical play sets an important psychological as well as physical foundation for later adulthood.

Physical play is sometimes a purely individual activity. Most children will simply enjoy developing the physical skills involved in swinging on a bar, or clambering around a climbing frame. Indeed, the urge to climb on things is very powerful in small children, and may easily represent a strong internal drive to develop our physical skills to the full. Some physical play, though, is more social. Rough-and-tumble play between children, or between adults and children, is also something which children evidently enjoy a great deal; and it serves a social as well as a physical function.

Pretend play

Pretend play, on the other hand, is about a different sort of learning. It allows the child to explore its world and the possibilities which it offers. It is no accident that children's pretend play usually begins by acting out simple domestic situations, because the social world is so very important to children. Pretend play allows the child to practise different social roles, and to develop an awareness of the wider social world.

Pretend play also encourages the child to develop its imagination, and many children do this to quite a high degree. It isn't uncommon, for example, for a child to develop an imaginary playmate who accompanies the child and becomes the focus for its exploration of the world. These imaginary playmates may be human, or they may be humanized animals, such as a lion or a horse. Although parents sometimes worry when their child begins to talk to someone who isn't there, there is no evidence at all that it is harmful. Some psychologists have even studied the number of high-achieving scientists and public figures who had imaginary playmates when younger, and have suggested that exercising the imagination in this way is actually a very positive thing for a child to do. But it is hard to obtain evidence for this idea one way or the other.

Play with words

Children also enjoy playing with words. Indeed, as anyone who has heard a toddler babbling knows, they seem to enjoy playing with speech sounds before they even have words; and this urge to experiment continues throughout early childhood. Many children talk constantly to themselves as they play. This type of talking, known as **egocentric speech**, doesn't have much to do with communication. Its main function is to help the child to think. Vygotsky (1962) argued that when a child is using egocentric speech it is actually thinking aloud – the language is a kind of running commentary on what the child is thinking about. As the child grows older, this way of using language becomes internalized – we think it to ourselves, but don't say it out loud (unless we have become too used to being on our own).

Children also engage in sociable playing with words. Opie and Opie (1969) went around children's playgrounds collecting the word-games which children use. They collected an enormous set of rhymes, riddles and puns, and argued that these form a verbal culture, passed on from child to child. The popularity of these word-games implies that they are an important part of how children learn to interact with one another; and they also help children to develop an understanding of how subtly words can be used. It doesn't stop with young children, either – the fascination with 'double-meanings' shown by adolescents who are just learning about sex is another example of the many different ways that people play with words.

Play with objects

A great deal of children's play doesn't actually involve toys at all. But some does, and even from quite a young age, an infant will play with an object, holding it, sucking it and being interested in it. Lowe (1975) discussed how play with objects becomes more sophisticated as the child grows older and its social awareness develops. Lowe's stages are presented in Table 10.2.

Toys which attract curiosity and interest in children seem to be preferred to toys that are simple representations of objects. Hutt (1966) suggested that exploratory play is linked strongly with both mental and emotional development in children, which suggests that it is a good idea for a child to have toys which encourage it to explore and to be curious. In one set of studies, Hutt used a 'supertoy', which was a wooden box with wheels, buzzers, bells, counters, pedals, and levers. Playing with different combinations of levers and pedals would produce several different outcomes – noises would sound and counters would be covered up or revealed. Children enjoyed playing with the supertoy, and would play with it for longest if it was set to maximum complexity.

Hutt also observed two- to three-year-old children playing with the supertoy, and then saw the same children four years later. Those children who had been most interested in exploring the supertoy were more confident and more social, and also had higher IQ levels than those who didn't explore it much. Nobody is suggesting from this that playing with the supertoy produced these differences, of course. But it does suggest a strong link between an inclination to explore, and later development. And this in turn suggests that toys which encourage exploration and curiousity in children are likely to be of positive benefit.

table 10.2 stages in playing with objects

Age of child	Activity
9 months	The child will hold, wave, bang and suck objects.
12 months	The child looks at things before sucking, waving, banging them about.
15 months	Familiar objects are used as if in everyday life e.g. 'pretend' drinking from a cup.
21 months	The child uses more than one thing together, e.g. 'feeding' a doll from a toy bowl.
24 months	The child's play with objects is becoming increasingly realistic, mirroring everyday life, e.g. driving toy cars along marked-out 'roads'.
30–36 months	The child begins to get toys to 'act' for themselves: e.g. a doll may put the other toys to bed.

Social play

Social play is another category of playing which has been studied by psychologists, although as we have seen, several of the other kinds of play are also social, at times. Essentially, there are three main kinds of social play: **free play**, which is worked out by the children themselves as they go along; **formal play**, which has clearly defined rules and procedures, such as skipping games or card games; and **creative play** in which children develop a new game together, perhaps involving imaginary characters or entirely new rules.

Early research into children's play tended to focus on children in playgroups, and so was all to do with how children of the same ages played together. But of course most social play actually takes place between members of the same family – brothers, sisters, parents and other relatives – that is, between people of different ages. Cohen (1987) used diary methods to record the play of his two young sons within the family, and found that even from a very early age, children would initiate different favourite games with different members of the family.

Garvey (1977) showed that when pre-school children are left to play with someone of the same age, they often begin a kind of dramatic play, involving familiar scenes and stories. Younger children, for example, often play games about mothers taking care of babies; while older children are more likely to play games which reflect their growing awareness of a wider context, like doctor–nurse games or acting out fairy stories.

We can see, then, that children's play is quite varied, and can take many different forms. Through playing, children develop skills and engage in exercising both their mental and physical muscles in preparation for adult life. What is very striking, though, is how much of children's play is social in character. Even if a child is not actually interacting with other people directly, it is often rehearsing social roles or expressing its social awareness as it interacts with toys. The psychological study of play, like so many other aspects of psychology, shows us just how powerfully we are influenced by other people and our social worlds.

Social competence and social influence

How is it, then, that the young child comes to be able to understand its social world? In the middle of the twentieth century, psychologists tended to believe that a child's developing understanding of its world occurred simply as a result of interacting with things – people or objects, it didn't matter which. The child would build up its schemas through assimilation and accommodation (see Chapter 9), and gradually become capable of formal abstract thinking as it matured. These ideas were based on the thinking of the famous Swiss psychologist, Jean Piaget. But in the last 20 years of the twentieth century, psychologists came to realize that Piaget had underestimated the power of social influences on children and, as a result, had failed to realize how sophisticated even a young child's thinking can become.

Developing social competence

In the 1980s, a group of researchers based at Cambridge University carried out a large-scale ethological study of young children in their families. They explored how small children interact at home, and found that in this context, children are far more socially competent than they had thought. Dunn (1988) argued that the play, humour, emotions and conflicts of family life are part of the way a child learns. It doesn't just pick up what it is supposed to do from praise or punishment – it takes part, actively, in a series of dynamic and emotional exchanges.

Some of those exchanges consisted of **teasing** older brothers or sisters. Dunn found that children often deliberately provoke their siblings, sometimes to the point of tears. Every family is different, and some families quarrel more than others; but teasing is a very common activity among pre-school children, and one which they become more sophisticated at as they grow older. Up until the age of about two, the child tends only to tease its older or younger siblings; but from age two onwards, it is just as likely to tease its mother – often by deliberately beginning to do something forbidden while she is watching, and seeing how she reacts.

Children don't just tease, though, they also comfort their siblings, and even their parents, when they are upset. Even children as young as two years old will respond to a brother or sister's **distress**, and try to comfort him or her by offering toys or stroking. Comforting was particularly evident among the older pre-school children in Dunn's study. By 14 months or so, younger children will also comfort their older brothers and sisters when they are upset, or their parents when they have accidents or minor upsets.

Dunn (1988) identified four features of social competence which young children evidently possessed, and which implied that they were far more competent than people often assume. These four features are: understanding others' **feelings** – that is, 'tuning in' to the moods of others, and responding to distress, amusement and other emotions; understanding others' **goals** – that is, developing an awareness of other people's intentions and personal plans; understanding **social rules**, in terms of what is and is not permitted, when rules will or won't apply, the idea of responsibility, and the use of excusing and justifications; and developing a **theory of mind** – that is, understanding that other people have minds of their own and may know or not know things that the child knows.

There is, of course, much more to the child's social cognitive development than this, but the information that researchers have gained from studying children's social competence has told us a great deal about what we can normally expect from a child, at what age. By and large, a child becomes fully aware of other people as independent individuals, with minds and feelings of their own, round about the age of three and a half. This awareness is the basis for empathy, social responsibility and all sorts of other qualities which are such an important part of belonging to society – and we acquire it far earlier in life than researchers used to think.

Social influence

Children continue to develop, and later childhood is an important period for the formation of friendships, physical and linguistic competences, and all sorts of other abilities. But that learning doesn't happen in a vacuum. It is structured by school, by parenting, and by other social interactions that the child experiences. The Russian child psychologist, Vygotsky, emphasized the importance of other people in the child's cognitive development, and argued that their influence is essential if a child is to realize its full cognitive potential.

The **zone of proximal development**, according to Vygotsky, is that part of the child's potential which the child is able to achieve with structure and guidance from others; and this is far greater than a child can manage on its own. It includes abstract thinking, reasoning, problem-solving, complex language use and the development of sophisticated memorizing. And the informal teaching which happens in families, schools and neighbourhoods is an important part of the child's cognitive development.

Adolescence

Adolescence is often thought of as a turbulent period – a period of upheaval and rebellion from parental authority. This image of adolescence has been very popular with Hollywood since the 1950s, and it has passed into our everyday consciousness. But it's questionable just how realistic this impression of adolescence is. Although some people, undoubtedly, do have a turbulent time in this period of their lives, others pass through adolescence quite smoothly, and without major upheavals. These differences have been reflected in psychological theories, too. Cockram and Beloff (1978) identified four major perspectives on adolescence, which are manifest in psychological theorizing.

Adolescence as 'storm and stress'

This view sees the adolescent as inherently rebellious, rejecting the authority of parents or other representatives of 'the establishment', and looking only to the peer group for social influence. Adolescents in the films of the 1950s and 1960s were portrayed as moody and emotionally unstable, and as implicitly difficult for adults to interact with. Various explanations were put forward for this phenomenon, including the ideas that it was a throwback to the animal passions of an evolutionary past, that it resulted from the hormone imbalances of puberty, and the psychoanalytic notion that it was an emotional reworking of early childhood sexual conflicts.

Some anthropologists and psychologists, such as Margaret Mead (1972) and Bronfenbrenner (1974) argued that it arose as a result of the alienation of young people from adult culture in Western capitalist societies. In non-technological societies, Mead argued, adolescents were fully participating members of their communities, and so were not left to their own devices and regarded as a separate culture. Even in Soviet Russia, Bronfenbrenner argued, young people were more integrated into their society than they were in America, and showed fewer signs of alienation.

All of these theorists, however, were working on the assumption that a turbulent adolescence was the normal state of affairs for young people in Western societies. But gradually this view was challenged as psychologists such as Bandura (1972) began to study 'normal' adolescents, rather than adolescents who were attending clinics or courts because they were disturbed or troublesome. Bandura found that most adolescents didn't particularly oppose their parents' values or show hostility or rebellion. Rather, for many people, adolescence was a period in which they developed a more trusting and positive relationship with their parents, rather than the reverse.

Research by other psychologists confirmed Bandura's arguments, and the 'storm and stress' model of adolescence became increasingly regarded as one which had only a limited usefulness – appropriate for some adolescents, but not for most. So different models of adolescence began to emerge.

Adolescence as role transition

One of the most popular of these alternative models was the idea that adolescence can most usefully be seen as a period of role transition – a time when teenagers are changing how they interact with society in general, and with the other people around them. Moving from school to work, or from school to higher education, involves adopting different social roles, and these in turn can produce changes as different sides of the personality emerge.

There are several different aspects to the changing roles of adolescence. Sometimes, we retain the same roles, but there are changes in how we are expected to perform them. We would expect a ten-year-old older sister to act differently from a sixteen-year-old older sister, for example. But there are entirely new roles, too, which appear during adolescence, and these have to be learned. A Saturday job in a shop, for example, involves learning a way of interacting with people which is entirely different from the styles which we adopt with family or friends.

Part of being an adolescent, then, involves balancing out the different demands of the social roles that we are called on to play. Sometimes, these result in widely differing expectations: someone might be regarded as a responsible adult in their Saturday job, as a child by members of their family, and as an irresponsible teenager by their schoolteacher. Each of these expectations will bring different 'selves', or aspects of the personality, to the fore, so balancing their different demands is something which takes a bit of learning.

Adolescence as a developmental stage

A third way of looking at adolescence identified by Cockram and Beloff, is to see it as a **developmental stage**. This idea is based on Erikson's theory of life-long development (Erikson, 1968), which identified a number of different conflicts which each individual has to resolve as they pass through life. These are listed in Table 10.3. The successful resolutions of early conflicts, Erikson argued, set the foundation for the later ones, so all the stages are important in the person's psychological development.

The particular conflict which needs to be resolved during adolescence, Erikson argued, is that of identity versus role confusion. In a sense, this relates to the perspective on adolescence that we were just looking at – the way the adolescent needs to come to terms with the many new social roles that they are expected to play. In terms of the individual's own psychological development, Erikson saw it as important that the adolescent could accept the fact that they had a single, integrated identity, despite the fact that they played so many different social roles and acted differently in each one.

Only by maintaining or developing a coherent sense of identity, Erikson believed, would an adolescent form a firm foundation for a later productive adulthood, and for mature and satisfying relationships. If the different role demands which they experienced were too stressful, the person would experience what Erikson called a state of **identity diffusion**, in which they

10.3 Erikson's stages of lifespan development

Early infancy **trust vs mistrust**
The infant has to strike a balance between trusting people and risking disappointment, or being mistrustful and unable to relate to other people fully.

Later infancy **autonomy vs shame and doubt**
The toddler has to develop a sense of personal agency and control over behaviour and actions, rather than mistrusting its ability to do things.

Early childhood **initiative vs guilt**
The child has to develop an increasing sense of personal responsibility and initiative, rather than simply feeling guilty and uncertain.

Middle childhood **industry vs inferiority**
The child has to learn that systematic effort will overcome challenges, rather than just giving up and accepting failure.

Puberty and adolescence **identity vs role confusion**
The adolescent needs to develop a consistent sense of inner self, rather than being swamped by the range of roles and choices available.

Young adulthood **intimacy vs isolation**
The young adult needs to learn to develop intimate and trusting relationships with others, rather than avoiding relationships because they can become threatening and painful.

Mature adulthood **generativity vs stagnation**
The adult needs to develop a productive life, recognizing their personal achievements and abilities, instead of stagnating psychologically.

Late adulthood **integrity vs despair**
The older person needs to be able to look back on their life positively, rather than to feel that it has been meaningless and futile.

would have difficulty forming relationships with other people and would also find it difficult to make coherent plans for the future, and work towards achieving them. Without a clear sense of who we are, such things would be very difficult, and yet adolescence is often an important time of preparation for adult life, and can involve a considerable investment in work, effort and planning.

The lifespan approach to adolescence

The fourth type of theory of adolescence described by Cockram and Beloff is the **lifespan** approach to adolescence. This model presents the adolescent as an active agent in their own lives – unlike the other ones, which tended to see the person as passive, merely suffering or experiencing all these different demands. But adolescents are very active in interacting with their own environment, and can shape what happens to them to quite a high degree.

Lerner (1985) argued that adolescents interact with their environment in three ways. The first of these is that they act as a stimulus to other people, and people respond differently to them. Secondly, adolescents process information mentally: they think about what they are experiencing, interpret it, and respond accordingly. And thirdly, adolescents act as active agents in their own lives, making their own choices, and deliberately influencing what is likely to happen. All these combine to mean that the adolescent is much less passive than the older psychological models implied.

Changes and stages

So what can we conclude from all this? Essentially, it seems, there is no single way of looking at adolescence which will explain what everyone experiences. There are a lot of role changes which take place during adolescence, and a great many major life changes too. But each person will cope with them in their own way, and according to the awareness and understanding that they have developed as a person in their own right. Throughout this book, we have been looking at mechanisms which influence people, and which give us clues to understand why people are like they are. They apply just as much to adolescents, too!

Adolescence has its own internal stages – a young adolescent is faced with different types of challenges and transitions than someone in later adolescence. So it may not be very helpful to think of all adolescents as going through the same kinds of experience. Some psychologists, in fact, question whether it is actually useful to think of development in terms of stages at all, since so much development happens within stages, and each period of development tends to blend with the one before and the one after. People develop in complex ways, and rarely show an abrupt transition from one stage to another. So it's important to remember that stages may not really exist! They are just a shorthand way of describing that particular time in a person's life.

In the next chapter, we will look at other times in people's lives – the times when they become adults, have families, grow older, and eventually retire.

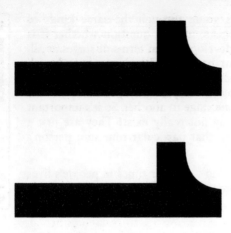

adulthood, retirement and ageing

In this chapter you will learn:

- why research into adulthood may be regarded as 'culturally specific'
- about recent changes in retirement theories
- to differentiate between 'cross sectional' and 'longitudinal' methods of studying ageing.

Contrary to popular belief, our development doesn't stop when we become adult. We continue developing and changing throughout our lives; and in recent years the study of lifespan development has become extremely popular. In the last chapter, we looked at childhood and adolescence. Here, we will look at development throughout the rest of the lifespan – that is, development in adulthood and during the ageing process.

Adulthood

It is only relatively recently that psychologists have begun to study adulthood in its own right. Of course, psychology is about people, and so the various aspects of how human beings function which we have looked at earlier in this book are all relevant to understanding adulthood. In that sense, psychology has always studied both adults and children. And work psychology, which we will be looking at in the next chapter, has a long history too, which is entirely concerned with adult life. But the idea that the period of life which we know as adulthood might also be worth studying in its own right is a relatively new one. To date, much of this research has been concerned with looking at the various phases which people pass through in the course of their adult life: charting what happens to us – or at least to many people in Western industrial societies – as we grow older.

Life transitions

Gould (1978) developed the idea that adult life consists of a series of **transitions,** or life changes, which occur at different times in our lives. The first of these is that of adjusting to the responsibilities of being independent and living away from parental care. Looking afer ourselves without someone in the background is quite different from the kind of independence which occurs when living as part of a family group, where there is always someone to fall back on, or to look after you if you become ill.

This transition, Gould argued, takes place usually between the ages of 16 and 22. Then there is another transition, which takes place during our twenties, in which we develop our own competences and autonomy, and choose our own rules to live by, rather than simply conforming to our parents' rules and principles. A third transition, according to Gould, happens between 28 and 34, as we come to know ourselves better, and learn to come to terms with aspects of our nature which we weren't really aware of before. And the final transition involves accepting that life isn't going to last for ever – that is, developing a sense of our own mortality. This final transition, Gould argued, happens between the ages of 35 and 45.

There are some big problems with this type of approach to studying adulthood. One of them is that it is very culturally specific – it is probably fine for describing the lives of middle-class white North American men, but things may be rather different for people of different backgrounds, where the normal course of living takes different forms. Another is that it doesn't account for individual differences. Some people don't leave home until much later in life; some people don't experience a lengthy period of independence but marry from their family home; and some come across these transitions at very different ages. So it would be difficult to say how the model applied to them.

If there are so many problems with this type of model, why should we bother with it at all? Well, mainly because it's a start. By identifying the kinds of things that are missing from a model like this, we can move towards developing better theories. Psychology doesn't have all the answers: it is continually changing, and trying to improve its theories and ideas. When a new area is first opened up, the initial theories are often quite limited; but they provide a useful basis for further research which can help us to develop a deeper understanding.

The family life-cycle

Sometimes, even if a theory is a little bit limited, it can still be useful. For instance, Duvall (1971) developed a model of the different stages of marriage which has been criticized in similar ways – it is culturally specific and it doesn't take account of the experiences of single parents, or of divorce, for example. But even with its shortcomings, the model can still help us to understand how a consistent long-term marriage goes through different phases; and how these phases actually involve different behaviour on the part of the couple, and different assumptions about what they are actually doing.

Duvall identified eight different stages of marriage in all. The first of these is the **honeymoon period,** in which the married couple are learning to live together, without children. At this time, they are getting to know each other and setting the foundations for their later life together. Statistically, a couple whose honeymoon period lasts for two years or more before children come along are much more likely to stay together in the long term than those who only have a brief interval before starting a family. This may partly be because they have the time to get to know one another as people much better.

The second period in Duvall's model is the **nurturing period,** when the oldest child is less than two years old, and the couple are learning to cope with being new parents. It can be a stressful time for both of them, and it isn't made easier by lack of sleep, and anxiety about how the child or children are progressing. So at this time, the couple are likely to need to give one another quite a high level of both practical and emotional support; and knowing each other well can make for fewer misunderstandings and quarrels.

The third stage is what Duvall referred to as the **authority period,** in which the family are bringing up pre-school children, with the oldest between two and five years old. Essentially, the parents have to train their pre-schoolers to behave in a socially acceptable way, and not like tyrannical little monsters! This, too, can be a deeply demanding phase for the parents.

Things often ease up a little when the family enters the **interpretive period,** in which the oldest child is between five and 13 years old, and at school. (The reason why Duvall categorizes these stages from the age of the oldest child is mainly because this signals the need for the parents to learn new behaviours. They have already learned most of the behaviours they will need for younger children – although each child is different, of course.)

The fifth period in the family life-cycle is the **interdependent period,** which consists of families with teenagers. At this time it becomes possible for the teenagers to take more of a share in the emotional and physical aspects of the family, and the relationship between parents and child can become a two-way, interdependent one rather than a simple, one-way, dependent one.

Then there is the sixth period, which Duvall refers to as the **launching period,** as the young adults emerge to become independent in society. Typically, this period involves some degree of support from home – perhaps providing a home for a child who is away at college during term-time, or providing help with furnishings or a regular Sunday lunch for a young adult who is independent and working. This period lasts from the time when the first child leaves, to when the last child leaves home.

The seventh of Duvall's stages is the **empty-nest period**, when all the children have left and the parents are together at home. This can be quite a difficult adjustment for some couples, particularly if the children have been the exclusive focus of attention for most of their time together. Some couples, though, find it a pleasant relief, because it means they can simply enjoy one another's company again. They often begin a number of co-operative activities that they weren't doing before, such as redecorating, or travelling.

The final period in the family life-cycle, described by Duvall, is the **retirement period**, in which the members of the partnership who were working are now retired. This, too, can be a period of re-adjustment, particularly if one of the couple has been accustomed to having the house to themselves for most of the day.

We can see, then, that each stage of the family life-cycle involves different adjustments and new forms of learning. Although, inevitably, it doesn't fit every single family, identifying the different stages in this way has proved to be very useful for marriage guidance counsellors and other people who are either trying to help people to adjust to changes in their relationships, or who are trying to do the adjusting themselves.

Retirement

In earlier times, the period of retirement used to be a brief interlude before old age and death. But in modern living, it has become quite different. Changes in diet, lifestyle and general health mean that most people continue to live an active, productive life for a long period after they finish formal working – as long as 30, or if they have taken early retirement even 40, years. This period is very nearly as long as many people's working life, so the idea of retirement as a 'restful interlude' isn't really very practical. Instead, lifespan psychologists nowadays see retirement as a way of developing in new and different ways, that weren't possible under the constraints of working life.

Disengagement theory

The first psychological theories about retirement tended to take a rather negative position. Cummings and Henry (1961) saw retirement as a gradual process of separating off from society. Old people might be numerous, but they were less visible than younger people, and less involved in social activities. Cummings and Henry saw this as part of a natural mechanism, similar to a weakened animal withdrawing from its herd to die.

Cummings and Henry put forward a biological explanation for this. They proposed that, as people grow older, there is a kind of inherited biological mechanism which encourages them, gradually, to withdraw from society. They have fulfilled their evolutionary function by bringing up families and helping their offspring to survive, and now, Cummings and Henry argued, evolution has no place for them. As a consequence, they become less and less involved in social affairs, leaving decision-making and social organization to younger people and become increasingly withdrawn into their own lives.

This rather gloomy process is known as **disengagement**, based on the idea that there is an innate tendency to disengage from society with age. It reflects a tendency of psychologists at that time to look for biological explanations for all human behaviour. But there are many problems with this model. For one thing, the relative lack of social involvement of older people isn't anything like an animal creeping away to die, because the period of being 'an old person' or a pensioner is so very long. Nowadays, it isn't uncommon for people to live for 30 years or more after they have retired, and that's quite different from a couple of days of being ill and weak before dying – the normal state of affairs among wild animals.

Activity theory

That type of explanation also ignores the social factors involved in retirement. An alternative explanation for why older people don't seem to take as active a part in society as they might was put forward by Havighurst, in 1964. Havighurst attributed it to the fact that older people have relatively few opportunities to play meaningful social roles in society. When someone is active and working, they play a large number of different social roles. These include various roles at work as well as roles to do with the family. In other words, as Havighurst put it, their **role-count** is high. But when someone retires from work, their role-count drops dramatically, because all the social roles that they played that were relevant to work – even ones as simple as being a commuter – vanish. All that is left are social roles to do with family and home.

In other words, Havighurst was arguing, people become less visible when they retire simply because they don't have as many opportunities to play a part in everyday social living. And this has personal consequences, as well as social ones, because people can easily come to feel apathetic and useless as a result. The way to counteract this, Havighurst argued, is for people to replace their lost social roles deliberately, by adding new ones such as joining clubs and societies for older people, or working for organizations like Oxfam, which employ people over conventional retirement age. Keeping up one's role-count, according to Havighurst, is the way to ensure a positive experience of old age.

Social exchange theory

In 1975, Dowd proposed a different way of explaining this question. Dowd proposed that retirement is actually a sort of social contract that the person makes with society. They obtain increased leisure time, and an 'honourable discharge' from the idea that all responsible members of society ought to work as hard as possible – the Protestant Work Ethic – and in return, they give up their involvement in how society's affairs are run. This **social exchange** is seen, according to Dowd, as a fair trade, both by society and by old people.

More recently, however, people are showing signs of being less prepared to accept this type of social contract. After all, we live much longer now than we did when retirement was first introduced, and we keep our health for longer, too; so it is much more practical for people to continue to take an active part in society. Among business and professional people, it is not at all uncommon for retirement to signal the beginning of a second career, and a much more independent one that allows them to use their experience, such as working as a consultant.

In other groups of society, too, people are beginning to see retirement as an opportunity to do new things. Organizations like the University of the Third Age encourage retired people to develop new hobbies and pursue new interests, and are becoming more popular and successful all the time. Many psychologists now take the view that successful retirement is all about making sure that you acquire new social roles, to replace the ones that you have lost through work, and activities of this sort are exactly the way that people do that.

Social labelling

Dyson (1980) interviewed a large number of people about their experiences of retirement, and challenged the idea that people see it as a fair exchange. Dyson's respondents saw it as fair for old people in general, but not in their own personal cases. They felt that, for the most part, society had thrown them on the junkheap too early, when they were still perfectly capable of making an active and useful contribution to society. But they did think it was probably fair for other old people, and for old people in general.

Dyson's research gave some interesting hints about the emergence of a new perspective on ageing, which developed during the 1980s. This view sees the lower visibility of older people in society as a product of **social labelling**. We live in an ageist society, in which stereotypes of old people are very strong – even though most of us are personally acquainted with individuals who don't fit those stereotypes at all. But it is very difficult for an individual to break through the social stereotyping and be regarded as an intelligent person with something useful to contribute; because too often they are seen as someone who is old, and therefore useless. Or they think this is how they will be seen, and so they don't bother trying.

The stereotypes associated with old people are particularly unpleasant. They are often regarded as sick, stupid, or even dirty. Because a minority of old people become confused, or suffer from mental disorders such as Alzheimer's disease, it is assumed that any old person is likely to become mentally incapacitated – although, in fact, the evidence is very different. Because of this, the positive contributions which older people can make to social events and processes are often overlooked, or simply ignored. Recently, a number of organizations and individuals have begun to challenge these stereotypes about ageing, and there is some indication that attitudes are beginning to change. But there is still a long way to go.

Retirement and responsibility

Some people who reach retiring age, though, still hold to the old negative ideas about retirement. Sometimes they feel that society has simply thrown them away, even though they are as fit as ever. But sometimes they interpret any aches and pains as being evidence that they are becoming old and useless, so they stop doing activities which would help them to keep fit. Anyone will grow infirm if they do nothing all day but sit in the house and watch TV – muscles need exercise to keep toned, and a healthy retirement means an active one. Also, feeling socially useless is a major source of stress and helplessness. Without another source of self-esteem, such as a hobby or voluntary work, people can become extremely depressed, and appear to give up on active living.

People who take this view are actually much more likely to die in the first few years of retirement than those who take a more positive view. It seems that they find it much harder to find anything worth living for, because they feel so useless. This also helps to explain why women live longer than men (although there are other factors to be considered too). Women who are past retiring age now, grew up in a culture in which the home was considered to be a woman's primary responsibility. Even after they have retired, that responsibility still remains, so they still have something in their lives to be involved with. But men of the same age were usually brought up to believe that their primary responsibility was to work and be the breadwinner for the family. That responsibility vanishes with compulsory retirement and this can be emotionally devastating. Even people who have looked forward to retirement can find, after the first few months, that feeling socially useless is more than they can cope with, and they can become very depressed even, sometimes, to the point where they give up trying to live.

This is why it is so important for retired people to make sure that they have some other interest in their life, and more than just one if at all possible. Many retired people take up another responsibility where they can still feel needed, such as voluntary work. Gardening is particularly popular, because a garden needs to be looked after – it can't be neglected or it will quickly turn wild. So gardeners know that their efforts are necessary and worthwhile. Some people develop hobbies such as travelling, or learn a new sport, such as golf or bowls. All these are ways for people to develop other sources of self-esteem, to compensate for being without paid employment.

Ageing

As we've seen, many people live healthy, happy and productive lives for many years after the standard retirement age. But sooner or later, barring accidents, we all become old. It used to be thought that ageing was a steady decline in functioning, with people going inevitably downhill from the age of 50 or so. But now we know that is not so. The research evidence which suggested this pattern of ageing was seriously flawed in the way that it was done, and modern experiences show that ageing occurs quite differently.

The general pattern seems to be that we have only a very gradual decline in our older years, and that decline can be slowed down by exercise and activity; but that eventually we reach a period of more rapid physical decline, which rarely lasts for more than about five years. Usually, the person dies at some point during the five-year period. In some old people, that decline is brought about by an accident – a fall or some similar event – which damages them physically but, more importantly, shakes their confidence and makes them feel unable to cope with life as they once did.

How inevitable the decline is, once it has begun, is something nobody knows. We do know, though, that even old bodies can respond surprisingly well to exercise. In one study, 90-year-olds who began a programme of physical exercises were found to be putting on muscle mass as a result – in other words, their muscles were responding to the exercise and becoming stronger. This finding has been repeated a number of times now, and it shows that the saying 'it's never too late' may be even truer than we realize.

The real danger in ageing, more than any other, seems to be the person's own beliefs about it. Someone who expects to decline and become incapable as they grow older is not likely to face their body or mind with extra challenges. Without exercise, our bodies have no incentive to grow stronger or to maintain their normal levels of strength; so they become weaker. This, to the person who expects to be weak as a result of age, is 'proof' that they were right, and their belief in inevitable decline is confirmed. But really, it began as a self-fulfilling prophecy.

Intelligence and ageing

The same thing seems to happen with mental abilities too. For example, intelligence is often inaccurately cited as one of the areas which declines with age. For many years, people 'knew' that various abilities, including intelligence and physical strength, reached their peak in the early twenties, and then declined steadily from then on throughout a person's life. This knowledge was based on a series of studies, reported by Miles in 1931, which involved measuring various human characteristics in people of different ages. When they plotted the results of these measurements on a graph, Miles found a steady decline: the older the person was, the less strong, or intelligent (as measured by IQ tests) or able they were.

Other researchers found similar results, so for a great many years there was a strong belief in an inevitable decline with age. Indeed this belief is still held by a great many people, including some doctors and social workers, but when we look more carefully at the evidence, what we find is actually quite a different picture.

Cross-sectional methods

The problem was that all of these studies were done using **cross-sectional methods**. That is, the researcher tested several different groups of people, of different ages. But someone who was 60 in 1930 had experienced quite a different upbringing and lifestyle from someone who was 20 at that time. Their schooling was quite different, their life experiences were quite different, and their standards of living were different too. The same thing applied to cross-sectional studies that were conducted later in on the century: they failed to take account of the very major changes in education and health care which had taken place.

It wasn't surprising, for example, that older people did badly on intelligence tests in the 1960s, when they had experienced an education which consisted, in the main, of learning large chunks of information off by heart. Younger people, by contrast, had experienced a form of education which stressed reasoning and mental skills, and so they naturally performed much better on IQ tests.

Longitudinal methods

When psychologists actually began to look at how individual people developed, following them up through their lives, a very different picture emerged. Obviously, **longitudinal research** like this is quite hard to do because researchers need to follow it up over many years. So there are fewer longitudinal studies of lifespan development than there are cross-sectional ones. But there are some. For example, in 1966, Burns reported on a study of intelligence and ageing which had begun in the 1920s with a group of teachers who were just emerging from their training colleges. The researchers tested the teachers' intelligence throughout their careers and found that, contrary to what the cross-sectional research showed, their IQ scores had actually increased as they had become older. The apparently inevitable decline with ageing wasn't inevitable at all!

What was even more interesting was the particular scores which the teachers had obtained on their IQ tests. The tests assessed intelligence in two parts: **verbal intelligence**, which was to do with the use of words and knowledge of vocabulary, and **numerical intelligence**, which included the use of symbols and logical reasoning as well as arithmetical abilities. When the researchers looked at these scores, they found that the 'arts' teachers, who taught subjects such as English and history, showed an increase in their verbal intelligence scores, but a slight (though not very great) decline in numerical intelligence. The science teachers, though, showed an increase in their numerical intelligence but a slight decline in their verbal intelligence scores.

What this clearly implied was that, more than anything else, it is the amount of **practice** we have which is most important in whether we are likely to improve our intelligence as we get older or not. If we adopt a passive mental approach to living, just receiving information passively and not bothering to learn new things unless we absolutely have to, it's likely that our intelligence would decline. Our muscles waste away if we don't use them and, in the same way, our intelligence declines if we don't use it. But if we remain active in our thinking, and ready to learn new things or to challenge our previous assumptions, then we are likely to retain our intelligence, and even increase it. The more we use a skill, the better we get at it.

This is only one example, but both psychologists and doctors are finding, more and more, that getting old has almost as much to do with lifestyle and practice as it has to do with the number of years that we actually carry. Everybody gets older, of course, but ageing doesn't mean an inevitable steady decline from age 20, as people used to think.

Memory and ageing

The problem, though, is that we all have our own beliefs about ageing and sometimes, as we've seen, these can become self-perpetuating. For example, most people believe that memory inevitably declines as you get older. Because they believe this, they notice each time they fail to remember something, and take it as 'proof' that their memory is really getting worse. Their belief becomes a self-fulfilling prophecy, because they become convinced that there is less and less point in trying to remember things because they won't manage it anyway. And then they don't remember things, because they don't make any effort to store the information.

Harris and Sunderland, in 1981, decided to put this idea to the test. They obtained a group of people aged between 20 and 36, and compared them with a group of people aged between 69 and 80. When they tested their memories for events in everyday life, they found that the younger people in the study actually experienced more memory failures than the older people!

It was possible, of course, that the younger people forgot more simply because they had more going on in their lives. After all, the older group comprised all retired people. So Harris and Sunderland repeated the study, this time with a group of people who were still working, aged between 50 and 60. This time, they found an even stronger difference beween the two groups. Again, the younger people were much more forgetful than those who were older, even with information that they were trying to remember.

So why is it that older people are so convinced that their memories are poorer now than they were when they were young? It's possible, of course, that they really did have better memories when they are young, and that for some reason the younger generation studied by Harris and Sunderland didn't have very good memories at all – after all, this was a cross-sectional study. And the educational system which was current when the over-sixties were younger did involve quite a lot of memorizing. But what seems more likely is that it is much more to do with motivation and attention.

Attention and motivation

Young people, by and large, don't worry too much about their mental abilities. Older people, though, sensitized by society's belief in an inevitable decline in mental ability with ageing, do worry about it. So when a younger person forgets their key, or can't remember someone's name, or forgets what they came into the room to do, they hardly notice it because it simply doesn't matter to them. When an older person does the same thing, though, it sticks in the mind because they are always wondering if it is a sign of age.

So where the younger person simply shrugs off everyday forgetting, the older person worries about it, and notices it much more. This means that when older people look back on their own earlier lives, they don't remember being worried about forgetting things at all when they were younger, and they come to the conclusion that they simply had better memories. This reinforces the belief that their own mental abilities are declining, and so becomes a circular process.

A psychological decline with ageing, then, isn't nearly as inevitable as it once appeared to be. If we use our mental abilities, we are more likely to improve them than to lose them, at least until the very final years of our life. For people who lead full and active lives, and don't hesitate to make efforts or to stretch themselves a little, it seems that they can retain their abilities almost to the end of their lives, with only a relatively sudden decline in the last five years, rather than a continuous steady one.

Of course, your system responds to the demands that you make on it – which is why sports doctors and physiotherapists know how important it is to exercise injured muscles as soon as healing has begun. Resting simply means that the muscles adapt to limited demands, and become weaker. It's the same with ageing: people who believe in a continuous decline, and don't push themselves to make an effort, naturally become more and more frail and feeble, because they are never stimulating their bodies or minds to become stronger. There are limits, of course, but we haven't yet begun to discover what they are, and they certainly aren't encountered in most people's lives.

Principles of lifespan psychology

In the past two chapters, then, we have seen how lifespan development covers far more than just childhood. Sugarman (1986) identified four central ideas in lifespan developmental psychology. The first of these is the idea that development always needs to be seen in its **social context**. How people develop is influenced by their society, their family, their social class and their culture, and social influence can come from many other sources as well. So we can't really study development without taking these into account.

The second idea which Sugarman identified is to do with the fact that social influence isn't just a one-way process. People influence one another, and are influenced by others – it's a two-way process, which we call **reciprocal influence**. This influence isn't static either – it changes all the time. We are influenced by family members and by changes happening within the family, as well as by changes among our friends and work colleagues. And we exert our own influence on these changes as they develop.

Reciprocal influence is important, but it's far from being the whole story. We are also active **agents** in our own lives, making our own choices and decisions. In that sense, we are all active in shaping our own development, and how we understand what is going on is an important aspect of that. For example, as we saw earlier, we know that mental abilities don't inevitably decline with age, but someone who believed firmly that they did decline would tend to 'take it easy' and avoid challenging situations as they grew older, because they wouldn't think it was worth trying. And because of this, they would decline faster than someone who understood lifespan development in a more positive way.

Another fundamental principle that Sugarman identified in lifespan psychology is that of **complexity**. Essentially, this is the same principle that we have encountered so often throughout this book. People are not simple beings, and no single approach is going to be enough to tell us about human beings. We have to take into account different levels of explanation, and to explore connections and issues which arise from them, if we are to get any useful awareness of what human beings are really like.

In the next chapter we will look at another aspect of adult psychology – the psychology of working life.

12
working life

In this chapter you will learn:
- why a manager's theory of human nature can completely alter the way employees work
- to identify three styles of leadership
- how to define the term 'organizational culture'.

Up until now, we have been looking at just a small sample of psychological knowledge. There's much more, of course, but it gives us a general idea of what 'mainstream' psychology consists of. Since its very beginnings, psychology has been both a 'pure' and an 'applied' subject – that is, some areas of psychology are concerned with scientific investigation purely in order to understand what is going on; while other areas are concerned with the various ways that psychological knowledge can be put to use.

Applied psychology takes many different forms, and quite a lot of them are covered in *Teach Yourself Applied Psychology*; so we won't be going into them in so much detail here. But they are also part of psychology, and contribute to our understanding of day-to-day living; so in the next few chapters we will look at how psychology can help us to understand people in everyday situations. We will begin, in this chapter, by looking at how psychology can help us to understand people at work.

Why do people work?

For a human being, work is a deeply important part of life. Although we might daydream about a life of leisure, the reality is that most of us are psychologically, and physically, healthier if we are working. If we are prevented from working, by unemployment or redundancy, we are very likely to become depressed. If that unemployment continues for a long time, we are also liable to fall into a kind of learned helplessness (see Chapter 3), which can sometimes make it very difficult for us to find work again, or to make the sustained effort that is necessary if an opportunity does come along.

Unemployment has other negative effects as well. Warr (1987) found that between 20 per cent and 30 per cent of unemployed people showed a deterioration in their physical health. Binns and Mars (1984) found that unemployment often leads to difficulties in personal relationships as well, often because of the additional strain brought on by continuing financial difficulties. And, of course, the longer we are unemployed, the more these problems are likely to become exaggerated.

Latent functions of working
Jahoda (1982) suggested that the reason why long-term unemployment is so damaging is because working serves more functions for us than we realize. It doesn't just serve the obvious

functions such as earning money to live on, although this is important, of course. But working has other functions which are not so obvious. Jahoda identified five latent functions of working, which are listed in Table 12.1. We don't really notice these while we are working, but they are extremely important in helping to keep our emotional and psychological life balanced.

---

table 12.1 latent functions of working

1 Employment imposes a time structure on the waking day.
2 Employment brings about regularly shared experiences and contacts with people outside the family.
3 A job links the individual with goals and purposes beyond one's own.
4 A job defines aspects of personal status and identity.
5 Paid employment enforces its own activity.

Thinking of work in this way can be useful, too, because it can give us some hints as to how unemployment can be survived. For example, people who are unemployed but keep themselves busy by doing voluntary work don't usually suffer from the depression and learned helplessness that so many other unemployed people experience. This seems to be partly because they gain the same latent functions of working from their voluntary commitment. It can sometimes be like this for people who are committed to a particular hobby, as well.

'Scientific management'

Looking at what happens when people don't work can tell us a great deal about what working actually does for us. But what of people at work? What motivates them to continue working? One of the first psychological theories of working was the very straightforward one which has probably occurred to you already, as you read this chapter: people work for money.

F. W. Taylor, in 1911, believed firmly that money was the sole reason why people work. Given this, he reasoned that a work and pay system which allowed people to earn more by being more efficient would be useful, both to employees and to employers. Taylor developed an approach to work which became known as 'scientific management', and was based entirely on the idea of work being as efficient as possible.

Time and motion

Taylor began implementing his new approach with a labourer loading pig iron onto railway trucks. From observing the labourers' working, he became convinced that the work could be done much more efficiently. He got one man to agree to do exactly as he was told: lifting when he was told, resting when he was told, and so on. By the end of that working day, the labourer had loaded $47^1/_2$ tons of pig iron, instead of his usual $12^1/_2$.

Taylor went on from there to develop the principle of **time and motion** studies, in which production and labouring jobs were carefully observed and timed, in order to identify the most efficient ways of working. This 'scientific management ' approach became very popular in the first half of the twentieth century, because it seemed to represent a new and better way of organizing work.

Like many ideas of that time, though, it was simply too mechanistic for human beings to put up with for very long. The first half of the twentieth century was full of mechanistic ideas about progress, and the idea that the world was really based on very straightforward engineering principles. As a result, it was common for people to be seen as much like machines, and this affected psychology too. In fact, we've already seen something of this, in the behaviourist approach to learning which we looked at in Chapter 9. The problem, though, is that people are not machines, and when they are treated as if they are, they tend to rebel.

Sometimes that rebellion is unconscious. The rates of industrial accidents, for example, increased with the introduction of scientific management. Although some early industrial researchers (e.g. Greenwood and Woods, 1919) came to the conclusion that some people were simply accident prone, later researchers saw it as a simple consequence of expecting human beings to act in exactly the same way, day after day, hour after hour. Sickness and absenteeism rates also increased, as did rates of staff turnover – the number of staff who simply left.

Social aspects of working

In the 1930s, a group of psychologists showed that there are important social dimensions to working, as well. In a series of studies at the Hawthorne Electric Plant, in Chicago, Elton Mayo and his colleagues Roethlisberger and Dickson began by trying to find the best lighting levels in a particular workshop. They began by raising the lighting levels, and found that production increased. Then they lowered the lighting levels and production increased again. Finally, they put the lighting levels back to how they had been originally, and production was higher than it had ever been.

The Chicago researchers had hit on an important discovery about working life. Almost regardless of what they did, the employees in that area worked harder as a result. The one exception came when they varied the tea breaks, and had a condition with about eight short breaks throughout the day. The girls in that part of the factory complained that they didn't get time to concentrate on what they were doing. But apart from that single case, it wasn't their physical conditions of work that mattered. The fact that the researchers were taking an interest in what the employees were doing was enough to increase their motivation.

Group standards

In another part of the company, the researchers investigated a department called the bank-wiring room. This consisted of a group of people who were usually left to work without much supervision. Interestingly, the workers in that section of the factory seemed to be unaffected by the changes introduced by the psychologists. They had developed their own way of working, which produced a regular, steady rate of production. They didn't increase it much, even when paid extra, but then they didn't slow down either.

When they looked into it a bit more deeply, Mayo and the others found that this group had developed a clear code of practice about how each person should do their share, and not do anything which might get the rest of the group into trouble. The principles by which they were working are listed in Table 12.2, and all the members of that department held to them. As a result, it was one of the most reliable and dependable parts of the organization.

---

table 12.2 an informal 'code of practice'

1 You shouldn't work too hard – 'rate-busting' is not acceptable behaviour.
2 You shouldn't slack over your work – do your own fair share.
3 You shouldn't tell a supervisor anything which might get a fellow worker into trouble.
4 If you hold a position of authority, you shouldn't pull rank or act officiously.

Informal leadership

In some later studies, Mayo and his colleagues explored the idea of group leadership. They were investigating an aircraft factory in southern California which had serious problems with staff turnover – people were leaving, and new people were being taken on, at a rate which made it very difficult for the factory to operate properly. But in one department, there was very little staff turnover indeed, which attracted the attention of the psychologists.

When they investigated, they found that this department had an informal leader who took charge and sorted out disagreements between people when they arose. The leader also welcomed new people when they joined the department and took care that they should meet everyone, and get to know what each person was doing. Then they were taken on a tour of the whole factory, so that the person could see how their own job contributed to the production of the whole aircraft.

The outcome of all of this was that these people felt that they were part of the organization, and welcome, from the very beginning. They knew that there was someone to whom they could turn for help or guidance if they needed it. And they didn't find their work on the factory line alienating because they had a clear understanding of how what they did fitted in with producing the whole plane. The actions taken by the informal leader of the group were exactly what was needed in a big plant like this, and gave a number of useful pointers to the psychologists as to what would be useful areas of practice.

Each of these different studies, and several others, pointed to different aspects of work motivation, and showed that there was much more involved for people than simply earning money. The first study, on lighting, had shown that people respond to management or others taking an interest in what they do. The bank-wiring room showed that doing the right thing by one's colleagues was more important than simply trying to get extra pay. And the aircraft factory study showed the value of effective leadership, and also the value of people being able to see their own job in an overall context.

Expectations and management

As a result of the Hawthorne studies, work psychologists began to pay close attention to the social dimensions of working. What became apparent almost immediately was the way that people respond to the **expectations** which other people have of them. If managers distrust their staff, and show their distrust by close supervision and not allowing them to make even minor decisions for themselves, the result is that their staff will become unwilling to take responsibility, and sometimes even become untrustworthy. But if managers trust their staff, and show it by listening to their ideas and giving them enough autonomy to get on with doing their work properly, people almost always respond by acting responsibly.

Theory X and Theory Y

McGregor (1960) drew these, and many other observations showing the importance of expectations in management, together and concluded that how people behave at work has everything to do with how they are treated. McGregor argued that people like to feel valued and appreciated at work and, that if they are given the opportunity, they will generally work hard. However, some managers, McGregor argued, actually create irresponsibility among their employees by showing, through their everyday practices, that they don't trust their staff, and that they think they are naturally lazy.

McGregor argued that managers tend to have two different underlying theories about human nature which they apply to their employees. The first one, which he called Theory X, is the old-fashioned idea that people are really shiftless and lazy, and won't work unless they are made to. This type of theory, according to McGregor, is the one which leads to these self-defeating approaches to management and supervision.

The second theory, which McGregor called Theory Y, is the idea that people really like to work, and that the job of the manager is to provide a working context which will allow them to show what they can do. Managers who hold Theory Y, McGregor argued, set up working conditions in which staff feel valued and trusted. As a result, their staff really do work hard, because they know that their efforts are appreciated.

Human resource management

The early theories of what motivates people at work form an important background to the area of management known as **human resource management**. This, as the name suggests, is the branch of management which is particularly concerned with people. A great many modern organizational psychologists are involved in human resource management, and their concern is to ensure that the organization's practices are all operating to make sure that people are working well and positively together, and in a way which enables them to adapt to change when it is needed.

Working in teams

One of the important areas in human resource management has to do with helping people to work in ways which realize their potential. Sometimes, this involves giving them more challenging jobs to do; but, sometimes, also it involves organizing work so that it can be done by teams. Hayes (2002) discussed how effective work teams can be in helping an organization to cope with change and develop responses to challenges.

Team building

A team is different from a working group because it is task-focused and much more clearly structured. Organizational psychologists have developed various kinds of team-building exercises which can be used to help to train people to work together. Some of these exercises focus on helping people to get to know one another – they adopt an interpersonal approach, encouraging people to be honest with one another, and creating an open and safe climate in which people feel able to admit their weaknesses and identify their training needs.

In the 1960s and 1970s, many team-building exercises adopted this approach, focusing on **sensitivity training,** in which people learned to become more sensitive to one another. They would learn, for example, about non-verbal communication and the way that people can signal intentions or emotions by their body language or behaviour. They would also learn how to listen carefully to what people are really saying (something that most of us are bad at!). And they would learn how to offer support when people are doing something particularly challenging and needing help. In other words, they learned to respond to the interpersonal messages of other members of the group.

More recently, approaches to team building have tended to emphasize the roles and tasks which people in the group are concerned with. Adair (1968) argued that any given team has to take account of three sets of needs: **task needs** – the practical things which have to be done in order to do the job at hand;

group needs – to do with overcoming interpersonal quarrels or disputes, and making sure that people can act together effectively; and **individual needs** – to do with what the individual members of the team want to get out of it.

The job of the team leader, in this model, is to pay attention to all three types of need and to make sure that they are all at least partly satisfied. It isn't enough just to concentrate on the demands of the job at hand and to ignore the group's needs, because this could mean that tensions between members of the group become so strong that afterwards, those people couldn't work together again. And it isn't really a good idea to concentrate only on the task and the group's needs and to ignore individual ones. It might get the job done, but in the long-term people work much better when they benefit personally from being involved, too.

The personal benefits of belonging to a team, though, don't need to be visible ones. In Chapter 2, we looked at the process of social identification, and the way that people like to be able to feel proud of belonging to a particular group. Hayes (2002) argued that this is a fundamental aspect of team working, too. Belonging to a successful, achieving group, and being recognized as contributing to it, is sometimes enough on its own to satisfy individual needs. Alternatively, teamwork may be seen as a way of accumulating experience which will help in later promotion.

The important thing, really, is the attitude that management has towards teamworking. Imai (1988) showed how Japanese management systems involve all of the workers, at any level in the company, in a continuous drive for improvement. People are encouraged to feel proud of, and committed to, their company, and are treated as intelligent and responsible people, no matter what job they are doing. So if they are asked to join a specific team to solve a problem, they are often pleased to be involved, and to be recognized as someone who has something worthwhile to contribute.

In too many organizations in the Western world, however, contributions like this are still ignored or unrecognized by management, so they are seen as just an additional chore for the individual. Although a skilled team leader will be able to get around this, by ensuring that their team, at least, pays attention to people's individual needs, their job can be made a great deal harder or a great deal easier by the organization's general policies towards its staff.

Leadership

Organizational psychologists have also been involved in studying leadership. Much of the early research into leadership tended to look for particular people who had leadership 'qualities' – who automatically acted like leaders and took on leadership responsibilities when that sort of situation arose. Later, though, largely as a result of a particularly interesting study conducted in the 1930s, psychologists became more and more interested in the idea that effective leadership was actually a style of interacting with people, rather than a specific inherited personality trait.

Leadership styles

The study was conducted by Lewin, Lippitt and White (1939), and was actually done in a boys' after-school model-making club. The boys were divided into three groups, and each group was given a leader who acted in a different way. Later, the leaders were changed round, to make sure that it was really their influence and not just differences between the groups of boys. The different **leadership styles** and their results are described in Table 12.3. As you can see, they support McGregor's idea that leaders bring out particular behaviour in their subordinates and, in fact, this study and the other research which it stimulated was an important part of the evidence which McGregor used when he first developed his 'Theory X and Theory Y' model of management.

table 12.3 leadership styles and their effects

	Style	Effect
Authoritarian	Leader makes arbitrary decisions, doesn't consult group, gives orders, supervises closely.	Group works hard when leader is present, stops work when absent. Competitive and attention-seeking.
Democratic	Leader makes decisions on the basis of group discussions, delegates responsibility, gives requests rather than orders and expects co-operation.	Group works steadily whether supervised or not, is helpful with one another, and solves problems jointly.
Laissez-faire	Leader leaves group alone to get on with work, does not intervene or attempt to influence them.	Group disorganized, does very little work, and is easily demoralized by small problems.

Following this work, approaches to leadership became concerned with just how organizational leaders or managers influence the people in their working groups. Some theories have seen effective leaders as having preferred styles, which concentrate either on the job at hand, or on the people they are dealing with. **Task-oriented leaders** are people who focus on the job which has to be done, whereas **process-oriented leaders** are more concerned with making sure that everything in the group runs smoothly, and that people get along well together.

Interestingly, and contrary to what we might expect, the evidence suggests that process-oriented leaders actually get more done in the end. Although the task-oriented leaders are concerned with what needs to be done, they are less efficient overall because they allow tensions and resentments to build up in their teams and, in the end, this means that people work less productively. Process-oriented leaders, on the other hand, concentrate on making sure that people are reasonably happy with one another, and with what is going on, so that they are free to give their best efforts to the job.

Transactional leadership

This observation led to a focus on leadership as being all about the **transactions** which take place between manager and employee. Transactions are interpersonal exchanges between two people. Often, these take the form of 'strokes' – that is, ritual greetings or enquiries which signal that the two people have recognized one another. A habitual 'good morning' exchanged between two people at a bus stop or train station is a good example of a stroke. The words of the exchange are relatively unimportant, but the greeting signals that the two have acknowledged one another. As we've already seen, being recognized by other people matters to us, so the everyday strokes that we get from other people can be very important. We may not notice them much when they happen, but we certainly miss them if they don't.

The idea of transactional leadership is that effective leadership is essentially a joint thing, depending on both the manager and the employee. How effective a leader is depends on how both the leader and the employees interact. It doesn't just depend on the leader alone. After all, people won't co-operate with someone who doesn't seem to come up to scratch, so a leader who comes across as being ineffectual or incompetent isn't going to be able to influence other people very much.

What this means is that a manager, consciously or unconsciously, negotiates their position with the employees. It's an interpersonal relationship, and their influence depends on being respected or valued. This is where the transactions come in. Strokes, for instance, can be either positive or negative: they can help us to feel good, or they can make us feel unhappy. Positive leaders look for ways of encouraging their staff to feel good, by recognizing their achievements and helping them to work around difficulties. Negative leaders criticize their staff, and only notice mistakes rather than positive achievements. But as decades of organizational psychology have taught us, it's not a method that gets the best out of people.

Transformational leadership

An even more recent way of looking at leadership is to do with the way in which large organizations can often become very unwieldy. This can make them slow to respond to changes in society, which means that they are not able to compete properly with other companies in the same line of work. A great many organizational psychologists are involved in organizational change, and one of the outcomes of this has been to make it clearer what an influence some kinds of leadership can have.

Some leaders seem to be particularly good at getting their staff to deal positively with change and to approach their jobs in new ways. They are known as **transformational leaders**, because they have the knack of being able to encourage an organization to transform itself – to adapt a different style of working. In recent years, with so many organizations having to adjust to an entirely different economic context, this has become an important feature of leadership.

Getting people to deal positively with change isn't as easy as it sounds. People will often resist changes to the way that they work, but this isn't because they are simply being obstructive. As we saw in Chapters 5 and 6, we actively make sense of our worlds, and we act in ways that fit with what we understand is going on. So, sometimes, people will object to changes in how they work because they can't see how it will improve things.

A transformational leader is generally someone who realizes how important it is that people should understand what is happening, and who makes an effort to show them why, and how, it will be worthwhile to make the efforts. Transformational leaders help people to come to terms with organizational change by showing how the new approach can be linked with what people are already doing. Smith and

Peterson (1988) showed how these leaders often use metaphors and stories to help make these links clear.

Another feature of transformational leadership is that such leaders also encourage members of the organization to be involved in the changes. They listen to what they have to say, and take their ideas into account. In the end, of course, this means that the employees are much more likely to work effectively and to make the changes successful, because they, too, are aware that there are good reasons for them.

This doesn't mean, though, that all organizational change is always a good thing, or that it is always successful. Sometimes, attempts to change how organizations work are resisted by the people working in them because they really are impractical – they have been badly thought out, and nobody has consulted the people who are really doing the work. Sometimes, too, people have simply had more change than they can cope with, and need a period to consolidate the new ways and let the new ideas sink in.

Organizational culture

Transformational leaders are people who try to change the general culture of the organization in which they work. Organizational culture is all about the general assumptions, beliefs and practices in an organization – its distinctive style of working. Sometimes, you can find two organizations, in exactly the same line of work, but which go about doing that work in entirely different ways. The people working in those organizations have quite different approaches to what they are doing; they deal with problems differently, and they expect different attitudes from management. Effectively, they are participating in different types of organizational cultures.

Levels of culture

Although some organizational researchers have spent their time trying to classify different types of organizational cultures, organizational psychologists tend to be more interested in how cultures work, and why they influence the people working in them the way that they do. Lundberg (1990) observed that organizational cultures seem to have three different levels, and these are listed in Table 12.4. Psychologists have studied culture at each of these levels, but we tend to be particularly interested in the deepest level, of shared assumptions and beliefs.

> ### table 12.4 levels of organizational culture
>
> **The manifest level**   Symbols, language, stories, rituals etc.
>
> **The strategic level**   Beliefs about the company's direction, planning and expectations, internal management strategies.
>
> **The core level**   Ideologies, values and assumptions about human nature and what people and the world are like.
>
> *(Lundberg, 1990)*

Other researchers, such as Van Maanen and Barley (1985) showed how organizational cultures aren't really just single phenomena, with everyone in the organization thinking the same way. Instead, different groups within the organization have their own ways of thinking. In a strong organizational culture, these different groups overlap, so they all have something in common. But in other types of organization, different groups may have entirely different assumptions and beliefs.

Working groups

Any organization contains a whole host of in-groups and out-groups: there are friendship groups, departmental groups, working teams, and many others. People often feel more loyalty to some of these groups than to others. Some organizational change doesn't happen, for instance, because it is resisted by 'canteen cultures' that keep certain beliefs and ideas going among the workforce even when management are trying to change it.

The classic example of how a canteen culture can work against organizational change is in equal opportunities. An organization may adopt an official equal opportunities policy, but groups of employees may still perpetuate racist beliefs. So anyone from an ethnic minority background has a very hard time indeed. Officially, for example, the police force is trying to be non-racist. It has maintained an equal opportunities policy for many years now and has attempted to develop better community relations with ethnic minority groups. However, several studies have shown how canteen cultures in the police force perpetuate a high level of racism, which isn't really affected by official policy. And it is the canteen culture, of course, which new recruits encounter when they are learning practical policing. As we've seen, we develop our schemas and our understanding of the world from our experience, and we use them as a guide for action. So first experiences like this are important in shaping future working practices.

Hayes (2002) discussed how an understanding of the kind of **social identity** processes which we looked at in Chapter 2 could help us to understand how canteen cultures work, and why they are so influential. Knowing about **social representations**, too (see Chapter 3) can help us to understand how these shared beliefs develop. People tend to take more notice of people who they think are like themselves, or who belong to the same in-group. So it's particularly easy for a group in an organization to develop shared beliefs about their work, and about life in general. Applying these two social psychology theories, therefore, can help us to understand how to tackle this sort of problem.

What we have covered in this chapter has been only a brief glimpse of psychology at work. There are many more areas of working life that work psychologists have studied. For example, ergonomic psychologists study the human–machine interface – in other words, they design machines which people can operate easily, and which will reduce the likelihood of mistakes. **Ergonomics** is a branch of work psychology, that has had a powerful presence in industry for many decades, but there isn't really enough room to write about it here. See *Teach Yourself Applied Psychology* if you are interested.

Occupational psychologists are also concerned with psychology at work, and particularly with the ways in which people and jobs come together. They are involved in selecting people for jobs, and developing tests and other techniques for identifying which people appear to have the personal qualities required by a particular job. They are involved in vocational guidance, which is all about helping people to find the right type of occupation for their own particular personality. And they are also involved with managerial strategies, such as job enrichment, which help people to become more satisfied with their working experience, and so become able to contribute more to their organization, and develop more personal skills. You can find out more about psychology at work in *Teach Yourself Applied Psychology*. But in the next chapter, we will look at some aspects of psychology and leisure – what we do when we aren't working.

13

leisure

In this chapter you will learn:
- to identify the positive and negative effects of watching television
- why computer games are psychologically appealing
- how to differentiate between external and internal motivation.

In this chapter, we will look at some of the psychology which underlies leisure activities. The concept of leisure has become increasingly important in modern society. By comparison with pre-industrial society, or even with the industrial society of 50 years ago, we spend far less of our day-to-day lives working (even though it may not always seem like that!). And for significant chunks of the week, we have specific times when we are not actually working at all.

It is difficult, really, to define leisure activities, because many of the things that some people regard as leisure are regarded as work, or at least chores, by others. Shopping is one of those things. Some people enjoy it, and treat it as a leisure pursuit; while others detest it and treat it as an unfortunate necessity of life. It certainly happens during 'leisure' hours; but whether it is truly leisure is open to question. So we will not look at consumer psychology here. If you are interested, there is a chapter on it in *Teach Yourself Applied Psychology*.

What we will look at in this chapter are activities which are more self-evidently the kinds of things that people regard as leisure. People have varied interests and hobbies and, as we saw in Chapter 2, it's possible to see them as an expression of our basic need for self-actualization. We enjoy developing our skills and interests, but we also sometimes spend our leisure time in less active pursuits, such as watching television – which may sometimes involve learning things, as in the large number of DIY and cookery programmes, but may equally well be nothing more than passive entertainment.

So we will begin this chapter by looking at television watching as a leisure pursuit. Then we will go on to look at a slightly more active way of interacting with a video screen, in the case of computer games; before concluding our sampling of psychology and leisure by looking at sport psychology. Of course, for some people sport is a profession rather than a leisure activity, and many of the insights from sport psychology have been developed with professional sportspeople in mind. But equally, many people play sport as a hobby or pastime, and so it is appropriate to look at it briefly here. If you're particularly interested in this area, there is a more detailed chapter on sport psychology in *Teach Yourself Applied Psychology*.

Watching television

In Western society, watching television is a very large part of our relaxation activities. Over 98 per cent of homes in Britain have televisions, and over half have more than one television set. People spend on average about four or five hours a day watching television, which makes it a significant cultural activity. But ever since television became popular, people have been concerned about it. So psychologists have been studying its effects for some time.

The effects of television viewing

One common debate, of course, is whether television increases antisocial behaviour, and particularly aggression, or not. Most psychologists firmly believe that it can do so, although it is hard to obtain definitive evidence, since there are so many other things which also influence people's lives and can lead to increased aggression – notably the frustration which arises from constant poverty.

The earliest studies of television's influence on aggressive behaviour were laboratory experiments. These were designed to assess an immediate change in behaviour as a result of people being exposed to aggressive images on television. Typically, research participants would be shown a piece of film which showed distinctively violent behaviour, and then they would be observed to see whether they mimicked that behaviour, or showed heightened aggression in response to a stimulus or a questionnaire. These studies did show some modelling effects, although not as strongly as some people expected them to, and some other studies failed to find the same results.

Problems with studying television effects

But these laboratory studies were really very artificial. Even if people are influenced by violence on television, it's unlikely that it would show up straightaway. Rather, as Bandura showed in his studies of imitative learning, we wouldn't be likely to show the aggressive behaviour until it was somehow worthwhile – or at least appropriate – for us to do so. So one reason why laboratory studies of television violence often have contradictory results may be because of the methods which they adopt.

Another problem with these studies is that they tend to look for group influences, rather than for specific effects on individuals.

They study a large number of people and see whether, on the whole, their behaviour seems to be influenced by the type of programmes that they watch. By studying people as a whole, they aim to cancel out individual differences and just look at general trends. But when it comes to something as important as this, it is individuals who matter. Even if only one extremely disturbed person out of six million viewers imitates a television murderer, that is one too many.

Social scripts and social understanding

It is difficult, therefore, to obtain absolute proof that television violence directly affects people. But this doesn't mean there is no evidence at all. As we saw in the early part of this book, human beings are particularly ready to acquire social scripts and different types of social understandings, and people learn from any kind of social contact. Television has a capacity to define a form of reality for people and this can make a great deal of difference to how we live our lives. It acts as a window into the wider world, and tells people what that world is like. So studies of the amount of television that people actually watch can tell us quite a lot.

One thing they tell us, is that watching a lot of television can distort how we see the world. Gerbner and Gross (1976) compared heavy television watchers and people who don't watch very much. They found that heavy viewers had a very unrealistic perception of the outside world, seeing it as an extremely dangerous place. Sometimes, these people believed that they were likely to get mugged as soon as they stepped outside their own doors, even though the towns that they lived in made such an event extremely unlikely indeed. More recent replications of the studies have shown this effect to have become even stronger.

The way that television tends to concentrate on violent action, both in reporting news and in its drama, means that heavy television viewers see the world as a much more dangerous place than it really is. People who watch less television, on the other hand, generally have a much more realistic perception of the risks of everyday living. They are aware that dangers exist, of course, but they don't exaggerate them the way that the heavy viewers do. They can weigh up, realistically, the odds against something untoward happening, and so carry on with their lives in a positive way.

The problem isn't really the fact that violence occurs on television. It's more to do with the proportion of violence that is shown on television by comparison with the amount of other types of human activity. Most people go their whole lives without ever coming across a murder in real life; yet the average television-watching child has seen something over 600 television murders by the time it reaches ten years old. Such an unrealistic proportion can't help but distort any child's picture of what the world is like.

Positive television

Not all television is bad, of course. Some nature and science documentaries or historical programmes can be educational, broadening our awareness of the world in which we live. For many people living in modern industrial societies, television has replaced books as the main way that we come to know our world. It's become a major agent of socialization, showing both children and adults how the world works.

Television also contains positive messages in terms of humour and fun. Entertainment programmes such as quiz shows may appear trivial to those who look for high-culture entertainment, but they actually show a friendly and positive approach in their dealings with people – most of the time, at any rate – and this is as useful in modelling behaviour as the more aggressive behaviour shown in soap operas and dramas. Sports and music programmes, too, serve positive psychological functions, stimulating people's interest and enthusiasm.

Teaching prosocial behaviour

There have been a great many studies of the influence of children's programmes in teaching children prosocial behaviour (prosocial is the opposite of antisocial). For example, in 1976 Rubinstein and others found that five- and six-year-olds who saw an episode of *Lassie* in which a boy helped a dog were more likely to help puppies in distress than children who hadn't seen the programme.

There is some evidence that the early soap operas, or at least the British and Australian ones, had prosocial effects on children – and possibly adults too. The Australian soap *Neighbours*, for instance, used to contain a number of clearly positive messages in its content. It contained ideas such as: if you see your friend is in trouble, try to help them out; or if someone has upset you, try to work out the problem with them so that you can be friends again. Soap operas of this type used to portray people as belonging to a community in which people helped one another out – a very different message from the competitive aggression of so much television drama.

Unfortunately, however, recent trends in television drama have meant that the positive messages of soap operas have become lost, and there is much more of a focus on the negative aspect of human interaction than used to be the case – aggression, murder, jealousy and so on. So what used to be a positive viewing experience, both for children and adults, has now become as negative as other forms of television drama; with the result that many parents are beginning to restrict their children's exposure to these programmes too.

Television and reading

There is quite a lot of concern regarding the influence television has on children's reading. Gunter (1982) showed how heavy television viewing can seriously impair a child's learning to read, particularly during the earliest years of the child's education. The reasons for this are all tied up with the child's own perceptions – of what reading is for, and why it should make the effort to learn to read in the first place.

As we saw in Chapter 9, the experience of an expert is quite different from the experience of a novice, and this applies to reading too. Expert readers see reading as a doorway into another world of information; but children who are only just learning to read have quite a different experience. One reason why some children find it hard to learn to read is because they haven't actually realized that it will be much easier once they are good at it. Novice readers are often so concerned with the mechanics of reading that they hardly notice the story. To them, reading is very hard, and they sometimes can't see any point in doing it.

This is made even more extreme by television, because the child sees television as similar to reading, but much easier. Reading needs a lot of practice: it takes time and effort before you recognize words at a glance, and are free to concentrate on the meaning of what you are reading. Television, on the other hand, gives you instant access to information. Moreover, it tells you stories, and lets you know about the outside world. So some children simply can't see the point in learning to read, and unless someone takes the time and trouble to show them what the point is, they will never put in the effort needed to become fluent readers. This is one reason why reading stories to children is so important – it shows them the kind of experience which they will be able to get in the long run, if they carry on making the effort to read.

And television isn't really a substitute for reading. It's an entirely different type of cognitive experience. For one thing, reading trains children's imagination, because children need to create their own mental pictures about what they are reading. Reading also introduces children to abstract ideas, that can't really be portrayed in a concrete form – and that forms an important basis for later understanding and analytical thinking. Television, as we have seen, can have some positive effects on children's development – it isn't all negative. But reading is an entirely different skill, which trains different mental abilities. So it is important that young children see it as such, and not as an equivalent to television.

Computer games

Computer games are another aspect of modern leisure life which have influenced a great many people – not quite as many as television, but a sizeable proportion of the population. They have become a major sector of the leisure market when it comes to children and teenagers; and many adults also have computer games which they enjoy playing. Unlike most other leisure activities, video games are relatively new – the very first game, Pong, was invented only in the early 1970s. Since then, they have continued to develop, and each year sees the launch of new games and new ideas.

Types of computer game

Computer games are tailored for several different interfaces, ranging from ordinary domestic computers to specialized games consoles. The accuracy of representation which they provide also varies, from very simple games such as Tetris which can even be played on a small-screen mobile phone, to highly complex ones with realistic, film-like backgrounds and characters, which require specialized consoles to operate them. So there is quite a range of possibilities available to those who enjoy playing computer games, and most people have their own favourite types. Table 13.1 lists the five main types of game; but game designers are inventive and often come up with new ideas, so there are always a few which don't fit exactly into these categories.

Table 13.1 Types of computer game

Action/adventure games

Simulations

Sports games

Strategy games

Arcade games

Action/adventure games

Action/adventure games are those in which the main character (or characters) is involved in some kind of quest or challenge. This might be seeking out something, such as hidden treasure; or simply defeating 'baddies' of one sort or another. Characters in these games often become well-known as popular figures – a process which again has been going on for almost as long as computer games have existed – and their fame continues long after people have stopped playing the game. Many people, for example, still remember Sonic the Hedgehog, even though the game itself is completely outdated; and the character of Lara Croft has become known by many who have never even attempted the Tomb Raider games.

Simulations

Simulations are another popular form of computer game, which generally involve some quite elaborate construction. One of the earliest of this type of game was Sim City, in which the player had to construct a viable city – putting in place features such as sanitation, factories, schools, residences and the like. Other games of this type may require the player to construct their own robot, empire, spaceship; or give them similar types of challenges. Effectively, they are problem-solving games, requiring the player to put together various types of information; and quite a few of them have a hidden educational content.

Sports games

Sports games mimic the kinds of pastimes which people might engage in as part of their more active leisure pursuits. They require the person to simulate the same kinds of skills as they would in carrying out these skills in real life, and often to make the same kinds of judgements, although with a very different set of controls. Everyday sports such as golf or tennis are popular in this category but, overall, the most popular are driving games. Driving simulations were among the very first games to be marketed. Their development may have owed something also to their potential for real training; in that those training to master complex types of controls, such as in flying an aircraft, or the sophisticated aspects of car driving, can often learn real skills from a well-designed simulation. So this area of computer games has always been well-researched and, as a result it developed more quickly than many of the other areas.

Strategy games

Strategy games have an even longer history, but used to be played with models and props rather than computers. Many of the traditional war games were converted into computer games, and have proved very popular. The first, of course, were familar domestic strategy games – computer chess games were developed almost at the same time as home computers themselves; and other popular board games such as Risk or backgammon have lent themselves successfully to computerized versions.

But the computer strategy game goes much further than that. The additional effects which they offer, such as 3D or explosions, have meant that many games in this category have been developed explicitly for gaming platforms. Some strategy games are specifically designed as team games – they are played over the Internet, often between groups of players who have never personally met, and they involve close co-operation in order for difficulties to be overcome. They are often referred to as 'Dungeon' games, because one of the earliest of these games was a fantasy-based one called 'Dungeons and Dragons'.

Arcade games

Arcade games are played purely for fun, without any particular goal apart from scoring as many points as possible. They include the shoot-'em-up video games, which typically involve chasing, firing missiles and causing opposing screen artefacts to explode or self-destruct; and skill games which involve catching or hitting objects. These games have a long history (in computer game terms), dating right back to Pong and Space Invaders; although their modern-day equivalents are, of course, far more sophisticated. What is interesting, though, is how popular they continue to be; and that in itself can give us several insights into the psychology of computer games.

The psychology of computer games

Whether someone enjoys a particular computer game or not will depend on a number of factors: their own personal interests, their personality, the structure of the game, the equipment they have available, and the skills which they already have in handling that equipment. Some games, for example, require more sophisticated handling than others, or more experience. But game designers are very careful to gauge the levels of difficulty within the game itself, to ensure that players can develop their skills and advance from one level to another as they get better at playing it.

Rewards and incentives

This carefully staged learning is important, because it helps to keep up players' motivation. By providing **manageable goals** for people to aim for and achieve, the game designers help to build a player's sense of competence and excitement. Added to this, when each new goal is reached, some kind of reward or recognition is offered. Sometimes this is an extrinsic reward within the game, such as obtaining a new type of weapon or a points bonus, but sometimes, it is an intrinsic reward that comes about as the person recognizes what they have managed to do. As we saw in Chapter 9, learning through rewards is a fundamental form of learning which has been studied in detail by psychologists, and is very effective. The popularity of video games gives us yet another example of just how effective it can be.

Self-efficacy beliefs

The idea of staged learning and the acquisition of more sophisticated skills taps into other aspects of human motivation as well. In particular, it helps to build up the person's self-efficacy beliefs – their sense of competence at being able to undertake particular challenges or perform particular tasks. We looked at self-efficacy beliefs in Chapter 6 and saw that they can be important in building up our personal self-confidence, as well as affecting our preparedness to learn. Computer games encourage success through perseverance, and so encourage children (and adults) to recognize that they can achieve things if they work hard at them – a useful message in any walk of life!

Sensation-seeking

Another aspect of human psychology which is activated by many computer games is that of sensation-seeking. Many people enjoy activities which are exciting, or which provoke a certain level of anxiety. The popularity of fairground rides is an example of this, and computer games tap into some similar types of psychological mechanisms. They don't do it in the same way as fairground rides do, of course; but the level of concentration which they require, and the skilled control, means that they can become quite thrilling and absorbing for the person playing them. The effect is increased, of course, by the background music of the game, which has been designed to heighten these emotional responses and to keep the player absorbed in what is going on.

Social interaction

A fourth aspect of human psychology which is involved in many computer games (although not all) concerns the way we respond to other people. The team-based 'Dungeon'-type strategy games involve co-operation between players, and those who play them find this type of interaction very rewarding – perhaps because it avoids the challenges and ambiguities of other types of human contact. Some people have expressed concern that teenagers with social problems may use this type of contact to avoid more direct face-to-face interactions; but the evidence seems to suggest that such teenagers have always devoted themselves to hobbies in any case, and at least these activities do bring them into contact with like-minded others. So they may actually result in such teenagers becoming more social than they would, had they been engaging in a more isolated activity such as model-building.

More commonly, though, games tend to tap into the psychological mechanisms activated by competition. Most games offer some opportunity for comparison with other people, even if it is only on the high-score board; and many games are designed explicitly so that two or more players can compete directly with one another. By offering a social dimension as well as a personal one, computer game designers allow for the game to be an interactive event between people, as well as between the person and the machine.

Are computer games harmful?

Just about any form of new technology raises social concerns about whether it is beneficial or harmful. When computer games became popular, many people worried about whether children would be damaged by playing them. Effectively, these concerns took three forms. Firstly, the fact that many games were based on violent concepts, such as beating up 'baddies' or shooting things, was thought to encourage a culture of violence among young people, or to make them more aggresive. Secondly, the fact that children spent so much time playing computer games raised concerns about damage to their physical health. Thirdly, the obvious enjoyment and preference which children showed for computer games games was considered to be potentially harmful in terms of their future learning.

Violence and aggression

Griffiths (1998) reviewed the evidence of various studies which have attempted to explore whether the violence of computer games is harmful or not. The general idea is that the violence in the games encourages children to model their everyday behaviour on the type of behaviour demonstrated in the game; and also that the gory nature of much computer violence will brutalize children so that they come to regard it as normal. However, most of the studies which have attempted to investigate this effect are inconclusive. Certainly if children are put in situations where they can act out the type of behaviour shown in a game, soon after playing it on the computer, then they will do so. But that is short-term imitation in rather artificial situations. Studies which attempt more realistic evaluations are much less clear-cut.

Griffiths (1998) pointed out that the evidence is inconclusive, but that overall there does not seem to be as much of a damaging effect as some people imagine. As a general rule, children are well able to distinguish between computer simulation and reality, in much the same way as they distinguish between the violence in cartoons and reality. Although they may sometimes act out the behaviour of some characters in video games, this is imaginative play, which they are not likely to confuse with real life.

Time spent game playing

Concerns about the amount of time that children spend playing computer games are another matter. Computer games, as we have seen, are designed to keep the person playing; and children may not realize how long they have been spending on that particular activity, without the intervention of an adult. Physical exercise is important for healthy development – and for healthy adult life, for that matter – so it is important for a child to have a balance of activities, with some time being spent in physical play or sport, and some time being spent on more passive activities.

This doesn't mean, though, that computer games are the worst offenders in this respect. The interaction between the person and the computer is a much more active and, in many ways more psychologically healthy form of engagement than the passive receptivity required by television watching. Rather than simply watching, the child who is playing on the computer is acting and thinking, which is preferable to being passive. If it comes to a choice between watching television and computer games, then computer games have a definite advantage – depending, of course, on the game and the television programme. Too long staring at any kind of screen, though, can be damaging to the eyesight, because eye muscles need exercising in the same way as any other type of muscle; so the ideal is always that children have a balance of activities rather than doing just one type of leisure activity.

Harm to learning

The third main objection to computer games is that they might be harmful to children's learning, because they encourage children to fritter away their time on the games instead of reading or doing things which are more obviously educational. This objection is more complex, because children learn in many different ways and, also, because there is relatively little research evidence. Overall, what evidence there is suggests that children who like to read still read for pleasure whether they play computer games or not – they appear to regard them as separate activities, not as substitutes for one another. Also, as we have seen, the perseverance which children devote to video games is regarded by some psychologists as a valuable form of learning in itself.

Many educational programmes, too, use children's enjoyment of computer games to convey educational messages. There is a range of educationally based CD-ROMs available for children of all ages, which combine educational information with engaging activities and challenges for the child; and several other games, as we have seen, have an educational undercurrent. So some video games and other computer activities can actually enhance children's formal education rather than interfere with it. Computer-based learning of this type may be regarded as different from the classic computer game, but it can equally well be argued that the popularity of video games helps to create the climate for the children's enjoyment of educational activities, and its readiness to learn. Again, it depends on the game, and this is definitely an area which needs more psychological research.

Computer games, then, are a significant part of the leisure activities available to most people. There is an ever-increasing range of games, and increasingly complex control systems, ranging from sophisticated driving simulators to film-quality displays. But some other new developments, such as 3D-based virtual reality devices, have been less obviously successful. Home-based virtual reality equipment did not take off in the way that its designers originally expected, partly because of the personal vulnerability experienced by people cut off from their immediate surroundings. DVD-based realism, by contrast, caught on very fast. This may have been the result of clever marketing on the part of the DVD people; but few inventions which have made people feel more vulnerable have been successful in the mass market. Whatever their form, though, computer games are likely to be with us for a very long time; and understanding the psychological mechanisms underlying them is interesting in its own right.

Sport psychology

Sport is another important way that people use their leisure time. Many of us are involved in sport in one way or another, whether we do it ourselves, or whether we just watch other people do it. Sporting activities range from everyday exercises such as walking or jogging, to team sports such as playing football, rugby or hockey, to performance sports like skating, athletics or cycling. In many ways, it is difficult to draw a hard and fast line between exercise and sport, but when the full range is taken into account most of us do something vaguely sport-like, even if it's only to go swimming now and again.

Some people, though, engage in sport much more seriously. They decide, from a relatively early age, that they are going to compete seriously in their particular sporting activity, and from that point they devote tremendous amounts of time to improving their skills, learning new techniques, and ensuring that their physical and mental condition is as perfect as they can get it. Some people do this as amateurs, aiming to participate in sports as a serious hobby, but not intending to make a living from it. Others aim to take sport up as a profession, by achieving international standards of performance or, possibly, by training others. Whatever their ultimate aim, these people devote a considerable amount of their lives to perfecting their sporting performance.

Music and dance

Sport isn't the only area of human activity which is like this, of course. Exactly the same things could be said about both dance and music. To become a professional dancer or musician doesn't just require a personal talent. It also requires devoting a large part of one's daily life to learning and perfecting performance techniques. This is particularly true if someone aims to take up music or dance as a profession, but it is also true if they want to aquit themselves competently as an amateur. Many of the findings of sports psychologists also apply to the psychology of music and dance.

Sport psychology is all about using psychology to help people to learn skills, keep motivated, and perform as well as possible. It draws from psychological knowledge and experience of sporting practice to try to understand how different factors can influence sportspeople in their performance, and what the best methods of training might be. One of the central aspects of sport psychology, therefore, is how we learn physical skills.

Learning physical skills

Learning to perform a complex physical action precisely is really quite a complicated thing. It involves hundreds, or even thousands, of different muscle groups, each contracting and relaxing at precisely the right moments. Each muscle contracts in response to a message from the brain, so the different messages which are sent from the brain to the muscles need to be highly co-ordinated if the movement is to be exactly right.

In Chapter 9, we saw how this involves automatizing the actions, so that they can be carried out without any conscious thinking, apart from the decision to perform them. This happens as the sequence of actions becomes controlled by the part of the brain that co-ordinates action, the cerebellum, instead of being controlled by the cerebrum, which is the part of the brain that we think with. And, as we saw in Chapter 5, drugs such as nicotine interfere with the messages from the brain to the muscles, which is one reason why high-performance sportspeople don't smoke. The other reason, of course, is that it also interferes with how efficiently we breathe, and with the amount of oxygen that the blood can carry.

The learning curve

When we are learning something new, we generally take quite a long time to do it successfully at first. But the more we do it, the easier it becomes. Someone learning to perform a new tennis stroke may fail entirely the first time they attempt it. As they practise, though, they are likely to succeed more and more often, until eventually they can do the stroke successfully all the time – at least, while they are practising!

It's the same with any physical skill. Someone who is learning to type will be very slow at first, but will become faster as they become more familiar with the positions of the letters on the keyboard. If we were to plot their speed of typing on a chart, measuring it against the amount of practice, we would find that it made a curve which picked up very steeply at first, and then rounded off more gently. And if we were to do the same with the practising of the tennis stroke, we'd find that it, too, made the same curve (Figure 13.1). This is known as the **learning curve**, and it shows how we go about learning any new skill.

Actually, though, the basic learning curve is only the beginning. In a complex sport or skill, we often experience several different curves, with a levelling out between them (Figure 13.2). We improve with practice a great deal at first, but then we hit what is known as a **plateau**, where we don't seem to get any better for a while. But if we keep on working at it, then eventually we begin to improve again. Most complex skills involve plateau learning, because they actually consist of many skills combined together, and it takes time to master each one. It's also possible that the time spent apparently not getting any better is useful because we consolidate those skills we do have, and make sure that they are fully under control.

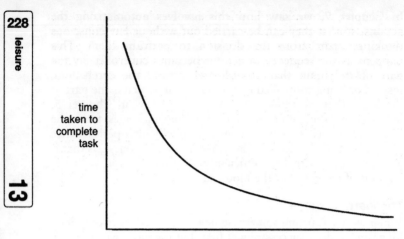

figure 13.1 a learning curve

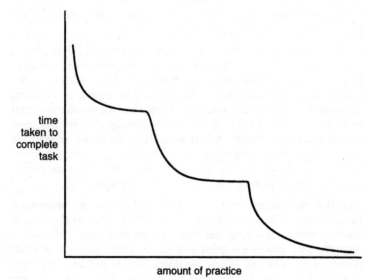

figure 13.2 plateau learning

The use of feedback

Another very important part of skill learning is **feedback**. Feedback is all about knowing what we have done – knowledge of results. If we didn't get any feedback about the outcomes of our actions, we wouldn't be able to learn anything. You couldn't get better at darts if you were blindfolded, and couldn't see where the darts had landed on the board! Instead, when playing darts, we use the outcome of our first action – throwing the first dart – to help us to aim the second one more accurately.

One of the most important tasks of a sports coach is to provide feedback. But the kind of feedback matters. Den Brinker *et al*, in 1986, investigated how important feedback is when learning to ski. They used a ski simulator, and asked people to learn how to make slalom-type movements while on the machine. The reseachers varied the kind of feedback, and found that the most useful type was when people were given feedback about the amplitude of their body movements – how much they swayed with the actions. They learned much faster from this than they did when they were given feedback about how often they moved, or how smooth their movements were.

Mental training

Another aspect of complex skill learning that sports psychologists have become very experienced at, is that of mental training. Mental training involves using the imagination, in a carefully controlled way, to improve performance. For example, Ainscoe and Hardy (1987) developed a training programme with gymnasts, in which they were asked to practise their performance not just physically, but also mentally – visualizing themselves going through each action successfully and smoothly. They found that using this method produced a noticeable improvement in how well the gymnasts learned.

Ainscoe and Hardy weren't the only psychologists to have discovered this. In 1983, Feltz and Landers reviewed 60 different studies of mental training of physical skills. They came to the conclusion that this method was a useful way of improving performance. Many athletes and other sportspeople use visualization as a regular part of their practice, and find that it doesn't just help their physical learning, it also helps their concentration.

Practice

Any new skill requires practice – it won't become a skill until enough time and effort has been put into perfecting it for it to have become virtually automatic. Some sports psychologists have investigated whether it is better to have long, concentrated sessions of practice, or whether it is better to break them up into smaller chunks. The answer seems to be somewhere between the two. Practice sessions need to be long enough for the person to get some physical control of the skill that they are working on, but it is also important to have breaks. These don't just give the person a chance to rest: they also seem to help us to consolidate the learning, physically, so that it comes more easily the next time we try it.

Gruson (1988) looked at how skilled pianists practised, and compared that with people who were still working through the lower grades. She found that the experts went about their practising in a different way from the novices. The experts, for instance, would spend much more time practising whole units. They wouldn't ever repeat single notes – if they made a mistake, they would repeat the whole section. Novices, on the other hand, would repeat single notes if they made a mistake, and this didn't really help them to learn the whole piece of music at all.

The implication, then, is that practising whole units is important for the development of fluent skills. If we wish to produce a performance which is polished and continuous, then we need to practise what we are doing in a way that is also continuous. It's obvious really, when you think about it, but it's surprising how many people don't do it!

Keeping motivated

Another important aspect of sport psychology is in studying how it is that successful athletes manage to maintain their motivation. Success requires continual training and striving to improve performance. And becoming a competent sportsperson involves giving up a great deal of free time, and putting oneself through a considerable amount of physical effort. For many people, such efforts would be too much. So what is it that distinguishes someone who is prepared to do this, from the rest of us?

Internal and external motivation

One of the most important distinctions which sports psychologists make is between internal and external sources of motivation. An internal source of motivation is one which comes from inside ourselves – which derives from our own intentions, ambitions and personal goals. An external source of motivation, as its name suggests, comes from outside. External motivators include rewards, avoiding punishment, and living up to other people's expectations.

Interestingly, there is quite a lot of evidence which shows that giving people external rewards, such as money, for achieving success in sport, music or exams, can actually be counter-productive. It can reduce someone's motivation, not increase it. For example, Orlick and Mosher (1978) asked children to carry out a balancing task on a bar, for ten minutes. Before and after the test, the children could spend as much time as they liked practising. The amount of time that they practised was taken as showing their level of intrinsic motivation.

Orlick and Mosher found that all the children spent much the same amount of time practising before the test. When they did the test, they gave one group of children a special award, saying that it was because they had done such a good job. Another group of children didn't get any reward at all, even though they were just as good. These children didn't know about the other group, so they didn't feel disappointed. But after the test, the children who had received the award actually spent much less time practising than the children who hadn't been given anything. Receiving the award had actually decreased their level of intrinsic motivation.

Of course, this doesn't mean that all awards are a bad thing. Sometimes, they can help motivation because they encourage people to feel competent, and that they are getting somewhere. When Orlick and Mosher told children beforehand that they could earn an award by doing the balancing task, those children didn't lose motivation at all. So things which tell us that our skills are improving as a result of our efforts help us to feel competent, and don't reduce our motivation. But rewards which aren't relevant to our efforts, such as money or unexpected awards, can sometimes reduce intrinsic motivation.

The reason for this seems to be that we tend to focus on just one explanation for why we are doing things. Even though, as we have seen, human beings often do things for more than one reason, we still prefer to identify just one reason at a time. So if someone receives an external reward for doing well, then they are likely to see themselves as being motivated by the reward, instead of by their own interest and commitment. If the rewards don't continue, or don't seem to be as important, the person loses motivation. Someone who knows that they are doing something for their own personal pleasure and ambition, though, isn't likely to lose that motivation unless their whole ambitions change.

Competence

This doesn't mean, though, that we could carry on putting lots of effort into mastering a sporting or musical skill if we didn't feel that we were getting anywhere. It is very important that we should be able to feel competent in our learning – that we should feel that our skills are improving, and that our own personal abilities to do things are getting better. Having good feedback is a part of that, because that shows us when we are improving. But another important part of this is the way that we set our personal goals. We need to have something to aim at, and that something must be something that we think we could manage. It needs to give us a challenge to rise to, but should not be so far ahead that we feel we could never get there. Setting manageable goals is an important part of retaining motivation, because the feeling that we have achieved another target helps us to keep going.

Achieving peak performance

Sport psychology is also concerned with making sure that people can perform to the absolute limit of their ability, at the times when it matters. Training and motivation are part of that, but there are other factors, too, which are the concern of sport psychology. On the training field, for instance, many athletes reach top performance. But when it comes to actual competitive events, some people consistently win, while others just don't seem to be able to manage that last, final edge which means success.

Positive thinking

Positive thinking is a crucial factor in distinguishing between people who are likely to be successful and those who aren't. Highly successful sportspeople don't allow themselves to think about failure. They don't just block it off – instead, they think positively about success. Not about winning the gold medal, but about actually doing the activity successfully.

This sort of approach requires a high level of mental discipline on the part of the athlete or performer. There are various techniques for doing this. One of them is learning how to concentrate your mental focus, so that you are aware only of the part of your surroundings which matter. The champion tennis player Billie Jean King described how her mental focus would change from a wide range, encompassing the whole court, while the ball was over the other side of the net, to a tight, narrow focus the minute the ball was hit by her oppponent. The gold medal-winning athlete Linford Christie used to limit his mental focus to the track in front of him during the few minutes before the race began, ignoring everything else except the starting pistol.

Another way that successful athletes use positive thinking is in visualizing success and achievement. The hurdler, David Hemery, described how one year he tried to prepare himself for disappointment, by imagining realistically how he would deal with failure. He lost. The next year, throughout his training, he allowed himself to think only about success, and didn't entertain the thought that he might not win. That was the year that he won his Olympic gold medal.

As with using visualization for training, Hemery's mental images weren't about standing on the podium. What he would visualize was completing the track without a single mistake, and in the best possible time. By creating a positive mental image of what he was capable of achieving, Hemery was able to build up his feelings of competence and confidence, and to make sure that his performance on the day was the very best that he could do.

Managing performance anxiety

Another aspect of making sure that you do the best you can, whether in a sporting competition or in an exam, is making sure that your anxiety levels don't get out of hand. We saw in Chapter 4 how being anxious or upset can interfere with how well we do things, so it is important for athletes not to allow themselves to get too worried. Using positive thinking is also a good way of doing this. By filling the mind up with positive mental images, there isn't much room for thoughts about failure or mistakes.

Athletes also manage performance anxiety by making sure that their bodies are not physically stressed in the wrong way. Anxiety can be increased by eating the wrong things, or by eating at too infrequent intervals. If we haven't eaten for several hours, for instance, we automatically become more anxious and aroused, because this is an ancient biological mechanism encouraging us to go out and look for food. Many athletes drink milk, because it contains naturally calming substances which work in the brain to reduce anxiety without interfering with our physical abilities. And, of course, they regard it as very important that they are properly rested and have a good night's sleep before a key competition.

Exactly the same principles apply to any sort of demanding human experience. It's just as important when you're doing an exam, for instance, to eat properly and to be rested, as it is when you are entering a sporting competition or taking a graded sports test. But it is astounding how many people ignore the physical demands of their bodies, and make their anxiety much worse by not eating properly, or by staying up the night before to 'study'. There is a physical aspect to managing any kind of performance anxiety, even exam performance.

Using setbacks constructively

Another feature which seems to distinguish the top performers from those who don't do as well, is how they handle failure when it actually happens. Many people respond to failing a test, or an exam, or losing a competition, by feeling upset and disappointed. But the top sportspeople don't do this. Instead, they react by being angry with themselves. They know that they can do better than that, and so they resolve to make sure that it won't happen again.

This has everything to do with the process of **attribution**, that we looked at in Chapter 3. Attribution, you may remember, is about the reasons that we give for why things happen. And this makes all the difference to how we respond to failure. If someone attributes their failure to lack of talent or ability, for instance, then they are unlikely to try very hard to overcome it, because they won't think there's any point. If they think it was just a 'bad day', or something temporary, then they will continue with their normal training, and not be too bothered about it. If they think it is because they were doing something badly, which they could do better, then they will work very hard to make sure that they don't make the same mistake again.

Sport psychology, then, like so many other aspects of psychology, brings together many different levels of human functioning. We have to perfect our physical skills, and ensure that they are fully co-ordinated. We learn by practice, accustoming ourselves to repetition and association. But we are also affected by our thoughts, beliefs and imagination – and these can make all the difference to how we learn, and how we perform, skilled actions.

14

education and health

In this chapter you will learn:
- what is involved in skilled teaching
- about two controversial aspects of dyslexia
- to identify three types of therapy used by clinical psychologists.

In one way or another, psychologists have been involved with both education and health care ever since psychology began. But the ideas which have developed in psychology during that time have changed considerably, as our understanding of the human being has developed, and, as these ideas have developed, so too have many of the social practices which emerged from them.

For example, in the middle of the twentieth century, a number of politically influential psychologists, particularly Sir Cyril Burt, believed that intelligence was a fixed, inherited quality. Since Burt was directly involved in giving advice to the Ministry of Education, this ultimately led to the introduction of a school system in which children were sent to different schools, offering different types of education, depending on their performance in an examination and intelligence test which they took at the age of 11.

Nowadays, we don't see intelligence in quite the same way. We see it as much more of an interaction between someone's own personal temperament and their experiences and environment. The experiences of mature students who were unsuccessful at school but who take exams, degrees and even higher degrees later in their adult lives, show that intelligence – in practical terms – can change dramatically with experience. And research evidence also suggests that as long as we use it, our intelligence increases as we get older, not decreases. So the old idea that a person has a fixed intelligence, which doesn't change through their lifespan, is pretty well discredited.

In the health field, too, psychological ideas and knowledge have developed considerably. During the first part of the twentieth century, this area of psychology was strongly influenced by the ideas of the psychoanalyst, Sigmund Freud, who believed that people were largely acting out the demands of unconscious parts of their personality. Freud believed that unconscious infantile conflicts could lead to both mental and physical disturbance, even in adults.

More recently, psychoanalysis has become pretty well separated from psychology. Although some of its ideas have been useful to clinical psychologists – in particular the idea of defence mechanisms, which we looked at in Chapter 6 – psychoanalysis as a way of seeing the world adopts a different style of reasoning, and takes a different view of scientific evidence, than modern psychology. For the most part, modern clinical psychologists draw on a different set of psychological insights and theories in their work. In this chapter, we will look briefly at some of the main ideas which psychologists working in education and health tend to use. Some of them may seem familiar, because quite often we will be looking at how the concepts which we looked at in the early part of this book are being applied in real life.

The psychology of teaching and learning

The idea of a rigidly fixed intelligence may have been discredited, but nonetheless, some of us are still quicker at understanding some types of things than other people are. People differ. We each have our own aptitudes, our own interests, and our own talents. But even if we have an aptitude for something, if we are not interested in it, then we are unlikely to put any effort into mastering it.

Student motivation

As we've already seen, being interested in something can make all the difference to whether we remember it or not. And, as we've also seen, becoming skilled at anything, whether it is an intellectual skill like reading or a physical skill like skating, takes practice. So a vital part of the psychology of teaching and learning consists of understanding how students come to be interested in what they are learning, so that they have the motivation to keep working.

The learning environment

In Chapter 6, we saw how human motivation can operate on several different levels. Our behaviour is sometimes energized and directed by how we think about things, sometimes by the situation itself, and sometimes by social and cultural factors. All of these are relevant to education too. For example, if we take one of the more basic levels of explanation, we are all influenced by the environment around us. A formal classroom layout produces different behaviour from the people in it than an informal setting.

Partly, this stems from our social understanding of what a formal layout is intended to convey: it is a kind of **non-verbal communication**. But partly, also, it is a learned association between stimulus and response. Our past experiences have formed that link, and so we act in the same way when we find ourselves in the same situation.

This might seem trivial, but it is one of the things that we need to take into account when we are considering the psychology of teaching and learning. For instance, many people who take qualifications in further education colleges are returning to study as mature students. Although they do want to study, often their first experience of being in a classroom again brings back unpleasant associations of school and feelings of inadequacy and failure. A teacher who is aware of this process is able to make sure that these feelings can be replaced quickly by ones which will help the student to learn, by providing more positive learning experiences in that setting. But someone who was unaware of what was going on could easily dismiss these people as not having the necessary motivation or ability to learn.

Programmed learning

Stimulus-reponse learning can be important in other ways, too. The behaviourist, B. F. Skinner, developed a system known as **programmed learning**, which used the principle of learning through positive reinforcement. Skinner, as we saw in Chapter 9, believed that it is better to reward appropriate behaviour than to punish inappropriate acts. So the learning system which he developed was based on the idea that the more people could get right, the more they would learn.

In a programmed learning system, information which needs to be learned is divided into very small chunks, each of which leads on to the next. By dividing it up like this, it is relatively easy for a student to get each answer right. If they don't, they go back and relearn the section until they do. Skinner believed that maximizing the chances of gaining right answers would provide the motivation for learning – unlike the conventional educational programmes of his time, which tended to emphasize failure and wrong answers rather than rewarding right ones.

Personal dimensions of teaching and learning

Skinner's ideas have been incorporated, in a modified form, into many educational systems. But not all of them. Skinner, as a behaviourist, believed that the stimulus-response level of explanation was enough to explain all human behaviour. So he believed that just the association between the information and the right answer would be enough for people to learn – and he also believed this could be provided just as well by teaching machines as by anything else (Skinner, 1966).

But this ignores other aspects of how human beings function. Our social knowledge and the expectations of other people are equally important in how we learn, if not more so. We have already seen how important expectations can be in educational performance, through Rosenthal and Jacobsen's work which we looked at in Chapter 2. And there are many other aspects of teaching and learning in which interpersonal relationships and social interactions are extremely important.

Achievement motivation

For example, as any teacher will tell you, some children seem to have a much stronger need for achievement than others. These children often learn well, because success is important to them and so they put a great deal of effort into studying. They aren't the only children who learn well, of course: some others do it purely because they are interested in what they are learning. But it is helpful for children to have a reasonably high level of **achievement motivation**, because this will see them through temporary difficulties and setbacks as they come to terms with new things.

Rosen and D'Andrade (1959) showed that achievement motivation seems to have a great deal to do with the way that parents interact with their children. In one of their studies, they gave a child a difficult task to do, while its parents were watching. The child was blindfolded and asked to build a tower, as high as possible, out of building bricks. The researchers took note of how hard the child tried to do this – how much effort was put in to getting the tower as high as possible – on the grounds that this would give them some idea of the child's general level of achievement motivation.

Rosen and D'Andrade also observed the parents closely, while the child was trying to complete the task. They found that those children with the highest level of achievement motivation had parents who consistently gave them praise and encouragement. Their parents also had quite high expectations – they anticipated that their child would do quite well in the task, and the children often lived up to those expectations. Parents of children who had low achievement motivation, though, didn't expect their children to achieve very much, and didn't particularly encourage them either.

Self-efficacy

Psychologists of that time tended to think of achievement motivation as a general trait, which would be roughly the same for anything the child encountered. Nowadays, many psychologists see achievement motivation as being linked with **self-efficacy beliefs** – our personal beliefs about how effective we can be (see Chapter 6). Since our self-efficacy beliefs vary, depending on which type of activity they are concerned with, this means that achievement motivation, too, can be variable.

For example, someone might have very high self-efficacy beliefs when it comes to maths – they know they can do it, and so they try hard in maths lessons and are successful in exams. The same person, however, might have much lower self-efficacy beliefs when it comes to learning history. If they have low self-efficacy beliefs for history, then they are less likely to put in the effort that is needed to master the subject and pass the exams.

But self-efficacy beliefs are not fixed. They can be changed by experience. As we saw in Chapter 2, experiencing repeated failure often leads to **learned helplessness**, and giving up. But if we have the experience of learning effectively, and realize that we are able to do so competently, our self-efficacy beliefs rise, and we are more likely to work harder. So a successful teacher, in this respect, is one who makes sure that students experience success from time to time, and also see that success as a result of their own efforts. This raises their self-efficacy beliefs, and provides them with the motivation to work at the subject, achieving things competently.

Personal constructs

Personal constructs, too, are important in the classroom. Personal constructs are the individual theories and ideas about the world that we develop from our personal experiences, and apply to new situations. Driver (1983) showed how these can be extremely important when people are trying to understand information at school. If our own personal understanding of the world doesn't fit in with what we are supposed to learn, then we will absorb only part of what we are learning. We will adjust the information so it fits with our own personal construct system.

This, Driver argued, is the source of most of the common factual errors which schoolchildren – and adults – make. She looked at children's everyday understanding of scientific ideas, such as heat or falling (gravity), and showed that if we develop knowledge of these things purely from our own experience, then the conclusions we come to are not the same as those developed by physicists. By the time children learn about these things in school, they have had plenty of time to develop their own theories and ideas about how the world works. As the children try to understand what they are learning, these theories get in the way.

Driver showed how understanding how students develop and apply their own personal construct systems to what they are learning can help teachers to teach more effectively. Mistakes don't come from stupidity, or an unwillingness to learn, but from applying the wrong kind of ideas to what they are supposed to be learning. Understanding this helps teachers to know what kind of explanations will be needed and why some students are having difficulty.

Levels of processing in remembering

In Chapter 7, we saw how we remember things far better if we have processed the information deeply. Being interested in something means that we do process the information, because we think about what it means, and what effects it might have. So we don't usually have any trouble remembering things that we are interested in. But knowing about levels of processing in memory can also help us with other aspects of educational experiences.

For example, taking examinations generally means learning a great deal of information, not all of which is scintillatingly interesting. But it is possible to use the idea of **levels of processing** to remember the information, even though we may not be totally thrilled by it. By changing the form of the information – drawing up charts, or diagrams, or making summaries – we force our minds to process the information and think about what it actualy means. And once we are aware of what it means, it is much harder to forget it.

In fact, books about how to revise are full of advice about working with the material. Drawing on their own good experience with students, the authors recommend various different methods for revising, all of which actually add up to processing the information more deeply. The problem, though, is that they don't usually explain why we should do it. Unless we can see a good reason for doing something, we don't usually bother. So understanding the psychological processes of memory, and why drawing up a table or a chart helps us to learn, are important.

Positive emotions

Another aspect of psychological knowledge which is important in understanding teaching and learning is how emotional states affect learning. In Chapter 2, we saw how people need a positive interpersonal climate if they are to be open to learning new things and developing their ideas. Nobody learns well in a climate of hostility or sarcasm, but if they feel approved of and safe, people often surprise us with what they can achieve.

So one of the things which a skilled teacher learns is how to create an atmosphere of interpersonal warmth in the classroom, which will encourage their students to become confident and to learn positively. Although many non-psychologists, including, unfortunately, some teachers, believe that we can learn when we are tense or anxious, the psychological evidence all points the other way. We are far less open to new ideas when we are tense and anxious. About all we learn in those situations is how to avoid pain, which is a basic and primitive form of learning. But there is plenty of psychological evidence for the oppposite: that in education as well as in everyday hobbies and interests, people learn best when they feel safe, confident and approved of.

Social dimensions to teaching and learning

There are also social dimensions to the psychology of teaching and learning. As we've already seen in this chapter, we can't really separate the personal and social aspects of learning, because we are all personally influenced by social factors. But there are other issues too. For example, in Chapter 2 we saw how **social identification**, or belonging to groups, is an important part of how we see ourselves. The attitudes which our friends and family take to education will affect us, as well as whether the teacher encourages the class to feel special, and a social group in their own right.

Social identification

A knowledge of social identification is useful for a teacher because it shows us how intergroup conflicts can develop. If students feel that their group identity is being disparaged or threatened, they may respond by reacting against classwork, or even against being in school at all.

But people can have many different social identifications, and these don't have to be in conflict. A student may be a member of a teenage gang, yet still work hard when he/she is in the classroom

– as long as that working hard isn't seen as a threat to his/her gang identity. Many extremely effective teachers have worked successfully with students who, on the surface, appear to be directly opposed to what they are trying to do. They have been able to do this because they have made it clear that there is no conflict between them.

A vital part of this involves knowing how important social identity is to our self-esteem. This helps a teacher to see why the student's social group is so important, and why it matters that the student should see how working for the future – which is what school or college work really is – is not a threat to their social identity in the present. Without such an understanding, many teachers are either dismissive of their students' social groups, or see them as inevitably in conflict with educational values. And the result is that these students, on their part, often feel misjudged and unfairly stereotyped.

We can see, then, that the psychology of teaching and learning spans a number of different levels of explanation. It ranges from the personal and emotional aspects of human psychology, to the cognitive, social, and even cultural levels of explanation. As with so many other aspects of human behaviour, we can gain insights from each of these levels of explanation; but if we are to get a more rounded picture of how human beings are, we need to take them all into account.

Educational disadvantage

Psychologists are also involved in helping children and adults who are experiencing some kind of educational disadvantage. Such psychologists are known as **educational psychologists** in Britain, although they are called school psychologists in the United States, where educational psychologists are more concerned with the applied psychology of teaching and learning. In Britain, educational psychologists are responsible for assessing children who are thought to need a special type of education, and recommending what sort of education that should be.

Specific learning difficulties

There are several different kinds of educational disadvantage. Sometimes children have specific learning difficulties, which means that they find certain kinds of information very hard to learn. If they experience a special school environment, in which the teacher pays particular attention to training them to handle the things which they find difficult, they can often learn a great deal more than they would do in an ordinary school.

Other children who also have specific learning difficulties, though, might benefit more from being in an ordinary school and mixing with the children there. The educational psychologist's judgement as to which type of schooling will be best for that particular child will take into account as many different facets of the child's experience as possible.

For example, we have already seen how much **social expectations** can influence us. They can affect our self-image, our interactions with other people, and how well we learn. If a child attends a special school, it is possible that people won't expect as much from him/her as they would do if he/she went to an ordinary school. So in some cases, if a child's problem isn't very extreme, then it may be better for him/her to go to an ordinary school and perhaps have some additional tuition which will help to overcome his/her difficulties than to go to a special school. The decision about whether to send a child to a special school depends very much on the child itself, and on how severe his or her problems are.

Educational psychologists undergo rigorous training in diagnosing learning difficulties. Some problems have a physical source: certain kinds of brain damage, for example, can produce very specific effects on how a child learns. Sometimes, it is possible to overcome these effects with the right kind of training. Most children recover very well from accidental brain injury, for instance, and often if they have the right kind of therapy, the effects disappear completely.

Sometimes, though, the problem isn't the kind you can get over. In such a case, the psychologist might decide that **amelioration** is the best approach, so the child will be taught how to cope with, and get around, the problem. By developing training which is relevant to the kinds of situations that the child is likely to meet, the child can learn how to live a relatively normal life, even though the child may have some difficulties.

Dyslexia

One of the specific learning difficulties which educational psychologists often need to diagnose is the problem known as **dyslexia**. Dyslexia used to be known as word-blindness, and people who experience dyslexia often have difficulty in identifying letters, or recognizing how they should be written. For example, a dyslexic person might write a letter like y or r back to front, but not realize that they had done it. They seem to be 'blind' to the image of the letter. Other dyslexics have difficulties recognizing words.

Sometimes dyslexia comes about as a result of some kind of accident which causes an injury to the person's brain. This is known as **acquired dyslexia**. Shallice and Warrington (1980) described two kinds of acquired dyslexia. One of them, which is known as surface dyslexia, is when someone has problems with the forms of words, such as difficulty recognizing letters, as above, or problems with spelling – like writing 'lurn' instead of 'learn'.

The second kind of dyslexia isn't about the forms of words, but about understanding them. People with this type of dyslexia have difficulty with words that are hard to visualize: they can understand words like 'tree' easily enough, but have problems with words like 'and'. Shallice and Warrington called this deep dyslexia, because it relates to a deeper understanding of words.

Acquired dyslexia isn't particularly controversial in psychology. It is a recognized outcome of some forms of brain damage, and there is a great deal of evidence which shows how people who previously had these abilities intact experience problems after their accident. But there is a second type of dyslexia – the kind that an educational psychologist would encounter – which is much more controversial. This is known as **developmental dyslexia**.

Developmental dyslexia is a problem which becomes apparent as a child develops and goes through school. A few children seem to be virtually unable to identify words and letters properly, and so have problems with spelling. Some psychologists believe that this problem occurs because of an inherent deficit in the brain, and some have even gone as far as to suggest that it is a genetic disorder, although as yet the evidence for this is a little sketchy.

So far, so good. There certainly do seem to be cases in which children have difficulties of this kind, which really do seem to result from some kind of inherent problem. The controversy comes, though, with the question of whether all children who are considered dyslexic really have these problems. Many psychologists (for example, Whittaker, 1982) see the word 'dyslexic' as a convenient label which is used in many entirely inappropriate cases. Whittaker and others believe that children are often labelled dyslexic when all they really have are problems with spelling.

The problem is compounded by the fact that the concept of dyslexia became popular in Britain soon after a nation-wide experiment on reading, which tried to teach reading using a special phonetic alphabet, known as i.t.a., or initial teaching alphabet. This was based on the principle that children learned to read by 'hearing' the words – a principle which we now know to be untrue. But as a result of the use of i.t.a., a great many children became confused about the need to spell accurately, and many schools almost gave up on teaching spelling formally.

In view of this social context, and the fact that spelling is something that doesn't come naturally to anyone – it always has to be learned by heart, and that takes effort – there is a great deal of anxiety that too many children have been labelled as dyslexic when really they could overcome their problem with a different kind of teaching. This is also exaggerated by a tendency to see a diagnosis of 'dyslexic' as a message that there is no point trying to teach this child words or spelling. As with may other educational disorders, special training programmes which recognize the difficulty, and address it directly, can often overcome the problem, at least if it is in a mild form.

So there are two aspects to the controversy about dyslexia. It isn't really about whether dyslexia exists. The first aspect is about whether all the children who have been labelled dyslexic really are, or whether the label has been given to them simply because they are finding words or spelling hard. The second part is about whether an accurate diagnosis of dyslexia means that the problem is permanent or fixed. Special training programmes suggest that it isn't, and that it can be overcome, but many people seem to see such a diagnosis as if it were a life sentence.

Childhood autism

Sometimes, the problems that educational psychologists encounter are broader than straightforward learning disorders. For example, the problem known as childhood **autism** seems to be a broadly based emotional and personal disorder, which results in such children being unable to relate effectively to the people in their lives.

Autism was first identified as a general syndrome by Kanner (1943), who pinpointed four characteristics which autistic children possess. The first, and probably the most important, is that they are unable to form relationships with other people. Although they may interact, they seem to be aware only of the way that another body impinges on them, not of the person as a human being.

The second characteristic is that autistic children rarely play spontaneously and, in particular, they don't engage in play which involves pretending. Ordinary children, though, begin pretend play from quite an early age, and don't need to be taught it at all.

Autistic children also show differences in how they learn to speak. Some of them never actually learn to talk at all. Others will talk quite a lot, but when they do, they don't speak in the same way as ordinary children. For instance, they may not quite get the hang of reversing the pronouns which we do automatically in conversation. Although ordinary children learn this quite easily, autistic children say what they have heard other people saying, so they tend to refer to themselves as 'you', and to the other person as 'I'.

The fourth distinctive characteristic of childhood autism is that these children often have an almost obsessive insistence on certain routines or repeated activities. They seem to enjoy repetition and routine, and can become very upset if their routines are interrupted for some reason.

Harris (1988) discussed how a range of psychological evidence all points to the idea that autistic children don't have a **theory of mind**. In other words, they are not aware that other people have a mind of their own, and may see things differently. Baron-Cohen (1992) described an autistic girl, Jane, who had no problem remembering people or information, but who had absolutely no awareness of the fact that other people were independent, thinking and feeling human beings. Her inability to empathize, or to understand someone else's point of view, resulted in a great many of her autistic symptoms.

Counselling and therapy

A different area of activity for psychologists is in health care. Psychologists are involved both in mental and physical health care, in one way or another. Clinical psychologists have been concerned with helping people who suffer from emotional disorders or mental illness since the early part of the twentieth century. More recently, health psychologists have become increasingly concerned with aspects of our physical health care, as it has become more apparent that so many aspects of our physical health depend on psychological, rather than medical, factors.

Clinical psychology

Clinical psychology, for the most part, has been concerned with people who are suffering from some kind of mental or behavioural abnormality – people who we might call mentally ill, although often, thinking of them as 'ill' isn't the best way to understand what is going on. Clinical psychologists often work alongside psychiatrists (doctors who specialize in mental illness) in psychiatric hospitals or clinics, but their approach to dealing with the patients is very different. Where a psychiatrist draws on a knowledge of physiology, which means adopting treatments such as chemotherapy (drugs) or physical treatments such as electro-convulsive therapy, clinical psychologists use their knowledge of human psychology to tackle the problem.

Behaviour therapy

For example, some of the types of problems which clinical psychologists might deal with are what we know as **neuroses** – fears or anxieties which have become so extreme that the person has difficulty living a normal life. In the 1950s, psychologists who were interested in conditioning approaches to learning took the view that many of these problems could be understood entirely as problems of behaviour. These people, they argued, had learned inappropriate ways of dealing with their environments, and this inappropriate learning was causing them problems. So the way to tackle those problems was for them to learn appropriate ways of dealing with their environments instead.

This led to the development of a number of different, behavioural, methods for dealing with neurotic problems. As we saw in Chapter 9, psychologists began to use conditioning techniques for dealing with the irrational fears known as **phobias**. By treating the feared object as the stimulus, and substituting new, learned associations such as relaxation for the fear reaction, people could learn to deal with their phobias, and overcome them.

Other psychologists used approaches which derived from operant conditioning, or from social learning. Bandura (1977) showed how **modelling** could also be useful in teaching people to overcome everyday fears. Seeing someone handling a snake harmlessly often gave those who were frightened of snakes a role model to imitate, and they found that their own level of fear became much less as a result.

Behaviour shaping

Many psychologists working with disturbed people adopted the idea of **behaviour shaping**, which comes from operant conditioning theory. Using this, a person becomes able to carry out an entirely new type of behaviour by learning it a little at a time. This principle was very successful, for instance, in helping people with agoraphobia – a fear of open spaces. Rather than forcing them into dealing with the whole problem all at once, a psychologist would gradually help the person to build up their abilities, a little at a time. They might begin, for instance, by getting used to standing in the open doorway of their own home. Once they could do this easily, then they might venture out for just one or two steps; and each time a little more would be added until eventually they could manage to deal with the outside world easily.

Another way in which behaviour shaping was used was in **token economy** systems, introduced to help long-stay psychiatric patients to take more responsibility for their own lives. In the 1960s and 1970s, some patients had been in psychiatric hospitals for decades, and they had become thoroughly institutionalized – dependent and unable to look after themselves. Psychologists developed training systems which would allow them gradually to learn how to do basic things, like sweeping a floor or taking care of their own clothes.

Since it is important for operant conditioning that the reward or reinforcement should happen immediately after the person performs the behaviour which is to be rewarded, the patient would be given a token when they did something right. In very severe cases, this might at first be for something as simple as holding a broom and making vague sweeping movements. Once they had learned this, behaviour-shaping techniques would be used, so they would only be rewarded for sweeping a bit more thoroughly. At the end of the day or week, they could exchange their tokens for privileges of one kind or another. In this way, long-stay patients were gradually taught the kinds of behaviour which they would need if they were ever to leave the institution and live in a hostel.

Cognitive therapy

In the late 1970s and early 1980s, as psychology changed its emphasis, clinical psychologists began to develop new approaches, which drew on other areas of psychological knowledge. A new form of therapy, known as **cognitive therapy**, emerged. Psychologists began to work on the self-defeating beliefs of many of their clients, showing them how to recognize negative attributional styles and how to develop realistic and positive self-efficacy beliefs. Research into stress management showed how important it is for people to have a sense of control over their own lives, and many clinical psychologists adopted these principles in their work.

Counselling psychology

Another form of clinical psychology first emerged in the 1950s, with the work of the psychologist Carl Rogers. As we saw in Chapter 2, Rogers believed that human beings had two basic needs: the need for positive regard from others, and the need for self-actualization. From his experience with his own patients, he came to the conclusion that providing an environment in which people would experience unconditional positive regard would allow them the security to be able to explore their own potential and to make their own choices.

Client-centred therapy

Rogers's work became the foundation of what was later to become counselling psychology. He developed an approach which he called **client-centred therapy**, to emphasize that it was the client who held the responsibility and made the decisions, rather than the professional who was supposed to be helping them. In client-centred therapy, the therapist provides a supportive, warm environment in which the person explores their own options and makes their own decisions.

Following on from this, Rogers concluded that it was equally possible for other people to provide a supportive and warm environment. He developed the idea of **encounter groups** – groups in which people would share their problems, and encounter one another openly, as individual human beings. It was this which provided the basic principle of the self-help groups which have become such an important part of Western societies.

Rogers's ideas became extremely influential in many areas, and were taken up by many people, both psychologists and otherwise. Counselling as a profession was developed on the basis of Rogerian principles, although it has since developed other approaches as well. Although many counsellors are not psychologists, the area of applied psychology known as counselling psychology has been growing considerably in recent years, and it consists of qualified psychologists who apply their professional skills and training in counselling work.

Health psychology

Psychologists are also involved in working to enhance physical health. Health psychology is a very broad area because it is concerned with the psychological aspects of our physical health, and there are a great many of these. Maintaining physical health isn't just about avoiding illness: it's also about making sure that we stay well, so lifestyles and beliefs are very important in health psychology.

Doctor–patient communication

Some health psychologists are interested in doctor–patient communication. For example, people often don't give their doctors all the information they need to make an accurate diagnosis because they feel intimidated by the doctor's manner, and by the formal setting of the surgery. Health psychologists use their knowledge of non-verbal communication and social appraisal to help doctors to communicate more effectively, so that they can overcome these problems.

Another aspect of doctor–patient communication concerns the issue of following medical instructions. Surveys show that as many as 60 per cent of people don't actually use medical treatments in the ways that they have been told – and this is important, because this can make all the difference to whether the treatment is effective or not. A drug which has to be taken with food will not do its job properly if it is taken on an empty stomach, because it interacts with the chemicals involved in digestion to have its effect.

So health psychologists look at the various reasons why people do or don't follow medical instructions. They explore issues such as lifestyle – given the person's everyday life, is it actually difficult for them to do what they have been told to do? They also look at people's beliefs about medicines and how they work, and at how instructions can be misunderstood. Research of this kind has produced a number of recommendations for medical personnel which have improved how accurately people use their treatments.

Behavioural treatments

Another aspect of health psychology is concerned with behaviourally based treatments. In some physical illnesses, such as diabetes, there is no known cure. All that patients who have diabetes can do is to manage their disorder by behavioural control of some kind. Health psychologists help people to do this, by looking at aspects of behaviour such as diet control, lifestyle and how people monitor their own health.

By now it should come as no surprise to discover that one of the most important factors in managing diabetes, as well as other behaviourally based disorders, is that people should have a sense of control over their own health. People who see their illness as not under their own control are likely to suffer more, and to do things which will make the situation worse, than people who see what happens to them as the outcome of their own actions. A passive approach to an illness such as diabetes has demonstrably worse outcomes than an active management of the problem. So health psychologists are also involved in training people in techniques for managing their own lifestyles, stress levels, and the like.

Health education

Another aspect of health psychology is in health education programmes: public campaigns which are designed to encourage people to take up healthy behaviours and minimize risks. Anti-smoking campaigns, AIDS avoidance campaigns and, more controversially, advice about what constitutes a healthy diet are the kinds of area in which psychologists have been involved.

Persuading people to take up healthy lifestyles is not as easy as it may sound. Simply giving people information doesn't really work, because there is often quite a difference between what we know and what we do. We may be aware that something is risky, and yet do it anyway. And there are also social factors involved, which can influence what we actually end up doing. For example, there is a big discrepancy between the number of young people who are aware that they should use a condom when they are having sex, and the number who actually do.

Even though the risk of AIDS is high, and the consequences of contracting HIV can be tragic, many people still engage in extremely risky behaviours.

Psychologists studying this area have identified a number of factors which maintain this risky behaviour, such as the belief that sticking only to one partner will minimize the risk – even though the partnership later breaks up and the person then enters another relationship – or the idea that it detracts from the spontaneity of the experience, and makes it seem too 'planned'. There are questions of habits: many older people are reluctant to adopt condom use because they have established sexual habits without them. And there is also, of course, the question of a power imbalance between men and women, since many men oppose the use of condoms and many women do not feel confident enough to insist on their use.

It is these kinds of factor that show how complex the problem of risk avoidance really is. It goes much deeper than simply providing people with information, and an awareness of human psychology is necessary to tackle these complex issues. As we have found so often, health care and the promotion of healthy behaviour involves understanding the human being on a number of different levels. It is far from being simple and obvious.

We can see, then, that psychologists are active in a great many different aspects of education and health. If you are interested in these topics, you may like to read the relevant chapters in *Teach Yourself Applied Psychology*, which go into a little more detail about them. In our next chapter, however, we will turn our attention to the question of psychology and the environment.

15 living in the world

In this chapter you will learn:
- how an understanding of proxemics might help us to reduce vandalism
- to identify four psychological aspects of environmental stress
- how psychology can be useful in the prevention of disasters.

This chapter is about environmental psychology, which is the study of how our surroundings and circumstances influence how we act and how we feel. It isn't just physical surroundings which are important in this: environmental psychologists study the social environment too, in terms of the other people who are around us and how their presence makes a difference.

Our environment can affect us in more than one way. For example, it can act as a confining, or restricting force. We adapt our behaviour to our surroundings, and those surroundings sometimes only allow certain kinds of actions. If you are a patient in a hospital, for instance, there are only a certain number of possibilities for action, partly because the environment allows you only to do certain things. The kinds of behaviour which are possible for someone out walking in the hills are entirely different from the kinds of behaviour which are possible for a mother at home with a small child.

Environments also have the power to produce particular kinds of behaviour from us. How a patient in a hospital acts is, to a very large extent, determined by the hospital environment. It isn't just that it restricts the possibilities, it's also that we realize that certain kinds of behaviour are expected from us and so we act accordingly. Similarly, we tend to speak in hushed tones in a church or holy place even if we aren't personally very religious, because just being in that environment produces that behaviour.

Another way that the environment affects us is that it can motivate us to act in certain ways. Different types of environment encourage us to do different things. Take going on holiday, for instance. When we are away from home, we often find ourselves exploring new places, or trying out new foods – behaviours which we wouldn't be nearly as likely to do at home. People are also sometimes motivated to stay in a particular part of the country, even if it means adapting to a less well-paid kind of work; or to live in a particular kind of house, even if it means hard work and struggle to get there.

Proxemics and privacy

Human beings are very conscious of space and places: it seems to be one of those things that is built deeply into our consciousness. For example, we automatically seem to use distance as a type of non-verbal communication, which says something about the relationship that we have with other people. Conventional distances are different from one culture to the next, but in all societies we stand closer to people that we like than we do to people that we don't like; we stand further away when talking to a stranger than to a friend, and we conform to cultural standards about what is the usual, or acceptable, distance for certain kinds of interaction.

Personal space

The area of psychology which is concerned with personal space and the distances which we keep between people is known as **proxemics**. Everyone seems to be surrounded by a little 'bubble' of personal space, and we only allow people inside this space if we know them well enough. But, as I've already said, different cultures have different ideas as to how big that bubble is. What is a comfortable conversational distance for someone from a Middle Eastern country will often feel too close to a North European, so if the two are in conversation, it is easy for tensions to arise. The North European will feel tense and crowded, because they feel that their personal space is being invaded; while the Middle Eastern person will feel that the other is being distant and hostile, and not particularly friendly.

Zones of personal distance

Hall (1966) proposed that we have four zones of personal distance, as listed in Table 15.1. When we look at this table, though, we have to remember that the distances which Hall provided as examples are drawn from Europe, Britain and the United States – and don't represent all of the subcultures in those societies either. We also need to bear in mind that one category can sometimes shade into another – our personal distance zones aren't really as rigid as they might seem from this description.

---

table 15.1 zones of personal distance

1 Intimate	(0–45cm)	For lovers, very close family (such as mother and child), or very close friends.
2 Personal	(0.5m–1.2m)	For friends, or family members.
3 Social	(between 1.2m and 3.5m)	For a business conversation, or a discussion with a relative stranger.
4 Public	(between 3.5m and 7.5m)	For public meetings and ceremonies, with speakers and audiences.

It isn't just the distances themselves which vary. Even when people are very close, the amount of contact that they actually make with one another depends on their culture. Jourard (1966) observed couples at pavement cafés in various parts of the world, and observed how often they touched hands, or made body contact in some other way. London had the lowest number: many couples didn't make any contact at all during the period in which Jourard was conducting the observations. Puerto Rico, on the other hand, had the highest, with as many as 180 contacts between couples in the course of a single hour.

Often we try to protect our personal space by using markers such as shopping bags or newspapers. You will often find, for example, that people reading in libraries will mark out a small area around themselves using bags or coats – establishing a kind of temporary 'territory'. In 1966, Felipe and Sommer conducted a study in which the researchers deliberately went and sat down too close to people working in libraries (it's interesting, isn't it, that we all have an idea of what 'too close' means?). Only one of the 80 people involved actually asked them to move, but the others all indicated that they were uncomfortable with the situation. Some people piled up papers and books to form a barrier; others used body posture to separate themselves, by turning away from the intruder and hunching their shoulders or putting an arm around their work; but most simply packed up their things and moved away.

Protecting privacy

Incidentally, this study is another example of the kind of research psychologists used to do, but which wouldn't be considered ethically acceptable nowadays. People are entitled to their privacy and to be allowed to work undisturbed, and it is important that modern psychological studies should not cause anyone to feel discomfort or distress. So a study which deliberately intruded on someone's privacy wouldn't be permitted by a psychology ethics committee, unless there was a very good reason indeed for doing it, and unless the people themselves had agreed to co-operate.

The concept of personal privacy is an important one for environmental psychology, although it is a hard one to define. Privacy means different things to different people. Some people see privacy as being entirely alone; others see it as being just with friends or family; others, as in the library study, see it as being left undisturbed to get on with what they are doing even if there are other people around. Personal privacy is linked closely with social respect, and we saw in Chapter 6 how important that can be for us. So even if it just takes the form of respecting personal distance, it's important to respect people's privacy.

This may seem to be a relatively unimportant point, until we remember that there are some situations in which people lose all right to personal privacy. One of the reasons why people find it so disturbing to be in hospital, for instance, is because hospital patients are placed in a situation where all of the normal social markers for privacy and personal space have disappeared. Nurses and other people can enter freely what would normally be an intimate zone for the person, and make bodily contact; and everyday actions become far more public than they were before. Sommer and Dewar (1963) discussed how this invasion of personal space and personal privacy is a serious source of strain for a hospital patient.

We protect our privacy in other ways, too. For example, even an ordinary family house has certain areas which are 'public', such as the sitting room, but other areas which are entirely private. In the normal run of things, a visitor to someone's house wouldn't expect to see the bedrooms, for example. And even the public access is restricted to certain people: strangers are excluded carefully, by physical barriers such as fences and locks, and the area of ground which represents the territory is carefully marked out. Protecting personal privacy is so important to us that, for most people, what is really upsetting about being burgled isn't so much what has been lost, as the knowledge that their personal territory has been invaded by a stranger who has no respect for them or what is theirs.

Defensible space
Newman (1972) suggested that having some kind of defensible space is important in minimizing urban stress, and even crime. From studying the incidence of vandalism on different housing estates, Newman found that most of it happened in public places, and not in areas which were clearly 'owned' by a resident or small group of residents. The most extreme amounts of vandalism happened in public areas which were also enclosed or hidden from view, such as lifts or stairwells.

Newman argued that housing developments ought to recognize the concept of **defensible space** – the idea that the people living in housing projects should have areas which were clearly marked out as theirs, and which they could look after. By doing so, Newman asserted, it would be possible to reduce the amount of vandalism. When existing housing estates were looked at, Newman argued, some of them seemed to have been designed almost to encourage vandalism, because of the way in which they used the space.

Newman identified four principles for developing areas of defensible space. The first is that there should be clearly defined territories, which people can see as 'owned', such as individual gardens and entrances. The second is surveillance: it is important, Newman said, that an area should be overlooked, so that other people can see what is going on in it. The third is image: a building should look secure and well-protected, because this will reduce the number of opportunistic crimes. A building which seems to be an easy target will attract people who are ready to take advantage of any opportunity, such as an open window; whereas one that looks secure won't attract them so much in the first place. The fourth principle is that the surrounding environment should also be open and easily surveyed. There's not much point in a well-designed housing development which can be reached only along dark, lonely roads!

Meeting strangers

A different facet of privacy is concerned with how we respond to the people around us. In modern industrial society, crowds are an ordinary part of everyday living. Yet this is a relatively recent development. For most of our history, human beings have tended to live in small village or nomadic communities, consisting of 100 to 200 people, so everyone would be known individually. In a situation such as this, encountering a stranger is a rarity, so anyone new would automatically be an object of interest.

The problem is that we still have many of our biological adaptations to meeting strangers, which evolved during the millions of years when meeting strangers was rare. We respond differently to strangers than we do to people who are familiar, and our response is more aroused and tense. Yet in city or town life in modern societies, we meet strangers all the time – in fact, we are more likely to encounter strangers than friends. So the mechanisms which evolved to adapt us for a life in which most people are known and familiar become overloaded and stressed, because they are continually being activated.

It is for this reason that so many people find crowds stressful. In a crowd, we are unable to maintain our usual personal space, which is a source of tension. People sometimes even bump into us, which we find even more stressful, and we often perform quite complicated dodging manoeuvres when walking down a crowded pavement, in order to avoid bodily contact with strangers. We are also liable to make eye-contact with strangers, and eye-contact is one of the most powerful signals of all.

Eye-contact – looking directly into someone's eyes while they are also looking at you – isn't a signal that we take lightly. Prolonged eye-contact is a sign of intense interest in the other person. At its extremes, it can signal love – or its opposite, hostility and threat (there is no chance of confusing the two, because the muscles around the eyes are arranged quite differently). We look at someone who is speaking to us, which is a signal that they have all of our attention. We look away from someone if we don't want to disturb them, or make them feel self-conscious.

So even fleeting eye-contact, of the sort we have with strangers, is stressful when it happens often enough. In situations where prolonged eye-contact might happen because the same strangers have to remain close by, such as in a lift or a tube train, we tend to look upward or out of the window in order to avoid it, which is why advertisements tend to be placed high up. City-dwellers learn to cope with this type of stress, of course, but it is present in the background nonetheless.

Crowding

Crowding can produce stress in other ways, as well. In a well-known study in 1962, Calhoun showed that laboratory rats that were allowed to breed freely and become overcrowded became much more aggressive, even killing one another as part of the competition for living space and food. Since this behaviour would normally be totally alien to these animals, it showed how much stress the crowding had created.

There are indications, too, that human beings become much more aggressive if they are crowded. Loo (1979) studied young children in a day nursery, and found a strong link between bad temper and crowding. The more children there were, the more quarrelsome the youngsters became. Similarly, McCain *et al.* (1980) showed that prison riots and also suicides were much more common when prisons were overcrowded than when they held their intended number of prisoners.

In another study, Kelley (1982) showed that there was a strong link between the density of the population in 175 American cities and the amount of crime. Even the types of area which were relatively low in crime showed more crimes as the population increased – and that included all sorts of crimes, ranging from car theft to murders. Kelley drew the implication that population density, in and of itself, is one source of environmental stress, which shows itself in increased crime rates – although there are, of course, other factors which influence crime as well.

Sources of environmental stress

Cassidy (1997) discussed the many different ways that our environments can affect us, psychologically. Most of us, for example, have had the experience of being in an environment which calms or soothes us. For many people, being out in the country is a particularly restful and relaxing experience. For others, being in a bustling, busy market can be an experience which lifts their spirits and makes them feel happy. But environments can have the opposite effect too. Our surroundings can make us feel tense, or anxious, or can simply represent an increased strain as we go about our day-to-day lives.

In 1982, Herzog and others surveyed a large number of people about which features of cities they found most pleasant. Trees, grass and water were popular, as was distinctive architecture which was in harmony with its surroundings. Old, untidy settings such as factories and alleyways were considered to be the least pleasant of all.

Noise

Other types of environmental experience can be deeply stressful. Whether we are aware of it or not, we are taking in information from the world around us all the time. If a stimulus is continuous, we become habituated to it, so that we are no longer aware that it is happening. You will probably have noticed this if you have a fridge that hums. You don't consciously hear the humming, but when it stops you become aware that it was there in the background before. This realization tells you that, even though you weren't hearing it, the noise was still being registered by your nervous system.

Background stimulation of this kind can be much more intense than we realize. People who live in small towns or in the country often find it difficult to sleep when they visit a large city for the first time, because they find the continual traffic activity too noisy. People who live in the city don't notice it as much, but their senses are still registering it. The continual background noise of traffic, machinery and household equipment is a source of minor, but continual, stress.

Loud noise is even more stressful. People who live close to airports often have to have special sound insulation installed to protect them from the noise of the aircraft taking off and landing; and those who live close to motorways often need a sound screen, such as a thick row of trees, to baffle the noise. Loud and prolonged noise at work can cause people to go deaf, which is why operators of noisy machinery are expected to wear ear defenders; and this sort of noise is a source of stress as well as a physical health hazard.

A high level of noise at work affects our level of arousal (see Chapter 4) so that we feel 'keyed up', and often irritable. It also makes it difficult for us to communicate with other people, which is stressful too. This affects some kinds of work more than others: in an investigation of the effects of work noise, Poulton (1976) found that it was skilled jobs, which require concentration or rapid action which are most affected by work noise.

Not all noise is stressful, though. The noise level at a music concert can be extremely loud, but doesn't produce serious effects – although it might, if we were trying to carry out a skilled task which required concentration. For the most part, though, the fact that we have chosen to listen to it, and also the fact that it is musical rather than simply noise, makes a lot of difference to our reactions. Also, the fact that it is temporary, lasting only for a few hours, rather than being part of our daily experience, makes a difference.

Control and stress

As we have seen so often, if we feel we have some control over the stimuli around us, then we don't find them nearly as stressful. And this can apply to loud, unpleasant noises too. Glass and Singer (1972) asked people to solve a set of problems while a loud, harsh noise occurred from time to time. Half of the people in the study were able to press a button which would stop the noise, at least temporarily, but they were asked not to use it unless they really had to. The others didn't have any way of stopping the noise. The group who could have stopped the noise if they wanted to, actually didn't stop it at all, but they performed much better on the problem-solving task than the others. It seemed that just knowing that they could control it if they wanted to was enough to remove the stressful influence.

There are other studies which show how important a sense of control can be in reducing stress. Lundberg (1976) investigated the levels of stress experienced by male passengers on a commuter train. The more people there were on the train, the more stress the passengers experienced, even though there were always enough seats for everyone. Lundberg also found that people who were first on the train, or who joined it at an early stage in its journey didn't experience as much stress as those who joined the train later, even though they had a much longer journey.

What seemed to be important in the passengers' experience of stress was whether they could choose their own seats or not. People who joined the train early had more choice in where they sat, and were more likely to be able to choose a favourite seat. It seems that feeling that they had some kind of control over their commuting experience made a considerable difference to the amount of stress people felt.

Temperature

Temperature can be a source of environmental stress, too. People working in an atmosphere which is too cold or too hot find it difficult to concentrate on their work, which is a source of frustration. However, we have to be a bit careful when we are looking at temperature as a source of stress, because there is quite a big difference between external high temperatures – warm weather – and an indoor hot stuffy environment.

Baron and Ransberger (1978) looked at weather reports and civil disturbances in America, and found that riots were most likely to happen when the temperature was hot – although not when it was unusually or extremely so. This doesn't mean, though, that rioting is caused by hot weather. As Smelser (1962) and many other researchers have shown, riots are sparked off by perceived social injustice, not simply because people feel like rioting. But in hot weather, more people are out on the streets, and so unfair or unjust events are more easily noticed and more easily communicated to others.

Pollution

We also respond more strongly than we realize to levels of pollution in the environment. Pollution represents a source of physical stress for our bodies, because they have to cope with semi-toxic substances, such as lead or nitrous oxides, as well as trace amounts of real toxins, such as those in commercially grown vegetables. These can also produce mental effects as well. Rotton and others, in 1978, showed that when people were experiencing high levels of air pollution they felt less happy, were more likely to dislike other people, and to see the negative side of things that happened to them.

On a more specific level, too, Bleda and Sandman (1977) showed that cigarette smoke could produce depression and anxiety in non-smokers. So it seems that environmental stresses of various kinds, whether that be noise, crowding or chemical pollution, can make a lot of difference to how we live our lives.

Disasters and accidents

Experiencing ongoing environmental stress is one thing: experiencing a disaster is quite different. From time to time, events happen which have massive implications, both for the people who are involved in them but also for the smooth and safe running of society as a whole. The nuclear explosion at Chernobyl, the Hillsborough football stadium disaster, the Zeebrugge Ferry disaster, the Kings Cross fire, the Hatfield train crash and many others were traumatic events of such magnitude that they affected the lives of thousands of people: not just those who were directly involved, but many others as well.

Systems and errors

Psychologists studying how these disasters have happened find, repeatedly, that they show a similar pattern. In each case, a large number of minor problems have occurred fairly regularly, but these are overlooked or tolerated because they are part of a much more complex system, because they would be awkward or expensive to correct, and because the chances of them escalating into a serious problem are considered to be low. However, eventually, these ignored minor problems combine, to produce tragic and disastrous consequences.

These problems are often a direct result of ignoring psychological factors in the situation. As we've seen in this book, psychological factors are many and varied, and so are the ways in which they manifest themselves in complex systems. The shiftwork practices in the ferry company, for example, meant that the people who were operating the *Herald of Free Enterprise* were unlikely to be functioning at their most alert, which became a major factor in how the error took place. As we saw in Chapter 4, people work better with some shift systems than with others, and this needs to be taken into account in any complex system.

Similarly, there are some designs which are likely to reduce errors, and some which make errors more likely to happen. Ergonomic psychologists investigate the best possible locations for warning and alert signals, and also which types of signals are most needed. The lack of alert signals on the bridge to indicate that the bow doors were still open was another factor which led to the *Herald of Free Enterprise* disaster. It might seem a trivial factor in itself, but combined with the other factors involved, it made all the difference.

The important thing about these kinds of factors is that they make the whole system more vulnerable. People don't act like robots: sometimes they make mistakes. So any type of complex system has to be able to allow for the occasional mistake on the part of its human operator, and it has to be designed in such a way as to ensure that these mistakes are less likely to happen. Having a shiftwork system where people on duty are overtired and less alert makes mistakes more likely; having a ship control system which doesn't point out vital information such as whether the bow doors are closed or not also makes mistakes more likely.

The kinds of mistakes which people make aren't random: they are ones which can be taken into account when complex systems are being put together. Reason (1990) performed a number of studies of everyday errors and mistakes and found that they tend to fall into three categories: those to do with skills, those to do with knowledge, and those to do with the rules that people are working by.

Skill-based errors
Skill-based errors are often concerned with the way that highly practised actions can become so automatic that we don't need to

pay conscious attention to them (see Chapter 9). This means that sometimes we fall back on habitual routines when really we intended to be doing something else. You've probably done something like this yourself, such as turning down your usual route to work or school instead of going in a different direction, because you weren't thinking about it.

Since this is quite a common type of human error, Reason argued that it needs to be taken into account when a complex system is being designed. If a mistake of this sort would be serious, then it is important to make sure it doesn't happen, by making sure that the kinds of routines that people are asked to follow in different circumstances are different enough from one another, that people don't just slip into automatic routines and habits. If two systems involve similar patterns of activity, then this sort of mistake is much more likely to happen.

Knowledge-based errors

Most kinds of knowledge-based mistakes come from the fact that people simply don't have the knowledge that they need in order to take effective action. An operator who has been trained only in one particular job, and who hasn't had special training for what to do in an emergency, can easily make a mistake simply because they don't know what the best thing to do is. So if the failure of effective action could result in a disaster – no matter how unlikely – it is important that people should be aware of how to deal with it.

Rule-based errors

Rule-based mistakes are often associated with tackling problems that haven't arisen before. Usually, people will try to deal with these by applying rules or principles which they have used in other situations. As we saw in Chapter 7, we use our existing mental schemas to direct what we should do in new situations. Sometimes, though, the rule the person tries to use is inappropriate, and this can have serious consequences.

Another kind of rule-based mistake happens when we are simply applying an inappropriate rule. To return to the Zeebrugge ferry disaster, Reason showed how the way that the directors of the company saw their job was an example of people working within an inappropriate rule. They defined the primary task as being to keep their shareholders happy, rather than being to ensure that the ferries ran safely on a day-to-day basis. This led to the adoption of practices which were cheap, but not safe.

This point may need a little explanation, because it is not saying that the company's finances don't matter. Ultimately, of course, a company which doesn't make a profit won't be able to run. But most similar companies would see running the ferries safely as their primary obective, on the grounds that it would ensure confident passengers and more profitability in the long run. The directors of the ferry company, though, aimed for profitability at the expense of safety and efficiency. As the outcome of the disaster showed, it was an ineffective policy in the end. But it is a clear example of applying inappropriate rules for the situation.

Post-traumatic stress disorder

Whenever we are involved in any kind of sudden loss or bereavement, we experience grief. Grief is an extremely disabling emotion, which can last for a very long time and has a number of complex elements. Ramsay and de Groot (1977) identified some of the main components of grief, and these are listed in Table 15.2. As anyone who has experienced the loss of someone they love knows, the complexity and intensity of the experience can be overwhelming at times.

For people who are involved in major disasters of this kind, though, the experience is even more severe. In addition to the grief which they experience as a result of the death and loss involved in the event, there is also the shock of the experience itself. This is often deeply traumatic and can have lasting effects. Clinical psychologists working in this area have identified a syndrome known as **post-traumatic stress disorder**, or PTSD for short. Although it has been known for some considerable time, it is only recently that PTSD has become acknowledged as a clinical problem in its own right.

Post-traumatic stress disorder happens in people who have experienced severe emotional traumas. It occurs in people who are engaged in prolonged and dangerous fighting, in people who have experienced torture, and in those who are involved in major disasters. If the stress is serious and continuous enough, it seems that most people will be affected in the end. Swank (1949) in a study of 4,000 survivors of the Normandy campaign, found that soldiers experienced what was then known as shell shock (but is now recognized as PTSD) if three-quarters of their companions had been killed, no matter how resilient they seemed to be.

table 15.2 components of grief

1	**Shock**	A feeling of numbness and unreality.
2	**Disorganization**	Being unable to perform even simple, routine tasks.
3	**Denial**	Refusing to admit that it has really happened.
4	**Depression**	Feelings of pining and despair.
5	**Guilt**	Blaming oneself for the death, no matter how unrealistically.
6	**Anxiety and/or panic attacks**	A frightened response to being overwhelmed by emotions.
7	**Aggression**	Hostility and anger at the unfairness of the bereavement, sometimes targeted at medical staff or relatives.
8	**Resolution**	Accepting the fact of the bereavement, as the worst of the grief dies down.
9	**Re-integration**	Beginning a new life without the dead person. Many people find it hard to do this straight away, but begin to manage it after a couple of weeks.

Emergency workers who have to deal with major disasters can also experience PTSD. Taylor and Frazer (1982) studied the people who helped out in 1979, when a DC10 on a tourist flight crashed into a mountain in Antarctica. All 257 passengers and crew were killed, and it took ten weeks to recover and identify the bodies. Several of the workers who had been helping to recover the bodies experienced persistent images of the disfigured corpses or suffered nightmares of air crashes. Those involved in recovering bodies from the World Trade Center in New York in 2001 were provided with special counselling, to help to minimize the effects of the trauma – an example of how widely recognized this syndrome has become.

Symptoms of PTSD

There are three main groups of symptoms in post-traumatic stress disorder. The first involves **re-experiencing** what happened. People suffering from PTSD often have recurrent nightmares of the event, and may also experience vivid memories of it during the waking day, which are extremely distracting as well as distressing. The second group of symptoms occur as the mind attempts to cope with the trauma, and these are known as **avoidance** or numbing reactions: people often feel detached or estranged from others, and distant from everyday life. The third group are to do with the increased **arousal** level of the body, so they include the inability to sleep or to stay asleep for very long, irritability, and a tendency to outbursts of anger.

These symptoms are similar to those which people would be likely to experience after any disturbing event, but what makes them distinctive in PTSD is how strong they are, and how long they last. Although sometimes the symptoms don't appear until some time after the event, they can go on for several months, or even years. They can also disappear for a while, and then reappear again. Archibald (1963) found that 15 years after a traumatic event had taken place, two-thirds of survivors still showed symptoms of PTSD.

Often, though, people don't recognize that what they are experiencing is actually post-traumatic stress disorder. Mitchell (1992) described how doctors were trying to treat the residents of the Scottish village of Lockerbie for some time after an American airliner exploded above the village, causing deep trauma and shock among the residents. But the doctors were not aware of PTSD, and so were at a loss as to how to proceed. When residents received insurance leaflets describing the symptoms, the local doctors realized that what they were treating was actually a specific and recognizable syndrome, rather than just a collection of individual reactions.

It matters whether the disorder is recognized, because it is possible to organize therapy which helps people to get over it – but only if people know what is happening. Some clinical psychologists specialize in this type of therapy, working with the victims of disasters to help them to overcome the problem and return to normal living. Although the symptoms don't disappear altogether, having therapy does help people to get over the most severe problems more quickly, and to cope with it better.

We can see, then, that psychology can be usefully applied, not just in understanding how disasters and accidents take place, but also in helping people to recover from the worst of their effects. The most important message, though, is the one which becomes apparent when we look at how these disasters happen in the first place: that if we take full account of psychological factors in the design and management of complex systems in the first place, they are much less likely to happen. This doesn't mean that they absolutely wouldn't happen, of course – nobody could promise that – but it would minimize the risks. And when the consequences of failure are so very extreme, anything which minimizes the risk of a disaster is worthwhile.

16

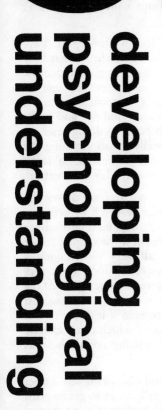

developing psychological understanding

In this chapter you will learn:
- about the five methods of collecting psychological evidence
- how 'theories' enable psychologists to be scientific
- why it is necessary to study human beings from several different angles.

If you've read this far, you'll have gathered that psychology is a pretty wide-ranging subject, covering a great many different aspects of human functioning. People are extremely complex, and understanding the ways that our minds work is never going to be a matter of one simple explanation. Everything we do is influenced by a diverse range of experience, from our biochemical state to the culture we were brought up in and the situation we are in right now. It's the psychologist's task to bring all these together and try to make sense of them.

Psychologists, though, are scientists, and most psychological knowledge is developed as a result of some kind of empirical research. As researchers, psychologists tend only to work in one small area at a time. It isn't possible to conduct research into the whole of human nature – we have to concentrate on just one bit at a time, or everything would be too complicated. So quite a lot of psychological knowledge consists of small bits of research, each of which can throw a little light onto a situation, but isn't enough to explain it on its own.

This means that it is very important for psychology to have ways of linking together those pieces of research, so that they can form coherent explanations for what is going on. Scientific explanations are known as **theories**, and they are just as important in psychological knowledge as empirical research. Without theories to bring together research findings and make sense of them, there wouldn't be much point in doing research in the first place, because it wouldn't really tell us anything – it would just be a collection of 'ooh-look-ain't-it-interesting' facts, and we can get those from quiz shows or everyday observation.

Actually, just about all psychological research is driven by theory in the first place. People conduct research in order to investigate whether a particular theory is true; and their findings are obtained in such a way that they can test the theory, to see how well it holds up in reality. It's all very well having a plausible idea, but lots of plausible ideas really don't work very well when we actually look closely at human beings. Part of the definition of a scientific theory is that it can be tested against empirical evidence, and challenged or refuted if it doesn't seem to work. There are other kinds of theories which don't exactly work in the same way, but we don't usually count these as scientific ones.

Even theories, though, can generally deal only with one aspect of human functioning at a time. If we really want to get to grips with what human beings do, we need to look at it using several different **levels of analysis** at the same time. Levels of analysis, which are sometimes known as levels of explanation, are all about the way that we choose to study something.

If we wanted to look into the human activity known as reading, for example, we might decide to study it by investigating what happens to the nerve cells in the brain as we read. This would be the **neurological** level of analysis, because we would be studying the neurones which are involved in that activity. Another psychologist, though, might choose to look at reading in terms of how we process the information that we receive, mentally. This would be the **cognitive** level of analysis, because it is concerned with our cognitions – how we perceive, remember and apply information that we come across in everyday life. A third psychologist might choose to study reading in terms of its functions in society – what children and adults learn from books and other publications, and how this influences social living. This would be the **socio-cultural** level of analysis.

All these levels of analysis, and quite a few others, are involved in understanding reading. Although we might conduct research into only one level at a time, getting the whole picture of what is going on when people read needs all of them. So if they are really about explaining human behaviour, the theories that we develop need to be able to bring together, or at least connect with, several different levels of explanation. We will be coming back to the idea of levels of analysis later in this chapter, after we have had a look at some of the different types of research methods that psychologists use to collect their evidence.

Conducting psychological research

Most psychological research is about gathering evidence, which will either support or refute the theories which have been developed to explain what is going on. Gathering psychological evidence is a bit like detective work. It is always easy to jump to conclusions about an answer. If a crime has been committed, you can always find someone who is certain who is responsible – but sometimes they are completely wrong. In the same way, when we are studying something in psychology, it is easy to jump to conclusions about it. After all, we all think we know about human beings. But sometimes, as with the crime, our conclusions are simply wrong.

So the psychologist, like the detective, has to put in hours of painstaking work collecting evidence, to find out what is really going on. Sometimes all that evidence will lead to the same conclusion we might have obtained by guessing, or from 'common sense'. But even though our conclusions might not be earth-shattering, at least we know that they are based on a solid foundation. Quite often, though, what we discover is totally unpredictable. Without collecting the evidence in the first place, we would never have known.

Psychologists collect evidence in many different ways. Psychology as an academic discipline has been around for nearly 150 years, and during that time it has passed through several phases. Each of these phases has left us its methods of research. As a general rule, these phases occurred because a particular group of psychologists believed that they had the best starting point for studying human beings. So the methods that they used can be helpful in giving us an insight into that particular level of explanation.

Introspection

Psychology began life as a special branch of philosophy, so in its early days the approaches it used were very similar to those used by the philosophers of the time. For the most part, this involved **introspection** – trying to understand the mind by analysing your own thoughts, feelings and experiences. Although this method fell out of favour for a time, because it didn't seem to be scientific enough, in a more systematic form it is used in psychology again today. Cognitive psychologists, for instance, sometimes use a method called **protocol analysis** to give them some ideas as to how people solve problems. This involves asking people to talk aloud about what they are thinking as they do a task, and analysing what they say. Some psychologists have found it a helpful way of gathering evidence about problem-solving, or even quite complex tasks such as musical composition.

The early introspectionist psychologists, however, were eventually overtaken by a different approach to psychology which developed round about the beginning of the twentieth century. This approach was known as **behaviourism**, and those who supported it argued that psychology needed to become more objective and scientific. Scientific, in their view, meant sticking to things which could be observed directly by other people, and that meant, effectively, restricting psychology to the study of behaviour.

Experiments

The behaviourists brought with them a rigorous approach to scientific method, which they tried to use to look at the 'pure' elements of behaviour. This meant that they were very concerned to cut out what they saw as 'contaminating' influences, and to design research which just dealt with the important things causing the behaviour, and nothing else. They believed that conducting tightly controlled laboratory experiments was the best way to do this.

An experiment involves manipulating a situation to bring about an effect. The behaviourists, in particular, tried to control their experiments very carefully. They would try to rule out all other possible influences, and then see what happened if the one factor that was left was altered.

This method of study has remained very important in psychology. Some research into attention, for example, has involved asking people to identify a single message or concentrate on identifying a signal on a screen, while different factors in the message have been adjusted. These experiments are carefully carried out under laboratory conditions, so that the researchers can be sure that their results really were caused by the factor they were studying.

Action research

There are other kinds of experiments though, which are much more loosely controlled. Research in organizational psychology, for example, often consists of **action research**, in which working conditions or communication systems are changed, and researchers observe how the change affects the people working in that particular place. Although field experiments like this can't be controlled as carefully as formal laboratory experiments, they can still tell us a great deal about people at work, and have done so, over the years.

Animal experiments

Unlike a modern psychologist, many of the early behaviourists believed that one single level of explanation could provide the key to understanding all human behaviour. This level of explanation was to do with habits and learned associations.

They believed that all human behaviour was really just chains of learned associations combined together, in the same way that atoms combine to form animals, plants, or minerals.

This led them to look for the 'atom' of psychology, or the simplest unit of learning which they could find. So they spent a great deal of time studying animal learning, because they believed that it was a 'pure' form of learning. They believed that animal learning, unlike human learning, was 'uncontaminated' by memories, ideas or imagination, so studying it would help them to identify how basic units of learning combined to produce complex behaviour.

Other psychologists, too, used animals to study basic units of human experience. In the 1960s, for instance, many animal experiments were conducted to investigate visual perception, and animal studies are still used to investigate some aspects of brain functioning. But animal experiments are much less common than they used to be in psychology. Nowadays, psychology is much more concerned with the ethics of animal research, which fortunately has meant that only studies which are serious scientific research and are likely to be of real value in adding to knowledge, are permitted.

Observation

The behaviourists, as we have seen, emphasized rigorous experimentation as the main research method for psychology. Gradually, however, psychologists with wider interests began to have more influence, and people began to use non-experimental methods for studying human behaviour. For example, it's not really a good idea to do experiments on children, but there was a lot of interest in the psychological aspects of child development throughout the twentieth century. So psychologists who were interested in this subject had to do their research by observing children, not by experimenting with them.

There are lots of different ways of performing scientific observations, but just looking at what is in front of you isn't one of them. Researchers need to know what they are looking for, and what they will know if they do actually observe it. Psychologists conducting observational research also need to make sure that their own unconscious biases don't affect how they make sense out of what they see. So many observational studies are conducted in a very systematic way, and sometimes under quite controlled conditions – such as watching children play in a specially equipped playroom which has video cameras or observation windows, so that they can be observed without interfering with their play.

Alternatively, psychologists sometimes conduct observational studies of behaviour in the natural environment. This approach is known as **ethology** and, nowadays, it has become one of the main methods of studying animal behaviour. But it doesn't just apply to animals – ethological studies are very useful when we are looking at families, for example. We have learned a lot about how parents interact with their babies by carrying out ethological observations.

Surveys

Sometimes, psychologists want to make large-scale observations of what people do or think, and they do this by conducting surveys. A survey involves a special **questionnaire**, which is given to a large number of people. By analysing their answers, the psychologist can observe general tendencies, or trends, in what people are doing or thinking. Surveys about AIDS, for instance, have helped psychologists to understand more about people's attitudes towards it – although they still don't tell us very much about what people actually do. They tell us what people think they might do, which isn't always the same thing.

Psychometrics

Another very special type of observation that psychologists use is known as **psychometrics**. Psychometric tests are tests which are designed to tell us something about the person's mind. They usually take the form of special questionnaires, which have been carefully contructed and tested, and which can sometimes give us useful clues about someone's personality, skills, or abilities. Intelligence tests and personality tests are examples of this approach to research. But it is important to remember that they only give us clues – psychometric tests don't have all the answers, and they don't give the whole picture. They can be useful in supplementing other information, but they are not complete research methods in themselves.

Case studies

Experiments and observational studies, for the most part, tend to deal with information from large numbers of people. This approach dates back to the first half of the twentieth century, when it was assumed that people, on the whole, were pretty similar. The general approach to society at that time involved understanding 'the masses', and the masses were not really seen as individuals. During the second half of the twentieth century, though, attention became much more focused on the individual person, and this in turn affected psychological research methods.

One outcome was that psychologists began to ask much more detailed questions about individuals and their experiences. To do this, they began to concentrate on just a few individuals, or single cases. **Case studies** weren't new to psychology: many famous case studies had taken place in the past. But they were regarded by the behaviourists as somehow being less scientific than large-scale studies. More recently, though, psychology has begun to accept the case study as a regular research method which can give us useful information.

For example, we have learned a lot about how the mind works through case studies of people with cognitive problems. One case study, for example, was of a respected academic who was completely unable to recognize people's faces. She was above average intellectually and, in all other respects, her mental functions were normal. Studying this single person in detail gave the psychologists undertaking the case study some useful evidence about how the mental skill of face recognition is organized in the brain.

Accounts and interviews

As we have seen, psychology in the twentieth century was deeply influenced by the behaviourist's insistence that studying behaviour was the only truly scientific approach. But in the later part of the twentieth century, it became increasingly apparent that this simply wasn't good enough. Two people can be in a similar situation, but each of them can interpret what is going on quite differently. Their interpretation will influence how they react, and that will influence what happens in the end. So if we really want to understand people, we also need to study how they make sense out of the world that they live in.

Towards the end of the twentieth century, psychology became increasingly concerned with social and personal meanings. After all, two people may experience very similar events, but it might mean something very different to each of them. Obviously, it is difficult to get at this kind of information using laboratory experiments or observations, and so a different research method became popular. This became known as **account analysis**, because it is all about analysing the accounts which people give of their own experiences.

Interviewing

Psychologists often collect accounts by conducting **interviews**. Interviewing is a skilled affair, because the person doing the interview needs to make sure that the other person feels relaxed and confident. After all, if you don't feel able to trust someone, you wouldn't be prepared to tell them much about your feelings or thoughts, will you? So an interviewer has to be good at encouraging people to speak, and at striking up a good rapport with the person they are interviewing.

There are lots of ways of analysing accounts. Some psychologists look at the ways that people express their ideas, and the metaphors and assumptions which they use. This is known as **discourse analysis**. Other psychologists look at the types of reasons, or **attributions**, which people give to explain why things happen. And some concentrate on identifying the main themes which emerge from what people are saying. Each of these methods is a type of **qualitative analysis** – a way of looking at the meaning of the information, rather than just collecting information about the numbers of people who reacted in particular ways.

We can see, then, that psychologists have a wide range of tools to help in their detective work. Incidentally, I have presented these research methods as if they were developed only at certain times during the century. This isn't really true. If we look back, we find that individual psychologists have used almost all of these methods at some time or other. But different methods are seen as important at different times, by psychology as a whole, and this is the process which I have been describing. It's important, because it affects how much influence a particular piece of research can have – both in psychology, and in society as a whole.

Levels of explanation

One of the most important lessons that we have learned from the history of psychology is that just looking at one single aspect of experience or behaviour isn't enough. People do things for lots of different reasons, and usually for several reasons at once. If we try to single out just one of those reasons, as if that were the only explanation, then straight away we hit problems. Just saying, 'Oh, they're really intelligent' to explain why someone became a research physicist doesn't answer the whole question, because it doesn't tell us why they became interested in science in the first place – or even why they went into an academic career at all, instead of becoming a politician or trader. Instead, we have to look at what people do from several different angles, to see how all the different factors and influences work together to produce the final outcome.

This is where we come back to the idea of **levels of explanation,** or levels of analysis. Anything that we do can be studied from several different levels. Imagine, for instance, that you came across someone reading this book. If we wanted to understand what was going on there, we could look at it from a number of different levels. We might ask what is going on in the actual process of reading. For example, how we can look at a set of marks on a printed page and respond to them as if they were words that someone has spoken to us. And that would be part of an explanation of what was going on.

But it wouldn't be the whole answer. There would also be the question of why the person was reading this particular book, rather than, say, a book about car mechanics. This would lead us into questions about their own personal experience and why they had developed some interests rather than others. We might also ask why they were reading in the first place, rather than, say, cultivating rice or watching television. This would lead us into a different set of questions, which would include questions about their particular culture as well as questions about personal habits, beliefs and moods.

In other words, we can look at the same thing using a number of different levels of explanation. We might use a very general level, such as looking at cultural influences on human behaviour. We might decide to approach a question from the point of view of social influences, by looking at how the people close to us affect what we do and how we conform to social expectations – or don't, as the case may be. We might look at it from the point of view of personal habits and past experiences, or we might look at it from the point of view of understanding how the visual system processes information in the brain. All of these, and many others, are levels of explanation that we can use in our attempt to understand human beings, and no single level of explanation is going to be enough in itself.

Emergent properties

The reason for this is that each level of explanation is more than just the sum of the lower level. Sometimes, for instance, you might hear people saying that once we know about all the different nerve cells in the brain, then we will know all there is to know about how the brain works. But this isn't true, because there are often entirely new properties which emerge when the different parts are combined into a whole system. And these **emergent properties** can make all the difference.

Perhaps this will be clearer if I take an everyday example. A cake is made up of everyday ingredients: flour, egg, butter, and so on. To understand what a cake is, you would have to know about these. But knowing about them wouldn't tell you everything about the cake, because a cake has properties which the single ingredients on their own don't have. At the simplest level, it has a taste and texture which are not present in the single ingredients. At higher levels, it may have cultural or symbolic significance, like the way that it can be given to someone on their birthday. None of these can be deduced simply by studying the ingredients.

It's the same with human beings. We can learn a great deal about people by studying the brain and how it works, but we can't learn everything. We may be able to trace which nerve cells in the brain are active when we are solving a problem, but this doesn't tell us how we are working out a solution, or why we are thinking about the problem in the first place. We need to look at human beings using as many levels of explanation as possible, if we are really to begin to understand what is going on.

Table 16.1 shows some levels of explanation which we can use in analysing problems. As you can see, psychologists use a wide range of levels of explanation in their work, choosing those ones which seem to be most appropriate for the questions that they are trying to answer. So the study of psychology involves looking at human beings from a number of different angles. A professional psychologist needs to be aware of each of these levels of explanation, and to be able to use insights from each of them when trying to solve a particular problem. An academic psychologist, though, generally conducts research within a single specialist area, and so often uses a more limited number of levels of explanation at any one time.

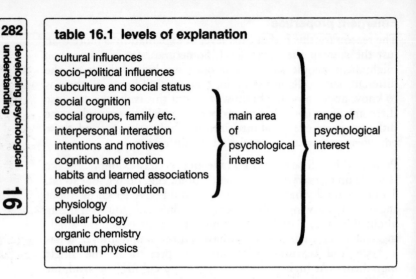

table 16.1 levels of explanation

cultural influences
socio-political influences
subculture and social status
social cognition
social groups, family etc.
interpersonal interaction   main area
intentions and motives   of   range of
cognition and emotion   psychological   psychological
habits and learned associations   interest   interest
genetics and evolution
physiology
cellular biology
organic chemistry
quantum physics

This book has only really been able to give you a very superficial 'taste' of modern psychology. But I hope that you have found it an interesting one. Psychology is an intriguing area of study and one which can give us many insights into why we are like we are. As long as we resist the temptation to go for simplistic answers, and bear in mind that there can be a lot of different influences on how we act at any one time, we can learn a great deal – and we already have! The companion book to this one, *Teach Yourself Applied Psychology* discusses some of the ways that psychological research has been used to help people in all sorts of different ways. If you're interested in learning more about psychology, you might enjoy reading that book as well.

It is my firm belief that understanding more about human psychology will also mean that we come to understand one another much better – and that is why I have devoted such a large part of my life to learning about it, and to writing about it and carrying out psychological research of my own. I personally have always enjoyed the study of psychology. I hope that you have enjoyed this sample of it, too.

Nicky Hayes

taking it further

Other books by Nicky Hayes include:

Teach Yourself Applied Psychology, London: Hodder & Stoughton Educational (2003)

A Students Dictionary of Psychology, London: Arnold (1998)

Foundations of Psychology, London: Thomson Learning (2000)

A First Course in Psychology, London: Nelson Thomas (1993)

Managing Teams: A Strategy for Success, London: Thomson Learning (2001)

You can find the academic references used in this book at http://www.nickyhayes.co.uk/nicky

Websites

Chapter 01

http://www.ryerson.ca/~glassman/approach.html

http://www.psychoanalysis.org.uk

Chapter 02

http://www.motivation-tools.com/workplace/social_prejudice.html

http://chiron.valdosta.edu/whuitt/col/regsys/self.html

Chapter 03

http://www.personalityresearch.org/attachment.html

http://faculty.babson.edu/krollag/org_site/soc_psych/moscovici_soc_rep.html

Chapter 04

http://www.infoaging.org/l-stress-home.html

http://www.trinity.edu/mkearl/spsy-emo.html

Chapter 05

http://tip.psychology.org/bandura.html

http://www.asdreams.orglidxeducation.htm

Chapter 06

http://www.scapegoat.demon.co.uk

http://www.users.globalnet.co.uk/~cfg/maslow_is.htm

Chapter 07

http://www.ted.ie/Psychology/Ruth_Byrne/mental_models/

http://www.socialpsychology.org/cognitiv.htm

Chapter 08

http://www.personalityresearch.org/evolututionary.html

http://www.wgbh/evolution/library/08/1/text_pop/1_081_06html

Chapter 09

http://www.hltmag.co.uk/mar01/mart1.htm

http://psycprints.ecs.soton.ac.uk/archive/

Chapter 10

http://www.sociology.about.com/library/weekly/aa091500a.htm

http://www.socialpsychology.org/develop.htm

Chapter 11

http://www.ace.org.uk/

http://www.sociology.about.com/cs/aging

Chapter 12

http://psychology.about.com/msub_ioleader5.htm

http://www.socialpsychology.org/io.htm

Chapter 13

http://www.psychwatch.com/sport_psychology.htm

http://www.ithaca.edu/cretv/research/tv_lives.html

Chapter 14

http://www.nickyhayes.co.uk/nicky/exams/examstress.html

http://www.psychwatch.com//healthpsych_page.htm

Chapter 15

http://www-personal.umich.edu/~rdeyoung/envtpsych.html

http://www2.mozcom.com/~mels/2/concern.htm

Chapter 16

http://psy1.clarion.edu/mm/General/Methods/Methods.html

http://www.socialpsychology.org/methods.htm

Disclaimer

The publisher has used its best endeavours to ensure that the URLs for external websites referred to in this book are correct and active at the time of going to press. However, the publisher has no responsibility for the websites and can make no guarantee that a site will remain live or that the content will remain appropriate.

index

teach yourself®

English for International Business
English Language, Life & Culture
English Verbs
English Vocabulary
Ethics
Excel 2002
Feng Shui
Film Making
Film Studies
Finance for non-Financial Managers
Finnish
Flexible Working
Flower Arranging
French
French, Beginner's
French Grammar
French Grammar, Quick Fix
French, Instant
French, Improve your
French Language, Life & Culture
French Starter Kit
French Verbs
French Vocabulary
Gaelic
Gaelic Dictionary
Gardening
Genetics
Geology
German
German, Beginner's
German Grammar
German Grammar, Quick Fix
German, Instant
German, Improve your
German Language, Life & Culture
German Verbs
German Vocabulary
Go
Golf
Greek
Greek, Ancient
Greek, Beginner's
Greek, Instant
Greek, New Testament
Greek Script, Beginner's
Guitar
Gulf Arabic
Hand Reflexology
Hebrew, Biblical
Herbal Medicine
Hieroglyphics
Hindi
Hindi, Beginner's
Hindi Script, Beginner's

Afrikaans
Access 2002
Accounting, Basic
Alexander Technique
Algebra
Arabic
Arabic Script, Beginner's
Aromatherapy
Astronomy
Bach Flower Remedies
Bengali
Better Chess
Better Handwriting
Biology
Body Language
Book Keeping
Book Keeping & Accounting
Brazilian Portuguese
Bridge
Buddhism
Buddhism, 101 Key Ideas
Bulgarian
Business Studies
Business Studies, 101 Key Ideas
C++
Calculus
Calligraphy
Cantonese
Card Games
Catalan
Chemistry, 101 Key Ideas
Chess
Chi Kung
Chinese
Chinese, Beginner's

Chinese Language, Life & Culture
Chinese Script, Beginner's
Christianity
Classical Music
Copywriting
Counselling
Creative Writing
Crime Fiction
Croatian
Crystal Healing
Czech
Danish
Desktop Publishing
Digital Photography
Digital Video & PC Editing
Drawing
Dream Interpretation
Dutch
Dutch, Beginner's
Dutch Dictionary
Dutch Grammar
Eastern Philosophy
ECDL
E-Commerce
Economics, 101 Key Ideas
Electronics
English, American (EFL)
English as a Foreign Language
English, Correct
English Grammar
English Grammar (EFL)
English, Instant, for French Speakers
English, Instant, for German Speakers
English, Instant, for Italian Speakers
English, Instant, for Spanish Speakers

available from bookshops and on-line retailers

Hinduism
History, 101 Key Ideas
How to Win at Horse Racing
How to Win at Poker
HTML Publishing on the WWW
Human Anatomy & Physiology
Hungarian
Icelandic
Indian Head Massage
Indonesian
Information Technology, 101 Key Ideas
Internet, The
Irish
Islam
Italian
Italian, Beginner's
Italian Grammar
Italian Grammar, Quick Fix
Italian, Instant
Italian, Improve your
Italian Language, Life & Culture
Italian Verbs
Italian Vocabulary
Japanese
Japanese, Beginner's
Japanese, Instant
Japanese Language, Life & Culture
Japanese Script, Beginner's
Java
Jewellery Making
Judaism
Korean
Latin
Latin American Spanish
Latin, Beginner's
Latin Dictionary
Latin Grammar
Letter Writing Skills
Linguistics
Linguistics, 101 Key Ideas
Literature, 101 Key Ideas
Mahjong
Managing Stress
Marketing
Massage
Mathematics
Mathematics, Basic
Media Studies
Meditation
Mosaics
Music Theory
Needlecraft
Negotiating
Nepali

Norwegian
Origami
Panjabi
Persian, Modern
Philosophy
Philosophy of Mind
Philosophy of Religion
Philosophy of Science
Philosophy, 101 Key Ideas
Photography
Photoshop
Physics
Piano
Planets
Planning Your Wedding
Polish
Politics
Portuguese
Portuguese, Beginner's
Portuguese Grammar
Portuguese, Instant
Portuguese Language, Life & Culture
Postmodernism
Pottery
Powerpoint 2002
Presenting for Professionals
Project Management
Psychology
Psychology, 101 Key Ideas
Psychology, Applied
Quark Xpress
Quilting
Recruitment
Reflexology
Reiki
Relaxation
Retaining Staff
Romanian
Russian
Russian, Beginner's
Russian Grammar
Russian, Instant
Russian Language, Life & Culture
Russian Script, Beginner's
Sanskrit
Screenwriting
Serbian
Setting up a Small Business
Shorthand, Pitman 2000
Sikhism
Spanish
Spanish, Beginner's
Spanish Grammar
Spanish Grammar, Quick Fix

Spanish, Instant
Spanish, Improve your
Spanish Language, Life & Culture
Spanish Starter Kit
Spanish Verbs
Spanish Vocabulary
Speaking on Special Occasions
Speed Reading
Statistical Research
Statistics
Swahili
Swahili Dictionary
Swedish
Tagalog
Tai Chi
Tantric Sex
Teaching English as a Foreign Language
Teaching English One to One
Teams and Team-Working
Thai
Time Management
Tracing your Family History
Travel Writing
Trigonometry
Turkish
Turkish, Beginner's
Typing
Ukrainian
Urdu
Urdu Script, Beginner's
Vietnamese
Volcanoes
Watercolour Painting
Weight Control through Diet and
  Exercise
Welsh
Welsh Dictionary
Welsh Language, Life & Culture
Wills and Probate
Wine Tasting
Winning at Job Interviews
Word 2002
World Faiths
Writing a Novel
Writing for Children
Writing Poetry
Xhosa
Yoga
Zen
Zulu

applied psychology
nicky hayes

- Are you interested in looking at psychology in day-to-day living?
- Do you want to know how basic psychological processes are relevant to everyday situations?
- Do you want to gain a better understanding of psychology to help others to resolve problems?

Applied Psychology is written by a leading author of psychology texts and provides a comprehensive look at psychology in a variety of contexts. It covers 20 different areas of the subject, including well-developed but unknown areas such as space psychology and eco-psychology.

Nicky Hayes is a well-known psychologist and writer. She has been writing psychology books for over 20 years and is a Fellow of the British Psychological Society.

teach yourself

philosophy of mind
mel thompson

- Do you want to investigate historical ideas about the mind?
- Are you looking to explore how the mind is related to the body?
- Do you want to examine the creative aspects of the mind?

Philosophy of Mind explores many issues about the mind, such as the concepts of memory and free will. It encourages you to consider the impact of information technology on our understanding of the mind and the way it works. It also considers issues relating the mind to religion and artistic creativity.

Mel Thompson is a freelance writer and editor, specializing in Philosophy, Religion and Ethics.

postmodernism
glenn ward

- Do you want to understand the basics of postmodernism?
- Are you encountering postmodernist theory for the first time?
- Do you need a quick reference to support your studies?

Postmodernism is an indispensable guide to this sometimes demanding terrain. It places the subject in a wide context by offering an introduction to the most important theorists in a number of different disciplines and by linking theoretical questions to a variety of examples from both 'high' and 'popular' culture.

Glenn Ward is an artist and lecturer in visual culture.

teach
yourself

politics
peter joyce

- Do you want to understand key political terms and concepts?
- Are you looking for an introduction to the study of politics?
- Do you want the ability and knowledge to develop your own opinions?

Politics gives you the background knowledge to enable you to consider and analyse important political questions. It focuses on key political themes and ideas complemented by examples from relevant countries. It also looks at the role of the media, international communities and pressure groups in relation to politics.

Peter Joyce is a senior lecturer in the department of Sociology at Manchester Metropolitan University.